D0372671

Breathing
Room

CREATING SPACE
TO BE A COUPLE

Elayne Savage, Ph.D.

New Harbinger Publications, Inc.

Publisher's Note

This publication is designed to provide accurate and authoritative information in regard to the subject matter covered. It is sold with the understanding that the publisher is not engaged in rendering psychological, financial, legal, or other professional services. If expert assistance or counseling is needed, the services of a competent professional should be sought.

Distributed in the U.S.A. by Publishers Group West; in Canada by Raincoast Books; in Great Britain by Airlift Book Company, Ltd.; in South Africa by Real Books, Ltd.; in Australia by Boobook; and in New Zealand by Tandem Press.

Copyright © 2000 by Elayne Savage
               New Harbinger Publications, Inc.
               5674 Shattuck Avenue
               Oakland, CA 94609

Cover design by Blue Designs
Edited by Carole Honeychurch
Text design by Tracy Marie Powell

Library of Congress Card Catalog Number: 00-134868
ISBN 1-57224-221-3 Paperback

All Rights Reserved

Printed in the United States of America

New Harbinger Publications' Web site address: www.newharbinger.com

02   01   00

10   9   8   7   6   5   4   3   2   1

First printing

For Jocelyn

We have a room for everything—eating, sleeping, watching TV—but we have no room for mindfulness. I recommend that we set up a small room in our homes and call it a "breathing room," where we can be alone and practice just breathing and smiling, at least in difficult moments. That little room should be . . . respected, and not violated by anger, shouting, or things like that . . . every home should have one room for breathing.

—Thich Nhat Hanh, *Peace Is Every Step*

Once the realization is accepted that even between the closest human beings infinite distances continue to exist, a wonderful living side by side can grow up, if they succeed in loving the distance between them which makes it possible for each to see the other whole and against a wide sky.

—Rainer Maria Rilke, *Letters to a Young Poet*

Contents

෨ "When I Give You More Space, You Think I Don't Love You as Much" ෨ "I'm Not Nagging, I'm Showing I Care About Us" ෨ "You Let Me Down"—Dealing with Betrayal ෨ "I Calibrate Myself to Your Emotions"

Acknowledgments

I have been joined in this book project by the participation, teamwork, and good energy of many incredible people. I sincerely appreciate of your support, perceptions, and wisdom.

I especially want to thank the students, workshop participants, and clients who have given so generously of their stories so that others may benefit from the profound and engaging vignette collages that evolved. I've learned so much from you.

Thanks to my literary agent, Victoria Shoemaker, of the Spieler Agency West, for believing in me, motivating me, challenging me, and helping me fight my many battles. And best of all, Victoria, you cleverly made *Breathing Room* happen. Thanks to the talented team at New Harbinger—to Carole Honeychurch for your astute editing skills, and to Kristin Beck, Lauren Dockett, Michele Waters, Kasey Pfaff, Tracy Powell, and Amy Shoup for your patience and good energy.

Then there were those of you who read (sometimes even reread) and edited the manuscript. My grateful thanks to Isaac Mizrahi, for your belief in this project and your perceptive and valuable editing and suggestions. To Gail Glassberg, what would I do without your keen eye, impressive editing skills, and long-time friendship. And thanks to my daughter, Jocelyn Savage, for the amazing insight and wisdom you have offered at various stages of the book's evolution. I'm also indebted to Roz Stein and Sandra Kistler for your perceptive feedback, to José Romero for your valuable additions, creative chapter and heading suggestions, and to Michael Litant for those wonderfully original ideas. Many thanks to Pro Sherman for your cleverness, good humor, and reminders that "perspective is everything" and to Michael Pritchard for your warmth and good humor.

I appreciate the support of long-time friends and colleagues—Marilyn Denn for your editing and wise contributions, Audrey Fain for sharing your knowledge and insights, Fran Wickner for your able expertise, and Mary Gullekson for your astute observations, especially regarding the importance of making the switch in thinking from an individual framework to a couple's perspective. I'm indebted to the wisdom of Eric Greenleaf and Karen Saeger, which has greatly influenced my thinking and writing about couples' dynamics. Others who have given so freely of their ideas and knowledge are my brother, Lee Raskin, Richard Friedlander, Norma Burdick, Stan Draenos, Stuart Oppenheim, Melanie Lawrence, Steve Salomon, Mollie Hazen, and Bob Nichol who introduced me to the relevancy of "horror vacui"—thanks to each of you for your valuable contributions.

I especially want to acknowledge those of who have supported my endeavors for so many years, especially my high school and college friends Sima Blue, Bette Cooper, Larry Grusin, and Andrea Kirby. And of course my Omaha high school English teacher, Marcia Blacker.

And thanks to Kerry King, John Goodman, Bruce Linton, Jim Byrd, Leslie Tibbets, Hal Savage, Lynn Taylor, Jeanine Harmon, Chris Raynham, Ruth Belikove, Frank Burke, Julie Kovitz, Harry Pasternak, Noelia Pereira, Les Fram, Bonnie Hall, Leonard Schwab, Rita Brenner, Lincoln Pain, Joel Klutch, Dave de la Vega, Phyllis Gorelick, Allan Gorelick, Marie Collins, Bob Collins, and Carol O'Brien. Each of you has been important in your own way to the completion of this book.

Thanks to Angi Spector and everyone at Mind-Body Connection in Oakland for opening my eyes to the importance of creating physical and emotional space. Special thanks to Carrie Peters for your significant observations about kinesthetic space. And I truly appreciate the interest and support of the Zen community at Green Gulch Farm—to teachers Norman Fischer and Reb Anderson, to Rafael Davidson who introduced me to the space/time work of Edward T. Hall, and to Cindy Bendelac, Michelle Bernard, Kat Fitzgerald, Paula Blaiser, Martin Lindner, Ron Gibbs, and Sidney Brinn. Thanks, too, for the encouragement from members of the National Women's Political Caucus.

I'm grateful for the encouragement of Herb Bivens, Kimn Neilson, Mark Liebenow—it's gratifying that book people not only believed in my ideas but contributed some of their own as well. I also appreciate the support from the Northern California Chapter of the National Speakers Association, especially Michael Larsen, Susan Page, Barry Wishner, Craig Harrison, and Sylvia Mills.

And I appreciate that special cheering squad—my family. Besides Lee and Jocelyn, thanks to Barbara, Lauren, and Jennifer Raskin, to Larry Raskin, and to all the Raskins, Wolfsons, and Walters—your caring and support have meant a lot to me.

A Different Kind of Space Odyssey

Introduction

Space is what keeps everything from bumping into each other.

—Wes (Scoop) Nisker

In our fast-paced lives, when we barely have time to breath, how can we make room for romantic relationships? Balancing needs for closeness and distance is difficult, especially when one of you needs to have more space or less space. If you don't get it, misunderstandings, hurt feelings, anger, and resentments arise. Sometimes there's too much closeness and you feel you can't breathe—especially when you're bumping into, stumbling over, or stepping on each other's toes. Other times there's too much distance, and you find yourself gasping and grasping—particulary if your partner is emotionally unavailable, withdrawing, or threatening to leave.

Creating a Comfortable Space

Some of us grew up hearing that space is the "final frontier." But. where intimacy is concerned, space is the first frontier to manage. Respect for comfortable personal space is crucial, but finding the right balance can be a real challenge. This need for comfortable space in relationships has become strikingly clear in my twenty-five years of working with couples who often find themselves bumping into each other. We all need some elbow room, but what's sufficient? How much space is adequate? How much distance is enough? How much intimacy is enough? How much is too much? Why are "needs" and "wants" and "personal boundaries" so confusing? In *Breathing Room* I will present ways to work out these complex issues with your partner. You'll learn how to recognize both strengths and problem areas in your relationship, create enough objectivity to step back and observe your interactions, and develop skills to sidestep the hurt feelings that can often result from misunderstandings about needs for space.

But this is not a book just for couples. It's for anyone who hopes one day to *be* a couple but instead keeps bumping into those disconcerting space issues. Relationships are the best teachers for moving past that often-overwhelming fear of intimacy and all that goes along with it: fear of rejection, fear of betrayal, and fear of abandonment. As scary as they can be, relationships are great for learning about yourself and how you interact with people you care about. Once you can learn to stand back a little, you'll get some great practice at acquiring objectivity about your process of interactions. You can learn a lot both from what goes right and what goes wrong.

Couples in Space—How to "Orbit" Around Your Partner

Sometimes it seems as if we're from different universes because we orient ourselves to time and space in different ways. But why wouldn't we? Each person has a very personal way of approaching space issues because of our cultural differences, our attitudes toward intimacy, and the effects of childhood experiences on us today. These factors can add complications to your relationship even if you're unaware of their influence. This book will help you gain a better understanding of how these dynamics interact and work for or against you.

Throughout this book, you'll find many examples of cultural differences that affect personal space. These can greatly influence your romantic relationships—especially if you and your partner grew up in different cultures that place dissimilar values on emotional closeness and distance. All too often couples take these differences personally, feeling their partner is "unfeeling" or "overly dramatic." But often these are only cultural style differences, and understanding their origins can save lots of relationship distress.

How you view intimacy is also greatly affected by family customs and cultural differences. Because your "models" were not the same as those of your partner, your expectations of intimacy also may not be the same. Your experiences in your family of origin affect the expectations that you bring to your relationship. You and your partner may have different needs for space and different ways of taking it. All of this affects how you experience intimacy. Or, as the case may be, how you *don't* experience intimacy.

But just what is "intimacy"? Often we find ourselves describing what intimacy is *not* rather than what it is, talking about what's missing, rather than what exists, and reciting what we don't want, instead of what we want. It's easy to complain about how distancing someone is, or how they pull away, or how we feel left out because they need their own space. Yet, when asked, many couples are at a loss to define what space and intimacy mean to them.

Breathing Room takes an in-depth look at what intimacy is and isn't and how it's affected by personal space. Just as each of us has different needs for space, we also have different styles of taking it. This can have a great impact on the quality of intimacy in your relationship. Differences in style where personal space is concerned can lead to hurt feelings, misunderstandings, resentments, bitterness, and distancing. Feelings can flare up with lightning speed, damaging the feelings of closeness that exist.

Breathing Room unravels the mysteries of how our early experiences influence these misunderstandings. Looking back to these experiences can give answers to some to our relationship problems. I once heard a commentary about how salmonella in our bodies can lead to arthritis down the road, because immune system cells that fight bacteria sometimes attack normal cells as well. In other words, our bodies have an overreaction that does collateral damage to our immune systems. It's much the same regarding early experiences. They, too, can do collateral damage to our psychological immune system and lead to emotional inflammation down the road.

In most instances, words or actions by peers, teachers, siblings, or parents were not intended to be harmful, but sometimes they were. It's not the "intention" that matters as much as the perception of the child—how we explained it to ourselves. Even unintended hurts can last a long time and affect adult relationships. I know this firsthand, because I was extremely sensitive to rejection as a child.

Words, looks, tones of voice, and even raised eyebrows all gave me shivers. I took everything to heart; I was thin-skinned rather than tough-skinned, and not very resilient. Some of you may have been highly sensitive as well.

> Each of you sees the world from a
> different but equally valid vantage point.

Perceptions that you carry away from your past into your present affect your relationships. All too often space gets filled with misconceptions and preconceptions, affecting the way people see the world. And remember, both you and your partner have unique experiences that contribute to your worldview, especially involving fairness, trust, and expectations. As a result, each of you sees the world from a different, although equally valid, vantage point.

Inner Space or Outer Space?

There are probably times when you let your inner space be affected by outside influences, namely your partner's likes and dislikes, expectations, preferences, and opinions. This is a big-ticket relationship issue—making enough room to be a couple and to be yourself, as well. This means being in a relationship and still keeping your autonomy—your independence, freedom, and identity. It means honoring your uniqueness. Usually there are powerful dual fears involved in this attempt: the fear of being yourself vs. the fear of losing yourself. It may feel to you that you have to choose between one or the other, but you really don't. In fact, the most intimate moments are when you can experience a balance of "I" and "we." *Breathing Room* will show you how to be both an "I" and a "we" without having to sacrifice either.

> You are dealing with two powerful fears: the fear
> of being yourself vs. the fear of losing yourself.

Through the "space" lens, we'll be looking at more than cultural and family-of-origin influences on intimacy, personal space, and maintaining autonomy. We'll also explore how personal boundaries, anxieties, stress and fears, power and control considerations, and life transitions influence closeness and distance. You'll learn about dozens of "space fillers" and "distance regulators" that interfere with relationships, and you'll come to appreciate the multifaceted ways in which space influences both sexual and emotional intimacy. And, finally, through illuminating stories and step-by-step suggestions, you'll learn how to take notice, take a breath, consider your options, and strategize how to make changes in the quality of your intimate relationship.

How to Use This Book

Breathing Room is easy to navigate. You can open the book to any chapter that appeals to you, but by starting with the introduction and chapters 1 and 2, you'll receive a foundation in the basic terminology I'll be using. You'll notice that some sections are overflowing with information, while others are fairly minimalist. This difference results from my intention to offer a "jump-start" on some new ways to think about space issues and how they affect your relationships. It would be too much of a digression to discuss some of the more minor points in depth, but I want to present an overview to you. In addition, there are many books out there on some of these areas, especially gender style differences and all the addictions such as cyber, alcohol and other substances. So, I've included some good resources in the list of Suggested Readings at the end of the book for you to refer to if you'd like more information.

Breathing Room is a natural progression from my earlier book, *Don't Take It Personally!: The Art of Dealing with Rejection*. Rather than finding ways to respect our partner's need for personal space, we all too often resent it and take it as a personal affront. Although I've tried to avoid repetition of material, I think some points in the first book are important in understanding the dynamics of personal space. You may find it useful to view the two books as companion pieces, especially if you desire more information about expectations and disappointments, personal boundaries, needs and yearnings, fears of rejection, perceptions of rejection from peers, teachers, or family, exploring options, and depersonalizing responses.

You'll find lots of stories in this book about generic "Joes" and "Janes," and you'll most likely recognize yourself or your partner in some of them. Using the "space" lens, you'll find yourself adjusting it for close-ups and stepping back for the wide view, much as you would with a camera. The closeups give you the ability to recognize snapshots of yourself and your actions. And the long shots provide the perspective to step back and give yourself enough breathing room to not always get caught up in the "drama" of the moment.

As you read, notice examples of sequence and reciprocity. *Sequence* in this context refers to problematic as well as positive behaviors in the relationship—what behavior comes before and what behavior follows. And what comes before that? And before that? Soon a pattern of interaction begins to emerge.

Related to sequence is *reciprocity*—the effect of behavior on subsequent behaviors, how one response begets another. In other words, every action is also a reaction, creating a *circular* rather than linear process of relating. For example, #1 says something to #2. And #2 thinks #1 means something negative or critical by what is said. Then #2 reacts protectively, that is to say, withdraws. And #1 reacts to the perceived withdrawal, perhaps getting hurt or angry. And on and on it goes, with no beginning and no end. In other words, #1 doesn't do it to #2. #2 doesn't do it to #1. They do it with each other. One person may indeed do some behavior that is not okay, but the other person *allows* it. In other words, each partner's behavior affects and is affected by the other person's behavior.

Reciprocity also describes how individual behavior affects the behavior in the relationship, which in turn affects the individual behavior. And this affects change as well. Individual change can lead to relationship change, which in turn can lead to more individual change. Let's say someone begins to understand that his or her partner's need for privacy is really a difference of style, and there is no need to feel threatened by this need. As a result, the relationship is less tense and more comfortable for both, and the other person no longer has to protect his or her space needs so fervently, allowing room for more closeness.

In addition, reciprocity includes *complementarity*—a dovetailing or fitting together by the couple where each one mutually supplies what the other lacks, filling out the relationship. For example: If #1 is private, #2 may be outgoing. Other dovetailing kinds of interactions include nurturing/dependent, assertive/compliant, giver/taker, dramatic/unemotional, and spontaneous/reserved. There are other ways we "fill out" the relationship, which include a bending of the lens of reality and which are discussed in chapter 2. For example, you may feel something is missing in yourself and, through glorification, seek it out in a partner, or you may project your own undeveloped, unacknowledged, or unacceptable traits onto your partner.

And yet another kind of reciprocity takes place when a couple negotiates an exchange of desirable behaviors, for example, "I'll be willing to tidy up the living room every day if you drive me to the metro station on your way to work." Unfortunately, as you'll see in chapter 11, these "agreements" are not always put into words, and sometimes they are not even in conscious awareness.

And as you read on you'll see that each of these reciprocity dynamics are related to the amount of personal space that each person takes up or gives up in the relationship. And you'll find more details and examples of reciprocity in chapter 2.

An extraordinary thing happened to me as I was working on this book. It started as a slight presence, grew more persistent over time, and soon became a flash of awareness that I could no longer ignore. As I was writing, I began to recognize myself in the stories and to realize how I'm more of a player in this drama than I knew. I have a big part in how the dance of intimacy gets played out by my choice of partners. But it is not just the "go away a little closer" messages that others give—I realize that I give them as well!

As you recognize yourself or your partner in the stories, you'll notice how space issues exist in ways you never before imagined. A new world will open for you, providing ideas that are unique to your own situation. Not only will you identify ways you may desire space or give up space, but you'll also notice ways you are respecting the sacredness of space for yourself and your partner. By following your own cues and instincts, you'll be able to see the world of relationships in a different way, enabling you to creatively fine-tune some adjustments or make some broad changes. Change happens best when you allow enough space for it to happen, and *Breathing Room* is about making enough space to find the breathing room every relationship needs.

1

Falling in Love
with Love

What Intimacy Is and Isn't

Defining "intimacy" is no easy task. This multifaceted concept has a personal meaning for each of us, as well as a uniquely special meaning for couples. Let's first take a look at what intimacy is. Then we'll examine some elements of an intimate relationship, and, finally, explore what intimacy *isn't*.

Intimacy?

Tim and Marie have been married for twenty-eight years, but when a series of stresses began putting a strain on their marriage, they sought couple's counseling. When Marie mentioned that she was a little worried about the level of intimacy they shared, Tim turned to her with a perplexed look on his face: "Just exactly what do you mean by intimacy?"

At first she thought he was joking. How could this man, who she had lived with all those years, be asking that question? But she quickly recovered from the surprise and gave him her definition.

"To me, intimacy means closeness. People coming together at a very deep level, sharing their thoughts—you know, a soul to soul kind of thing." She considered this for a few seconds. "It means being on the same page, being in sync—when you don't even have to say your whole thought because the other person can finish your sentence for you."

Tim looked surprised, and said quietly, "I've never thought about it like that." He hesitated a moment. "I'm not exactly sure what you mean."

She turned to him, an almost challenging tone to her voice. "Well, what does it mean to you?"

He thought for a bit, then looking a little sheepish, he offered, "I guess most men think it means sex, but I know it's really supposed to be more than that." Another long pause. "It also means working with one another—talking through things." He paused again and thought some more. "It's when I think you might be cold, and I put my arm around you to keep you warm."

Actually, in a way, they're saying pretty much the same thing. But the ways they express these ideas reflect their different ways of thinking. She sees intimacy as a sometimes-idealized, heart-to-heart, soul-to-soul closeness. He, on the other hand, sees intimacy as sexual and practical—a "taking care of things."

A Balancing Act

Intimacy is a balance between needs for closeness and needs for distance. In other words, it's not just the ability to feel close, but it's also the ability to say, "I need some space." Intimacy is also being able to respect your partner's need for space, not feel threatened by it, and, in fact, to welcome it as a sign of growing and changing. Intimacy benefits from the creation of breathing room, where each person gets to have their own space in their own way.

Intimacy has a myriad of meanings. When I first began to research the effects of childhood rejection on adult intimacy for my 1989 doctoral dissertation, I noticed that most authors defined intimacy in only a vague, amorphous (and often poetic) way. And, as we saw in the dialogue between Tim and Marie, "intimacy" seems to take on meanings unique to each individual.

Looking at the root of the word may shed light on its meaning: the Latin word *intimus* means "inmost" or "innermost." An example of this usage would be when you are granted access to someone's inmost character or innermost reality.

In the twenty-five years I have worked with couples, I've come to understand intimacy as the ability to have deep emotional closeness with another person—a closeness that allows you to be vulnerable to that person and to accept their vulnerability in turn.

But intimacy requires some risk-taking as well, as it is the ability to share your deepest fears as well as your highest hopes. It is moving past the fear of allowing someone to glimpse what is under that façade you may have been building for so many years. Intimacy requires another risk as well—making contact with your very core, standing in the center of your truth. At times, this means having the courage of commitment to stay in the same room with your partner and talk things out. At other times, it means sharing your secret thoughts and feelings, allowing yourself to expand, opening your heart so your truest essence is revealed. It means inviting another person into this sacred space and understanding that the other person is willing to allow you in, as well. And it is mutual respect and trust that allows this opening to occur.

Let's take a look at how some other relationship experts view intimacy. In *How One of You Can Bring the Two of You Together* (1997), Susan Page describes intimacy as an ease and comfort of being together—a flow between two people. In 1983's *Intimate Strangers*, Lillian Rubin describes intimacy as a reciprocal expression of feeling and thought that comes out of a wish to know another's inner life, and the ability to share one's own. In *Opening Our Hearts to Men* (1989), Susan Jeffers characterizes intimacy as being able to hear what the other is saying and feel what the other is feeling—at best, connecting at the level of the soul. And Maggie Scarf, in *Intimate Worlds* says it's being able to say who you are and what you need and being heard. It's having a place to go with bad news as well as good news (1995). Harriet Lerner, in *The Dance of Intimacy* (1989), offers this observation: "It's when we stay in a relationship over time ... that our capacity for intimacy is truly put to the test ... that we are called upon to navigate that delicate balance between separateness and connectedness ... without losing either when the going gets rough" (p. 2).

Another way to look at the facets of intimacy is to look at the basic areas it covers. One of my favorite descriptions of the components of intimacy comes from *The Intimate Marriage*, a 1970 book by Clinebell and Clinebell, where they identify seven areas of intimacy:

- *Emotional intimacy:* experiencing closeness of feelings

- *Social intimacy:* the experience of having common friends and similarities in social networks

- *Intellectual intimacy:* the experience of sharing ideas

- *Sexual intimacy:* the experience of sharing general affection and/or sexual activity

- *Recreational intimacy:* shared experiences of interests in hobbies, mutual participation in sporting events

- *Spiritual intimacy:* the experience of sharing ultimate concerns, a similar sense of meaning in life, and/or religious faiths

- *Aesthetic intimacy:* the closeness that results from the experience of sharing beauty (p. 50)

Although most commentators on intimacy identify reciprocal self-disclosing as a main ingredient, David Schnarch in *Passionate Marriage* (1998) points out that there are, in fact, two kinds of intimacy—one that expects reciprocity from the partner, and one that does not. *Other-validated intimacy* "involves the expectation of acceptance, empathy, validation or reciprocal disclosure from one's partner" (p. 106). One partner might think or say to the other: "I'll go first, and then you'll be obligated to disclose—it's only fair." *Self-validated intimacy* "relies on a person's maintaining his or her own sense of identity and self-worth when disclosing, with no expectation of acceptance or reciprocity from the partner" (p. 107). One partner might think or say to the other, "One day, when we are no longer on this earth, I want to know you *knew* me."

In differentiated relationships, when partners can honor their own and each other's uniqueness, other-validated intimacy occurs spontaneously, and the partners are not dependent upon it. "It's nice when you can get it," says Schnarch, "particularly when you don't need it—and, paradoxically, that's when you are most likely to get it" (p. 109).

The balancing act between closeness
and distance sometimes makes
intimacy an unpredictable proposition.

As you can see there are lots of ways to define intimacy. Using the preceding definitions as a basis, you may find yourself reforming your own definitions of what emotional closeness means to you.

But this book isn't only about achieving emotional closeness with another person. It's also about balancing that feeling of closeness with enough space to allow each person to remain an individual within the relationship, with an individual's sense of autonomy and freedom. It's this balancing act between closeness and distance that can make intimacy an unpredictable proposition for some couples.

Space

You may have an understanding of what emotional closeness in a relationship means, but what does "space" mean? I'll be using the term "space" to mean personal space—both physical and emotional. This would include individuality, personal boundaries, privacy, alone time, elbowroom, turf, and safe distances. It can also mean gaps and holes. And, yes, it means openings, too. The concept of personal space signifies something different to each of us because our needs are unique and our tolerances are individual. Each of us has a personal need for space that depends on two factors: our experiences growing up and the context and complexity of the present situation.

Personal space in a relationship is crucial but can often bring up anxiety when one partner desires more closeness than the other does. This may be because, as partners become more intimate, they feel compelled to open themselves up to each other (and perhaps even reveal things to themselves that they hadn't been aware of). They may find themselves uncovering things that they tend to keep hidden in more casual relationships.

This openness makes the disclosing partner feel vulnerable—prone to any action the other partner may take, from loving acceptance to hurtful rejection. This vulnerability can make romantic partners uncomfortable, especially when one partner wants more space than the other does. But it is this vulnerability that is essential to true intimacy

Vulnerability

Lillian Rubin in *Intimate Strangers* describes this aspect of intimacy as, "putting aside the masks we wear in the rest of our lives . . . believing we can be loved for who we *really* are . . . that our vulnerabilities will not be counted against us" (p. 68).

And isn't this often our bottom-line fear: "If you really knew me, you wouldn't like me"? We come to believe that no one could possibly love the *real* person under the mask. It is this learned overconcern about how we appear to others that interferes with our ability to be authentic: letting others see the person under the façade and allowing connection on an intimate level.

If only we could accept that showing vulnerability is really showing our humanity. It's our vulnerabilities that allow us to connect to someone, not our defenses. In fact, we're not really connecting unless we go to this vulnerable space. Allowing vulnerability is allowing entry to the soft, angry, scared, hurt, distrusting, needy, sensual, loving parts. It allows entry to that "young child" part that we are so afraid to let others see.

To be sure, we become so incredibly self-protective because feeling vulnerable represents feeling too exposed—showing our fragility, our fears, and our doubts. "Allowing" vulnerability is very different from feeling vulnerable or helpless and needing to defend or armor ourselves. But we're scared to show the vulnerable side of ourselves, so we cover it with layer upon layer of illusions.

Richard speaks honestly, "I have worn a mask since childhood, protecting myself. I can tolerate it if people reject my façade, but I wouldn't be able to stand it if they rejected the real me—that's too fragile." He pauses and adds sadly, "I guess I don't even know what's underneath anymore." If only Richard could give himself permission to get past that tough façade, getting access to his softer side and allowing others in, as well.

> It is our vulnerabilities that allow us to connect to someone, not our defenses.

But in order to let someone into this private place, you must first have some awareness of your own inner life. This means being able to check in with yourself, recognizing and validating your feelings, your thoughts, your needs, and your longings.

Even if you find yourself in attack mode, look inside to see what kinds of longings might be churning around. Once you have this awareness, you can choose to let your partner in on it. For example, if you find yourself chastising or assailing your partner, by looking honestly at the feelings inside, you just might realize that you're longing for attention, rather than actually angry about the argument at hand. Try acknowledging these hidden longings—it allows an opening for your partner to ask you what you need, and this awareness opens the door to intimacy.

As you can see, knowledge of your inner life is important. In other words, knowing yourself can be viewed as becoming intimate with yourself, recognizing your strengths and weaknesses, and being capable of self-acceptance and self-love.

> Knowing yourself means being intimate with yourself, recognizing your strengths and weaknesses, and being capable of self-acceptance and self-love.

Self-Acceptance

As Plato observed, "knowing thyself" is not an easy task. And accepting yourself is even more difficult. Acceptance means getting past blind spots, owning both your strengths and weaknesses, and acknowledging your "shadow" side, including those hard-to-face child parts. It means accepting yourself without judgments, without all those "shoulds" and "oughts," without being overly concerned about approval or disapproval from others. Sensitivity to disapproval from others seems to be related to how much we disapprove of ourselves. If you don't respect and accept certain parts of yourself, you probably don't want anyone else to see all those parts of you! In other words, you will reject yourself and worry that others will reject you as well.

Once we begin to see ourselves as worthless, unlovable, undesirable, or unacceptable, we tend to get wedged into that space, rejecting ourselves. It becomes difficult to take in positive, affirming messages. When there's so much self-rejection, self-acceptance doesn't have much room to exist.

This is especially true in moments of anxiety, when it becomes difficult to gain access to that "acceptance" compartment. You may know it's there but just can't get to it. It's simply not available. Gaining access to the accepting part of yourself is hard if you are loaded down with self-rejection. Do you sometimes find yourself too weighed down by negativity to open up to acceptance by others? How can you let in a positive flow of information, information you can really hear?

> Try on this motto: "Self-respect,
> instead of self-reject."

There are ways of breaking old patterns and moving from self-rejection to self-acceptance. One of the most basic tools I know for practicing self-acceptance is to practice accepting compliments from others. For example, if someone says, "I really like that jacket," out of habit you might respond, "Oh this rag? It's so old." What about responding with a simple, "Thank you"? No commentary, no excuses—just "thank you." Another tool would be to try on this motto: "Self-respect, instead of self-reject."

From self-acceptance springs self-respect, self-confidence, self-reliance, self-assurance, self-esteem, and self-satisfaction, but in order to accept yourself, you must first know yourself. And this inner intimacy is a prerequisite for sustaining intimate relationships with others. It has to be an inside job. If you don't know what is going on inside, how can you grant access to someone else? Once you become authentic with yourself, you can extend this self-intimacy to other intimate relationships. But, then again, one of the best ways to learn about yourself is to be in a relationship. You may learn about things like understanding, compassion, and having an open heart. You may also come to recognize a sprinkling of things like a tendency toward exhibiting "ownership," or jealousies, or an excessive dependency on your partner for validation.

Let's go back to the discussion of self-validated intimacy earlier in this chapter. This idea highlights the importance of achieving self-acceptance through acquiring the ability to maintain a solid sense of self-identity in intimate relationships. Self-validated intimacy offers the stability of relying on your own feelings of worth and self-acceptance rather than on your partner's approval. If you can fully accept yourself, you will not be so vulnerable to other-validated intimacy. You will be able to accept your partner's reactions without preconceived expectations. You can make yourself vulnerable to a partner without worrying that you will feel devastated by an unexpected reaction.

> Knowing yourself is a prerequisite for establishing intimacy with another person. It has to be an inside job.

Self-awareness allows you to have some objectivity about a situation and the people in it. It allows you to walk alongside yourself and make choices about what you say and how you react. Without self-awareness, emotions can swirl around you, take over, and spill over. This is "emotional flooding" when you become overwhelmed by your emotions. When you're "flooded," you're more likely to take things personally and overreact, and feel unable to think straight or sort out your feelings. You'll find examples of flooding and overreacting throughout *Breathing Room.* This kind of behavior interferes with being open and reasonable, which makes it tough on intimate relationships.

Ingredients for an Intimate Relationship

In my day-to-day work with couples and workshop participants, ideas have emerged about styles, issues, and implications of intimacy. Here are my top picks for the ingredients for an intimate relationship:

- Ability to give and accept respect

- Capacity for self-disclosure, including the ability to be sincere, honest, and authentic, and to show vulnerability and trust

- Capability for "teamwork" in the partnership—demonstrating flexibility, willingness to resolve conflicts, and the ability to work and play together comfortably

I very consciously put "respect" at the top of the list. Without it, you run the risk of amassing hurt feelings, misunderstandings, resentment, anger, and alienation. These sensitivities are off-putting and not conducive to feeling close to someone. In fact, you'll most likely find yourself creating protective distance.

"Respectfully Yours"

Mutual respect is essential to building intimacy. This includes respecting both your own and the other person's needs for space—individuality, personal boundaries, privacy, alone time, and turf. Without mutual respect there can be only limited closeness. If you sense someone isn't respecting you, you're receiving (and likely giving out) a message of pushing away or rejection, rather than a message of receptivity or acceptance.

> Without mutual respect, there can be only limited closeness.

Feeling respected means feeling accepted by another person, but what if you don't feel this acceptance? Nonacceptance feels like disrespect, which brings up a myriad of rejection issues.

In other words, feeling rejected equals feeling "dissed":

Disrespected	Dispensable	Dismissed	Disposable
Disclaimed	Disdained	Discounted	Disparaged
Discarded	Disbelieved	Disqualified	Displaced
Disregarded	Disowned	Disapproved	Disgraced

The list goes on and on. Disrespect often shows itself in the form of anger, which may erupt in rage or emotional outbursts. Or it may surface in baiting, teasing, sarcasm or cynicism, putdowns, judgments, or criticism. Or it may appear as manipulating others and making unreasonable demands.

Feeling rejected = feeling "dissed"

In *The Seven Principles for Making Marriage Work*, psychologist John Gottman describes the "Four Horsemen of the Apocalypse"—types of negativity that can be lethal to a relationship:

- Criticism (when a complaint turns into a character assassination)

- Contempt (when criticism turns into sarcasm, cynicism, namecalling, sneers, mockery, or eyerolling)

- Defensiveness (a protection against the attack)

- Stonewalling (the ultimate defense—tuning out, responding with silence, disengaging)

You may recognize that each of these "Horsemen" is wearing the cloak of rejection and disrespect. In *Don't Take It Personally!* I described how many of us grew up feeling rejected, invalidated, ignored, or discounted, and how, as a result, we suffer long-term damage to our self-respect, self-worth, self-assurance, self-confidence, self-esteem, self-regard, and self-acceptance. If we learned along the way to disrespect ourselves, we don't always know how to show respect to others

Disrespect is a form of rejection that pushes people away, hurts feelings, causes resentment and anger to grow, and plays havoc with relationships. Once these resentments grow, distance between two people grows as well. Small schisms can turn into deep chasms, leaving a gap to be traversed. Watch out—can a relationship abyss be far behind?

I'll Show You Mine, If You Show Me Yours

Mutual self-disclosure is often at the top of popular intimacy "lists," considered by many to be a prerequisite for developing intimate relationships. There's no question self-disclosure is a means of decreasing distance between two people, but self-disclosure can be tricky. We fool ourselves into believing we are good disclosers, but too often we *selectively* disclose. You might say this is selective intimacy. It's all too easy to disclose the things you're most comfortable with; sometimes, in fact, certain disclosures become more or less mechanical. You may tell certain stories that are safe to talk about, but the other person doesn't really know you. The ability to self-disclose means having enough self-awareness and strength to express our emotions, needs, thoughts, attitudes, beliefs, and fantasies.

But the capacity to self-disclose does not in itself guarantee intimacy—especially if it's one-sided. Have you ever been in a relationship where you can say just about anything to your partner, but he or she is not nearly as open to you? Or maybe it's a situation where, even though there seems to be a reciprocal sharing of thoughts and feelings, something is missing from the closeness and connection you yearn for. Again, expecting reciprocity can lead to disappointment.

> The capacity to self-disclose does not guarantee intimacy.

"Sincerely Yours"

Another way to improve intimacy is to show regard and respect by treating your partner with sincerity. "Sincere" means free from pretense or deceit, and alludes to demonstrating genuine feelings.

Our word, "sincere," comes from sixteenth-century France, and there is another, similar-sounding French phrase that has to do with being genuine. This phrase is "sans cire," which means "without wax." Here is a story I've heard told about this phrase—it may or may not be true, but it has a certain charm to it and is worth telling. In the olden days, casting bronze sculpture often resulted in imperfections. Artisans wanted to give the work a perfectly smooth finish, so they would fill the spaces with wax and color it to match. Perfect, yes. Smooth, yes—but surely not authentic. In order for a piece to be honest, it would have to be "without wax."

Some of us find ourselves doing that same wax trick. There are times when we fill our flaws with wax, presenting ourselves as something different than we really are, more refined, more polished—perhaps even real smooth operators. But, by attempting to smooth away our perceived imperfections, we are not being completely honest with ourselves or those closest to us.

Staying authentic is most certainly hard work. It's a lot easier to don a protective covering to feel more secure. Sometimes it might be wax. Other times it might be a façade or a mask.

Putting Aside the Masks We Wear

In the process of becoming intimate with another person, you may, at times, feel vulnerable and exposed. As a defense against this feeling, you may develop some sort of protective covering, or façade, because it feels safer. We tend to cover any feelings of vulnerability we may be feeling with a certain toughness, even an arrogance, that serves to push people away, or cause them to retaliate. And this disguise surely interferes with intimacy. It's hard for people to get underneath that self-sufficiency, and all that armor makes connecting difficult as well. Generating these self-protections and barriers creates pseudo-intimate situations, when people around you come close to your mask—what they think is "you"—without coming any closer to the real you inside.

> Armoring yourself with masks or façades
> makes connecting with another person difficult.

I'm reminded of the fake food in the windows of a nearby Japanese restaurant. It looks deliciously real, but you can't eat it, because it's plastic. Intimacy can be like that, too. It can look great on the outside, but all too often there's nothing real underneath.

There is an intriguing example of how we use masks in Eugene O'Neil's *The Great God Brown*. When the man lowers his mask to reveal who he really is, the woman continues to relate to the mask—her illusion of who he is. Relating to the real person is difficult for her.

Teamwork Works

Providing support and satisfactions for each other in mutually fulfilling ways is what I mean by "teamwork." This collaboration includes flexibility, willingness to resolve conflicts, the ability to work and play together, and consideration of the needs and goals of your partner.

In summing up what intimacy is, let's look to the wisdom of children commenting on their observations of adults in love. This perceptive list of comments by kids, four to eight, was compiled by Mary Ophanie P. Siatan, in the Philippine *Daily Inquirer*. Here are some of my favorites:

> When my grandmother got arthritis, she couldn't bend over
> and paint her toenails anymore. So my grandfather does it

for her all the time, even when his hands got arthritis, too. That's love.

When someone loves you, the way she says your name is different. You know that your name is safe in her mouth.

Love is what makes you smile when you're tired.

Love is what's in the room with you at Christmas if you stop opening presents for a minute and look around.

When you tell someone something bad about yourself, you're scared she won't love you anymore. But then you get surprised because not only does she still love you, she loves you even more.

Love cards, like Valentine's cards, say stuff on them that we'd like to say ourselves, but we wouldn't be caught dead saying.

Love is when you tell a guy you like his shirt, then he wears it every day.

Love is like a little old woman and a little old man who are still friends even after they know each other so well.

You really shouldn't say "I love you" unless you mean it. But if you mean it, you should say it a lot. People forget.

Now let's move from what intimacy hopefully is, to what it all-too-often isn't.

What Intimacy Isn't

By wanting to believe that a relationship is working, you may even fool yourself into it. This pseudo-intimacy gives the illusion of genuine intimacy, complete with the "look" and "feel," but it lacks the crucial depth of connection to another person. Let's say you find yourself "bonding" with someone around shared interests or activities. You may love the experience of talking at length with someone about these interests and telling yourself, "We have so much in common!" But that's not real intimacy

And speaking of bonding, have you heard of recent studies on oxytocin, the "bonding" hormone secreted by the pituitary gland and released during sexual orgasm in both genders? Here is an example in which our minds get outwitted by our physiology: Your mind may say, "No way is this a good relationship for me," but those hormones cry out, "Let's bond!" and we keep hanging in there, knowing the relationship isn't going anywhere. Maybe one day they'll package oxytocin, and we can put a few drops in our lover's coffee or tea. Voila! Instant bonding.

Do You Find Imitation Intimacy in the Dairy Case?

Another "pseudo" activity is the art of repetition, role behavior where you find yourself declaring certain words or phases to others so often that you begin to believe them yourself. An example might be: "I could fall for you," or "I think I've never felt this way before." You know that old saying: "If you repeat something enough times, you'll start believing it." You can end up fooling both of you, if you're not careful.

It's not exactly that you *mean* to be deceitful. Perhaps you don't know how to do it any other way. In fact, many of us grew up with a socialization process that teaches us to say what folks want to hear. So you may find yourself saying those varied "mantras" of socialcultural survival, those words that you've repeated many times before, to many other people.

You most likely know the expressions I mean when I talk about "imitation intimacy." Examples of these romantic platitudes are: "I've never met anyone quite like you," "I love the way I can talk with you, and you really listen," "This is magical," "I'd love to tuck you in every night," "I can really see us having a future together," "You're the best thing that's ever happened to me," "I'll always be there for you," and the hands-down favorite, "Oh, baby, you make me feel *so* good."

These declarations aren't *exactly* "lines," of course, even though there might be an element of the bullshit factor here. No, the chances are you may *think* you mean them in the moment and they just come trippingly off the tongue, so fluid, so tender, so romantic—and so phony.

Susan Page, in *If I'm So Wonderful, Why Am I Still Single?* (1990), exposes pseudointimacy as "intimate-type gestures and actions without any content beneath the dewy eyes and soft caresses. Just as a two-dimensional, black-and-white silhouette *suggests* a real person, so pseudo-intimacy is a shadow of what is possible in relationships" (p. 100).

Nurturing Is Not the Same As Intimacy

It's so easy to confuse nurturing with intimacy. Sure it feels great when your partner takes care of you, perhaps cooking for you, fussing over that burn on your hand, offering to massage your neck, or even making sure you have hot chicken soup when you're coming down with the flu. Sweet? Yes. Tender? Yes. Affectionate? Yes. But not necessarily intimacy.

As Lillian Rubin points out in *Intimate Strangers*, nurturance may be connected to intimacy and even be a result of it, but nurturance is not intimacy—nurturance is caretaking. Rubin takes a long look at men who can be nurturing but who have difficulty being intimate. Yes, nurturing men *do* exist; the market is not totally cornered by women. However, keep in mind that women who excel at nurturing could also have intimacy limitations. Nurturing is often a woman's way to intimacy through the back door. They think they are being intimate by being nurturers.

Women can get so confused by a nurturing man, too often mistaking the caretaking for intimacy. One woman I know actually married a man she had known for several years, but had never really considered a potential mate. Her feelings for him changed after she was attacked and robbed at an ATM. During the weeks he nursed her back to health, she watched her feelings for him shift. He took such good care of her during those long months of emotional and physical recovery that she found herself falling in love with him.

No question about it, he was very good in a crisis. He is a crackerjack caretaker because he's had lots of practice. As a child, his chronically ill mother depended on him to take care of her daily needs. He learned his job well and excelled at it because that was how he got validation. So, nurturing became a way of giving to get (his mother's love), and a way to fill up the empty space in his heart.

When he grew up, it was easy to transfer this acquired skill to his adult relationship. "Here I go again, putting my cape on," he'd laughingly say to himself. "I rescue damsels in distress—that's where I get my validation. But one thing's for sure: if you go around slaying dragons for damsels, you are going to get some blood on you!" This man had fooled himself into thinking his caretaking was intimacy, and he fooled his wife as well. Once her health improved, things deteriorated. He became less attentive, more distracted. She couldn't believe it. He seemed to change right before her eyes, thinking more about himself and his needs than about her. What happened? Both learned the hard truth: nurturing is not the same as intimacy.

However, the reverse *can* be true. Intimacy can, and often does, include the ability to be caring and giving. And it does offer an opportunity to nurture. After all, the care and feeding of a relationship is important for its continued flourishing. Remember, however, that the ability to be a caregiver is no guarantee that a person has the ability to be intimate. Don't shortchange yourself in relationships by assuming that your extraordinary expertise at caretaking assures the ability for intimacy as well.

Those of you who consider yourselves nurturers might find, as you read this, that you are building a defense in your mind, an argument against these ideas. It may challenge your image of yourself, and in response (or retaliation), you may want to challenge me on it. One man I know has already done that! His eyes flashed and he argued passionately with me—as if his very life depended on winning the argument. And, in a way, perhaps his life did depend on it. Certainly that part of him that needs to see himself as a nurturer.

So, how does someone acquire these special caretaking abilities? Many of you had that job description in your family when you were small. It provided an identity and role back then, and it still may. So, as adults, you may continue to glory in that job. Without it, you might feel as if there were a big hole that you would need to fill. So you continue to do what comes naturally. After all, isn't it a familiar role? It's a common enough role for women, but men have been known to fill that role as well.

> The ability to be a caregiver is no guarantee of the ability to be intimate.

On the surface, those little nurturing touches can feel so wonderfully caring. However, this doesn't necessarily mean the nurturer has the capacity to be open and intimate. Maybe you've found that all it takes is a little offer of "caring," and you quickly want to take it to another level, to raise the bar a little higher. And when these often-unrealistic expectations don't materialize, what a heap of disappointments it brings to the relationship!

Leslie came into a "check in" session with news that she had found the perfect man. "He can be so caring, so giving, so sensitive. I love the way he fusses over me. He seems to anticipate my needs. And he's such a good listener. Oh yeah, he's a very good cook, too. I find myself thinking, 'Wow, this is great. He's so tender—he must care for me so very much.' This guy is just what I've been looking for. I have to pinch myself to make sure it's not a dream."

A few months into the "dreamy" relationship, she asked for another session. She had a big question on her mind. "What happened?" she lamented. "Something is wrong here. Sure, he gives to me, but he doesn't seem to be able to open up enough space to let me in. When you get right down to it, he really doesn't say much about himself or his feelings. It's as if there's no room in his private life—I'm on the outside looking in, knocking at that damned door. I get so frustrated. Sometimes I wonder if there's anyone home."

When I saw her again the following year, she wasn't living the same dream. "It took all this time for me to realize that I didn't really know him. I woke up and started realizing that something crucial was missing. I couldn't seem to get below the surface with him. I didn't know what he was about. I didn't know what his concerns or worries were. I didn't have any idea what his fears were. I kept telling myself that he would open up sometime soon—it would happen if only I could be patient. But I finally realized he was letting me in as much as he could, and the relationship had gone as far as it was ever going to go. I was sure fooled there for a long while."

The nurturer gets fooled as well. He or she probably thinks they are being intimate because they are such good caretakers. But the thing is, nurturing is not always a giving to give—it's often a giving to get. This is an (often unconscious) "conditional" giving—hoping you'll get something back from the other person.

And, too, nurturing can be a way of controlling the relationship, reminiscent of the parent/child dynamic. It's a way of fostering dependency—bolstering your validation of yourself via encouraging someone to rely on you. And if your childhood job description was "the caretaker," this is an important part of your identity, and any validation you can get is important to your self-esteem. Because intimacy involves risk-taking—allowing yourself to be open, vulnerable, and even exposed—it's a lot easier to nurture than to be intimate.

In *Intimate Strangers*, Lilllian Rubin points out another intriguing characteristic of nurturing. There are times when it can actually be used as a defense against intimacy, a cover that screens the fact that intimacy really doesn't exist. She sees nurturing as a way of gaining love, obscuring fears of abandonment, and ensuring safety and security. But it can also be used manipulatively—as a means for staying in control, encouraging dependency, and insuring against the pain of loneliness. And, if someone nurtures out of fear and insecurity, it can, in fact, create a barrier to intimacy.

It Takes Two to Distance

It's so easy to blame the other person for having "intimacy problems." If only your partner or the person you wish you could have a relationship with would just get it together and grow up everything would be great. But it's more complex than that. Have you ever considered that part of the problem may lie with you? "Not me," you say to yourself (or whoever will listen). "Never me." But read on.

> Nurturing can be a barrier to intimacy; it's often
> easier to nurture than to be intimate.

Here is how one woman expressed it the day it dawned on her that she may play a part in all of this. "During my years of marriage, I had a very vague sense that I might have some problems. I experienced it as discontent, but I could never get close enough to it to see that it was *my* intimacy issue. I thought it was a one-sided thing—he had the intimacy problems, not me. But then I got a spark of awareness and realized that it takes two to distance, and I must play a role in it, too. And I can see it replaying in my romantic relationships now as well."

You, too, may be having a spark of awareness about your own role in relationships. One thing you may be saying to yourself is that intimacy problems are not only about wanting intimacy, but also a *fear* of it. The very phrase, "fear of intimacy," can really send chills down your spine, can't it? One woman was amazed at her newfound clarity on the whole intimacy situation. "I finally understand what fear of intimacy looks and feels like for me, and how it must look to the people in relationships with me. Because I manage to find people who are more afraid of relationship than I am, it feels like they are creating the distance and I'm reaching out for them. I tend to see myself as desirable and always available—if only *they* were willing.

"I used to think it was a one-sided thing, that I was the victim. But now I realize that I, too, play a role in this drama. I can see how I participate. Because I'm always expecting to be pushed away, I push away first. Some of the things I do to push someone away might be subtle, but the fact is, I do them. I guess it takes two to distance. I haven't seen my part in this before because I always thought that the other person was the one with the problem.

"So now I ask myself, 'Why would I repeatedly put up with the frustration of trying to be in a relationship with a frightened deer? Why don't I just walk away?' I realize now that I stay because I am all too familiar with emotional distancing, and even emotional abandonment. I realize that I learned to relate to people this way when I was a baby. It is who I *am*, not just something I do. Maybe one reason I was in such denial is that having a fear of intimacy was sort of like emotional leprosy. No one wants to admit they have an illness with no cure. Now I can see that choosing unreachable lovers has kept me from having to face my fear of intimacy. I really want to know what I can or can't do to 'fix it.' Even if the best that can be achieved is awareness with conscious effort, it would at least be helpful to know that."

And it is this "awareness with conscious effort" that will be the most helpful to you as well. In the following chapters, we will be colorizing some of the blind spots that you may have. It's pretty hard to change something if you are not even aware of it. So by recognizing, identifying, and becoming an objective observer, you can put yourself in a position to make some choices about how you want to "be" in relationships. And for starters, one way to be is to be your own person.

Your Intimacy Style

How did you get to be the way you are, intimacy-wise? Where do your ideas and behaviors concerning closeness and distance come from? What were the models of intimacy in your family? Did you get to experience closeness, or was there mostly distance? What do you remember about your early experiences? How were they reinforced?

Many messages have been passed along from generation to generation—our lives have been greatly influenced by the joys and struggles of out ancestors. Grandma passed down more than just her china. She and Grandpa passed down lots of "family ways" of looking at life and relationships—attitudes, beliefs, rules, values, and expectations. Included here are attitudes toward secretiveness, openness, trust, and displays of affection.

But our notions of intimacy are bigger than family. We also "inherit" cultural and societal ideas about the intricacies of time and space. In chapters 3 and 9, we'll be taking an expanded look at how these factors can result in hurt feelings and misunderstandings, affecting intimacy.

But it is the day-to-day growing-up experiences in our families that color our ideas of intimacy the most. It was here that we learned about closeness and distance, privacy and personal boundaries, respect, touch (good and bad), comforting closeness, or stifling overcloseness. And if conditions were optimal, some of us had the opportunity to learn how to be our own people with our own ideas and sense of self. This ability to honor our own differentness is the core of differentiation. And, as you'll see in chapter 2, unless we differentiate in our families, we will have big trouble differentiating in our romantic relationships.

Feeling Connected but Not Infected— Separating from Your Family of Origin

Because differentiation is about developing and honoring your own uniqueness, whether or not you learned respect for individuality and personal space depends on your experience in your family when you were growing up. In some families, kids grow up having to conform to what other people wanted from them. There, most likely, was an overwhelming feeling of "we-ness," making it difficult to learn respect for who you are as an individual, distinct from other family members.

Just as it is necessary in the family of origin to balance a sense of connectedness with a sense of separateness, it is also necessary in adult relationships to balance these qualities to create a sense of intimacy.

> Differentiation is about developing
> and honoring your own uniqueness.

Many of our ideas about differentiation come from the work of Murray Bowen, known best for his theories on differentiation as it relates to our family of origin. He theorizes that differentiation of self is determined in our childhood by two primary factors: our parents' degree of differentiation from their own families of origin, and the emotional climate in which we grew up. He goes on to say that this level of differentiation is replicated in our choice of romantic partners.

Because the opposite of differentiation is emotional fusion, Bowen developed a "Level of Differentiation Scale" (1978), which measures how much we might be "fused" with and caught up in the emotional process of our parents and siblings. Can we think things through, rather than being overwhelmed by reactive feelings? This ability to separate thinking from feeling is related to the degree that we have differentiated from what Bowen calls the "undifferentiated family ego mass." This is a condition of "emotional stuck-togetherness," with blurred personal boundaries and intense emotional closeness. Family members experience each other's thoughts, feelings, dreams, or fantasies. The relationships between family members can cycle from comfortable closeness to anxious, uncomfortable overcloseness to hostile, mutual rejection. Because emotional fusion can lead to confusion, is it any wonder people grow up feeling confounded about closeness and distance?

> Emotional fusion leads to confusion.

Some of you may have experienced some form or other of this emotional fusion as you were growing up. Did members of your family ever slip in and out of each other's physical and emotional space by speaking for each other, feeling for each other, or thinking for each other? Perhaps the brother gets yelled at and the sister cries. Or the mom is devastated that her daughter didn't get asked to the prom. Or the dad is beside himself that his son struck out in the game. One man tells the story of how, when he was a little boy, his grandmother slipped and fell down the stairs, and he cried uncontrollably because he felt her pain.

Well, if you happened to get conditioned in an emotionally interlocked family, what can you do about it? What are some steps you can take toward differentiation? How can you stay centered? Bowen describes opposing life forces—some toward growth and autonomy and some toward dependency and emotional overcloseness. He sees the process of differentiating as achieving a balance between these forces. This means developing a strong enough sense of self and not negotiating it away for the sake of conforming to someone else's expectations or demands.

Differentiation is a developmental process that continues throughout your life. It involves emotional emancipation in adolescence (and thereafter), while at the same time maintaining emotional connectedness to the family of origin. Once you begin to define yourself and become aware of yourself as separate from your family, a sense of self-identity can develop. This paves the way for intimacy. According to developmental theorist Erik Erikson (1950) this is the task of adolescence.

But in order to get to this place, postulates Erikson, basic trust must be developed. Trust is interactive—it connects our inner experiences to our outer world—and it refers to both inner trust of ourselves and outer trust of others. This trust (or confidence) leads to development of autonomy, initiative, competence, self-identity, and finally, intimacy. However, if basic trust issues are not successfully negotiated, there may be an impoverished sense of identity, and pseudo-intimacy or isolation may take the place of intimacy.

The Importance of Being Adolescent

We can think of adolescence as a practice period for adulthood. When we develop intimacy with friends, we pave the way for successful adult interpersonal relationships. Adolescence is not only the time for the young adult to prepare to leave home, it is also the time for the parents to let go.

One woman recalls how her parents acted right before she left for college. "It was as if they were cramming all their parenting into those last few months. An analogy would be like cramming for a test; if you don't know it by now, you aren't gong to get *that* much more done in the last couple of hours." The conflict comes when parents want a last chance to be parents, and adolescents want a first chance to be grown-ups.

> Parents want a last chance to be parents, and adolescents want a first chance to be grown-ups.

All too often we deal with our anxiety about dealing with our families by cutting off relationships. Psychiatrist Michael Kerr (1981), summarizing Murray Bowen's theory about emotional cutoff, points out that many people deal with unresolved fusion in their families "by insulating themselves or cutting themselves off emotionally from the parental family." "Emotional cutoff is an interesting paradox" he declares. "At one and the same time it *reflects* a problem, *solves* a problem, and *creates* a problem. It reflects the underlying problem between the generations. It solves a problem in that, by avoiding emotional contact, it reduces the anxiety of the moment. It creates a problem in that it isolates and alienates people from each other, people who could *benefit* from contact with each other, if they could deal with each other better" (pp. 249–50).

And this is precisely the problem. Unless you are able to successfully separate from your family of origin, how can you become your own person as an adult? And how can you move on to make a connection to someone new? Wouldn't your relationship be inhibited? Unless you learned to define an "I" within a "we," you may have some confusion about whether you really exist separately and distinctly from other people, with different feelings and different needs.

2

How to Be Two Without Losing You

Respecting Differences in Intimate Relationships

In *My Mother/Myself* (1997), Nancy Friday points out that in order to leave home and grow up separate and self-reliant, someone had to love you enough to give you a "self" first and then let you go. The words "I love you" cannot have meaning unless there is an "I" to love "you."

This "I" includes the ability to maintain a clear sense of oneself, even when loved ones are pressuring us to think or feel the same way they do. This is differentiation—the ability to say, "I might be similar to my partner in some ways, but I'm different as well. I have separate ideas, thoughts, feelings, likes, and dislikes." We visited the idea of differentiation briefly in the preceding chapter, and we'll be examining it even more closely here.

"I not only need time by myself — I need time to *be* myself."

Differentiation is about developing and honoring your own uniqueness. The opposite meaning would be terms such as "undifferentiated," "fused," "enmeshed," and "codependent." As one man observed, "The more I am able to define myself, the more I know who I am and what I need in a relationship." In autonomous relationships, differentiation means valuing freedom, whereas in dependent relationship, differentiation action means fearing abandonment.

In *Passionate Marriage*, David Schnarch describes how well-differentiated people can agree and not feel they are losing themselves, and they can also disagree without feeling embittered or alienated. He points out that "the less differentiated you are, the more likely (and severely) your marriage will bog down and require a crisis—or a therapist—to blast through emotional log-jams" (p. 17).

One American Indian saying describes intimate relationships as "two stones that rub together and polish one another." And Schnarch agrees that this "polishing" process smooths the rough edges through the expected frictions of long-term relationships.

> Intimate relationships are like "two stones that rub together and polish one another."
> —American Indian saying

Here are a few more very useful Schnarch factoids that may help you understand differentiation more completely. Differentiation is:

- Being able to stand up for what you believe

- Calming yourself down by self-soothing, not letting your anxiety take over, and not overreacting

- Not acquiescing to someone who has tremendous significance in your life

- Recovering quickly from arguments and not holding grudges

- Having the ability to tolerate intense intimacy

- Maintaining your day-to-day priorities

As you can see, differentiating allows you to respect and accept yourself, honor your uniqueness, and learn to trust yourself. Honoring your own needs does not mean that you care less. In fact, by differentiating you are also honoring the relationship. You hear lots said about "commitment" in intimate relationships, but what about letting it be okay to make a commitment to *yourself* and to allow your partner to have the freedom to be him or herself as well. This autonomy is the best gift you can give each other.

One young woman recalls the feeling of exhilaration when she first realized it was okay to be separate from her partner. "When we first started running together, we'd try to keep up with each other. It wasn't always easy. Then, one day, we began at our own speeds. I didn't feel I was alone, because I could feel his spirit with me as I ran. I felt connected to him, even though we were running at our own paces and in our own spaces."

Honoring your own needs does not mean that you care less.

But it can be hard to allow that separateness sometimes. We have feelings about certain "sacred" areas of our relationships. One man became distraught when his wife said she was curious about Buddhism and wanted to take part in a two-day meditation retreat. He felt she was being unfaithful to their shared religion. He was hurt because her curiosity felt like a betrayal of a belief that he felt they shared. A similar situation happened with another couple when he decided to change his political affiliation. She was stunned and felt hurt that he was "leaving my party." It was something they had in common for many years.

One couple spent a whole lot of time together in the early days of their marriage. They'd go grocery shopping, gift buying, and errand running together. It was a definitely a lot of togetherness. You can imagine how shocked she was when he announced one day that he wanted to start going to the Laundromat by himself. She felt confused and hurt, telling herself that he must want to get away from her. Telling herself that he didn't love her anymore, she fretted about it for days, yet she didn't try to talk with him. It had been a big deal for him to even suggest the Laundromat idea to her in the first place, but he was feeling stifled and desperate to have some space to himself. He had wanted to say something for a couple of months, but didn't know how. So finally, he just blurted it out. He had no idea, of course, how hurt she was by his declaration. Isn't it sad that all of this energy swirled around for each of them, and neither could initiate a discussion with the other about their feelings?

This story sounds all too familiar to me. When I was young, naïve, and first married, it felt more secure to me if we did everything together. I thought that was what married people were supposed to do—if we *did* things together, that meant we were a *couple*. I guess I took it for granted that marriage meant a kind of amalgamation. I never dreamed that marriage might benefit from creating necessary space.

I imagine something like this went through my mind: "If you care about me, you'll keep me company while I go to the dry cleaners or the supermarket or the post office." Now I can see how that was way too much togetherness. We both needed more room in the relationship to be fully functioning individuals, with our own interests and our own time and space. I can look back and see that what we really needed to do was to differentiate. In fact, during the time we were married, my husband wrote a play entitled *Breathing Room*. Yep—it's a story about a family atmosphere that is stifling.

It's Hard to Breathe When You're Breathing the Same Air at the Same Time

Friends, clients, and workshop participants often speak of growing up in families where security means doing lots of things together. "I can be intimate with friends," says Sophie, "but it's difficult to be intimate in romantic relationships. I equate intimacy with too much togetherness, because that's what I saw happen with my parents. Their idea of marriage was to do *everything* together. In fact, my mom would say she couldn't possibly sit and read a book if my father was in another part of the house. So she'd hang around him while he did whatever he was doing and, usually, criticize him. Here were two people who thought they had to breathe the same air at the same time. No wonder the atmosphere was so stifling. There was never enough oxygen to go around because it was *used* air!"

Sometimes we move all the way across the country to get away from our family's stale air, but the distance in miles is no guarantee that we will be able to separate *emotionally* from them. The decision to move away does, in fact, put physical distance between us and them, but the emotional overinvolvement frequently remains.

For some of us, differentiating from our families of origin would lead us to feel disloyal to them, perhaps even guilty. So, our primary loyalties remains with our families—we are still overly connected and overly dependent. In fact, we may even feel guilty or disloyal if we begin incorporating our partner's ways of doing things—preparing certain meals or celebrating certain holidays. I know of one woman who was afraid to tell her parents that she had joined her husband in his custom of opening Christmas presents on Christmas Eve instead of Christmas morning. She felt guilty because she was doing things differently than her parents.

This primary loyalty has to shift from our family to our partner. Unless this shift happens, it's difficult to truly connect with a romantic partner, and it becomes hard to develop an important sense of "we-ness" regarding your relationship.

Sometimes, however, the adult child is able to "leave home" both physically and emotionally, but the parent cannot seem to let him or her go. So, in order to protect yourself and "have a life," you may choose to keep your activities, friends, and romantic partners a secret from your parents. This is not an easy situation to be in because it may elicit feelings of guilt. It's that loyalty thing again.

Cultural influences are so very important here. Certain ethnic groups expect the children to be independent and leave home, while others count on the adult children to stay nearby and be "oncall" to the needs of the family. The point is made in *Ethnicity and Family Therapy* (1996) by McGoldrick and Giordomo that Anglo American families "are likely to feel they've failed if their children *do not* move away from the family, whereas Italian families generally believe they've failed if their children *do* move away" (p. 18). In fact, for the latter, "separation from the family is not desired, expected or easily accepted" (p. 574). And the authors point out that in the Jewish culture "after marriage, connections and obligations to the extended family continue to be important"(p. 614). In fact, Jewish family connectedness is so powerful in many families that if there's a perceived breach of commitment, a tendency exists to cut off all communication with that "disloyal" person.

It's true that some cultures are more enmeshed than others, but separating can be difficult in any family—especially if over-closeness exists. One woman I know was still living at home when she was thirty years old. She had a good job and contributed each month half of her parents' mortgage. Yes, they could use the financial help, but they would have been able to manage on their own if she left. Her parents made all the rules, and they were strict ones, too. The daughter had no room to be an adult there, but she was afraid to leave. Why? "I'm afraid they'll get angry if I move out. They might even disown me." At the moment she said this, she seemed to notice the irony, and added, "But wait a minute. Now it's as if they own me, so I guess maybe it would be a good thing if they *dis*owned me!"

There were some "ownership" issues for Jonathan as well. He described a recent visit to his family in the Midwest. When he mentioned "going home" (back to California) to his mother, she objected, "What do you mean 'going home'? *This* is your home. Right here. This is where your family is, and don't you forget it." This mother was unable to let go, unable to let him be his own person and have his own life. He moved fifteen hundred miles away, but in her mind, he still had not left home.

Based on her comments, it's not surprising how Jonathan remembers his childhood: "I always felt like a pawn in a chess game. It was as if my mind was a battleground for other people. There was no room for me to be me." When we did some guided imagery together, he described the intricacies of the chessboard. This time, using his imagination, it was *he*, rather than his parents, who took charge of the moves: "I choose to be a castle in the corner. What a powerful piece I am! If I want to, I can even change places with the king. But I really don't want to be king, because then I might have to constantly be dealing with other people's demands. Or I might be besieged from all sides. So I'll remain a castle—an ivory castle. I really like being this valuable piece. I have a center! I feel alive inside. I am strong and independent. I have emotional strength. I have soul. I am my own person. And I'm finding my voice.

Finding Your Voice

"It's hard for me to speak up," says one man. "My voice becomes kind of musty and crusty, and sometimes I have to go looking for it. So I've been practicing doing some voice warm-up exercises."

Many of us have lost our voices somewhere along the way. Probably it happened while you were navigating the twists and turns along the rocky road of childhood. Perhaps you've misplaced your voice. Possibly it's down in the basement, or in the closet, or under the bed. Maybe it's hidden beneath the same rock as the front door key.

There are lots of reasons you might have lost your voice. Most likely, it wasn't okay to have a mind of your own or to ask questions. Perhaps you weren't allowed to object or say "no" to your parents. If you did, they took it personally and then took it out on you. Probably it wasn't okay to say you were hurt or upset or angry with someone. "Like it or lump it," they might say. "Too bad if you don't like it. Who do you think you are anyway?" There was no room for your small, young voice to speak up.

> There are lots of reasons you might have
> lost your voice. Most likely, it wasn't okay
> to have a mind of your own or to ask questions.

Maybe you lost your voice because you were scared to death of someone or something. Or, maybe you just didn't want to hurt someone's feelings. Perhaps you didn't want to rock the boat—it was safer to remain silent. And, even if you did speak up, no one would pay attention to you anyway. Maybe you lost your voice because you were protecting someone and the only way to do that was to become small and insignificant. This would allow the other person to be big and important.

"I had to entertain my mom," recalls Heather. "After school, we'd sit and do homework for two hours, until Dad got home. I knew I was keeping her company, and I also knew that this kept her from getting into the refrigerator. But I could only be company for her if I pretended to need her to help me with my homework. I had to remain on the ground with Mom and pretend to be mediocre, because if I were to spread my wings and fly, I would leave Mom behind. She would still be on the ground, and the distance between us would be too great. I guess you could say that loyalty to her kept my wings clipped. I wasn't allowed to soar and be myself."

Sometimes it's simply that you don't feel heard or seen. "I seem to choose partners who can't see me, and now I realize that when I was a child my mother couldn't see me either," says one man. "For example, when I would bring up something that upset me, she'd say, 'It's not important,' and I'd translate it as, 'I'm not important.' Or 'other things are more important.'"

A woman I know says, "When I don't feel heard, I shut down even more. I really go silent." As an adult, you might withdraw and lose your voice when something happens in a present relationship that reminds you of an experience in childhood. Penny's story below is a good illustration of this.

Penny was an accomplished artist who could express herself very well on canvas, but in personal relationships she often struggled with being heard. If asked to describe her needs, she often would say, "I don't know." Yet, when asked to describe how she went about placing paint on canvas, she was able to offer this vivid account.

"I start with a mark, a dot on the canvas. Then I use my whole hand and arm to expand it. Because gracefulness is important to me, I paint with a flow. Whatever mark I put down first, I expand into a beautiful design. I have trust and confidence when I start out—I know it's going to go somewhere. I feel I can handle any problems that come up. And if something starts to look a little crowded, there is almost always a way out. I know I can figure a way to balance it into the design.

"By starting out really small, I can get a sense of the bigger picture, of bigger commitment to the work. I can be working on one small area and experience the whole design. This way I can enjoy the creative process and not get overwhelmed by what I *think* the big goals should be.

"I like simple contours, but it's important that the shapes look 'alive.' Even an unpredictable pattern can lead the eye around and end up being balanced—especially the way colors interact with each other. I put a lot of life and light into my work. You know, it actually seems to speak to me, saying it needs this or that."

And can Penny speak up as well? Can she say she needs "this or that"? Can she find *her* voice and transfer the self-confidence she enjoys in her artwork to her relationship with her partner? Can she not get overwhelmed by the thought of commitment? Can she stay with the flow of the process?

In one-to-one sessions, she speaks very quietly but steadily. Her eye contact is good, and she has a certain determination about her. But an interesting thing happens when her partner joins her. She does, in fact, tend to disappear. Her voice seems to evaporate, and she diminishes right before our eyes.

She says she doesn't feel heard or seen by her partner, that she feels invisible. Her small, soft voice reflects this. "My mother could never see me either," she recalls." I always felt as if I didn't exist for her. It's as if she saw me as some kind of a small, insignificant speck."

Penny's perception of herself as a "speck" is interesting if you recall her earlier account of how she begins an art project. Do you remember how she described starting with a "dot" on the canvas and expanding it? Is it possible that her art process is her way of expanding that speck?

Many of us find ourselves constricting into a speck. If we don't think our words are important, no one else will. If we don't listen to ourselves, no one else will. Others see us as invisible because we make ourselves invisible.

Now You See Me, Now You Don't

Withdrawing happens in other ways as well. Disappointments and hurt feelings can cause some of us to "leave the scene," to evaporate. And it's bewildering to our partners.

Frank finds himself getting upset at his new girlfriend, and his reaction is lightning fast. When his feelings get hurt, he "disappears" from the scene before either of them knows what's happening. Usually it occurs when he has some expectation in mind of how the evening will go, and it doesn't turn out that way. When he gets disappointed, he suddenly turns silent.

"One evening we were both at a meeting, and I offered her a ride home. I guess I had in mind that we could take a walk together once we got there and maybe have some time to talk. When she declined my offer, I was just crestfallen. I could feel myself getting silent and going into some dark part of myself. Yes, I know the idea of the walk was only a fantasy plan. My distress really goes beyond logic. So why did I get so upset?"

We did some exploring about Frank's growing-up years. It turns out that when his mom would get upset with him, she'd clam up and withdraw. She was truly an expert at giving him the "silent treatment," withdrawing her love. And when that happened what did Frank do? He, too, would clam up and withdraw. And this is the same thing he does as an adult—especially if he thinks other people are withdrawing from him. "I do realize that sometimes people just need their own space. But when it feels like they're withdrawing from me, I freak out, because withdrawing means withdrawing love—just as my mother did."

This situation gets even more complicated. Something else happens when Frank starts to disappear. Either he doesn't say anything at all or he puffs himself up and speaks quite loudly, even becoming unrelenting and obstinate. He's fond of saying, "In order to stand up for myself, I have to take a stand." Of course, his blustery demeanor often causes other people to flinch and retreat even more. And round and round it goes.

Allowing Space for Needs and Needs for Space

In *Don't Take It Personally!*, I noted how needs are a fact of life, whether we acknowledge them or not. The truth is, we all have them—and it really is okay. The trouble is, many of us grew up thinking it was bad to have needs. If we tried to express a want or need, we might have been told something like, "You're selfish" or "You're more trouble than you're worth." When, as a kid, I heard things like that, I'd tell myself that my needs didn't count, that I was too worthless to have any needs. I might as well have disappeared along with my needs.

Sometimes we confuse having needs with being needy.

Maybe you, too, got the message that there was no time or space for *you* to have needs. That sure left a mighty big hole that wasn't getting filled. Perhaps you began to fill the hole with longing. And perhaps you began to confuse having needs with being needy.

But you didn't even have any idea about how to go about asking for what you yearned for. How could you find words for something you weren't supposed to have? "I always wanted my mother to stroke my forehead and tell me everything would be okay," remembers one woman. "And now, I'd love it if my boyfriend would stroke my forehead once in a while, but I don't know how to ask him. So, I cross my fingers and hope he catches my hints." It's as if she's gambling to get what she needs. And, when her partner almost inevitably fails to read her mind and come through, she feels as though she may as well disappear along with her needs. And if you are not really there, how can you stay connected with someone in an intimate way?

Let's face it. Crossing fingers instead of speaking up doesn't work the way we'd like it to. Unrealistic expectations result in a lot of empty space filled with disappointments (more about this in chapter 13). By finding words to express your needs, you don't have to depend on someone reading your mind. Then you don't have to be disappointed or feel rejected. Being direct saves you from putting so much energy into being manipulative. A straightforward request will usually get you a clear answer such as "Yes," "No," or "I can't do that for you, but this is what I can do," or "I have to say no this time, but try me again." Sure, there's always the chance you might feel rejected if someone does say the dreaded "No." But, if you ask *directly* and get a direct answer back, it's somehow easier to tolerate. And, as motivational speaker Patricia Fripp says, "The answer will always be 'no' if you don't ask."

Being assertive, standing your ground, being direct—these are all ways of finding your voice and making space for yourself and your needs.

Can You Be Visible to Yourself?

One of the most difficult things to notice about ourselves is when we begin neglecting our own needs because we are so preoccupied with doing things for other people. One woman I know is a great list maker of all the things she has to do every day. But, chances are, the items are for the benefit of her mother or her husband or her friends or her clients. What about making a list just for her? It could include things such as a massage, a manicure, a facial, or a haircut.

And from where does this need to take care of everyone come? Most likely from her childhood experiences, where she took on the role of "space filler" in her family. Like many of us, she took this responsibility when she realized that there were spaces that needed filling in her family and her parents weren't capable. Two upcoming chapters offer more information about this dynamic. Chapter 3 discusses the idea of the overfunctioner/underfunctioner dynamic, and chapter 5 describes the role that perfectionism plays as a space filler.

If you, too, tend to *do* for other people and ignore your own needs, you may find the following reminder helpful. Remember that little airline spiel the flight attendants say at the start of each flight? You know the one, about how to use the oxygen masks in the event of an emergency. It goes like this: "For those of you traveling with small children, secure your own mask first, and then assist the child." Wise words. If you can't breathe, you can't be much use to anyone else—no matter how dependent on you they might be!

Yes, it is important to take care of yourself. Being heard, finding your voice, expressing yourself, and taking a stand are all important ways to be your own person. And, as we've seen, this differentiation is a necessary step in connecting in an intimate way with others. However, let's make an important distinction here. Knowing yourself, and honoring your thoughts and feelings doesn't mean you have to get stuck in a "Me, Me, Me" way of thinking.

From Solo to Duet

It's crucial to take care of yourself and your needs in a relationship, but that doesn't mean you resort to simple self-centered thinking. For a relationship to work, it's important to make the shift in thinking from an individual framework to a couple's framework. In other words, to think *relationally*, instead of *individually*. Individual thinking is more of the "Me, Me, Me" variety—what I need, what's best for me, what makes me feel good, exclusively.

You may forget to consider how your ideas or behaviors affect your partner. In relational thinking, you are able to be open to hearing concerns of the other person and to be empathic, putting yourself in his or her shoes, trying to understand what it feels like for your partner.

In individual thinking, you expend lots of energy thinking defensively. And this energy stays stuck, because you expend so much of it putting up and maintaining barriers. However, thinking relationally opens up an energy flow from one to the other, allowing growth for both the relationship and for the individual.

It's important to make the shift from thinking in an individual framework to thinking in a couple's framework.

Here is an example of what it means to think relationally versus thinking individually: If I'm thinking relationally, I'm open to your feedback. If I'm thinking individually, I'm not open to your feedback, and I shut down, taking it as a personal affront, as criticism, or a judgment. Thinking relationally opens the door for intimacy—you *want* to make yourself known to the other person and you want him or her to open up to you as well. Can you see how there is a flow of energy here allowing each of you to touch something meaningful in the other? Whereas, if you think individually, you try to hide who you are and you remain essentially closed to the needs of the other person. And then what happens to the energy flow?

Here's another example. If you have a tendency to be sensitive to feeling manipulated or controlled by someone, you will tend to be more adamant about it if you are in an individual framework. You may insist, "You're always trying to control me—I'm not going to let you control me anymore!" Whereas, if you're able to make the shift to a couple's framework, you will be more inclined to ask, "What is in the best interest of the relationship and not just in my own best interest?" You won't tend to take it so personally and become over-reactive.

To think relationally, it's important to move outside of your own world and see things from your partner's perspective, trying to understand their experiences, feelings, and point of view. Imagine a series of concentric circles, more or less resembling a dartboard. The innermost circle is *you*, and the ever-expanding circles around you are your universe and the people in it. When we were young children, we saw ourselves as the centers of our worlds, where everything revolved around us. And, yes, there is a sense of "specialness." Hopefully, as we grow up, we learn to step out of that center. But some of us have a hard time leaving that place of specialness. This can become a hard place to be as an adult, because, in that center position, all eyes are on you. It's no wonder you may be prone to taking things personally. In that center space, it's easy to feel like a target—just waiting for the dart's sting.

Taking things personally keeps us within ourselves. But when we can move out of that center space and look around, we gain some awareness of our own feelings and experiences and can begin to see things as others see them. Once we can develop the ability to see things from others' perspectives, we can begin to step away and depersonalize their words and actions. If we can outgrow the idea that the world revolves around us, then we can begin to realize someone else's thoughts and feelings are not necessarily the same as ours. We then begin to think relationally.

With this ability to have perspective about the actions of others, we can also begin to develop the ability to put ourselves in other people's shoes. This is *empathy*—the ability to walk around in the shoes of someone else. But it's more than imagining how *you* might feel in the same situation. Tapping into your own reservoir of experience to examine how you might feel in a similar situation is a good start, but be aware that this is your feeling and not theirs. If you only go as far as to imagine what you would be feeling, you are still stuck inside your own shoes. Empathy means trying to imagine how the *other person* might be feeling.

By seeing things from the other person's perspective, you can begin to understand what their experience is of a situation. You can begin to see that their behavior is, most likely, not intentionally directed at you, nor is it meant to hurt you, shame or embarrass you, or reject you. If you take things personally, you take up a tremendous amount of space, time, and energy dealing with the hurt feelings and misunderstandings that come between you and your partner. Not to mention the resentments and anger that can undermine intimacy. You can see why empathy is so important in a romantic relationship.

But developing empathy is not easy for some of us because we tend to get caught in the center of that dartboard. By outgrowing the notion that we are the center of our universe and the world revolves around us, we can begin to realize that someone else's thoughts and feelings are not the same as our own. This realization allows us to distinguish what belongs to "me" from what belongs to "you."

Confusing "I" with "Thou"

When you get right down to it, confusion about personal boundaries causes big problems in relationships. Having good personal boundaries means being able to recognize how our personal space is unique and separate from the personal space of others. It means knowing where you stop and the other person begins—regarding feelings, thoughts, needs, and ideas. You'll find much more information about personal boundaries in chapter 4.

Where does this boundary confusion come from? Perhaps because, when we were children, we absorbed our parents' feelings, and we tend to do the same with our partners later in life. For example, you might find yourself getting angry for your partner, who "never gets angry." Or depressed for the mate who can't acknowledge his or her own depression. Or fearful for the lover who shows a brave face to the world.

This reciprocal borrowing and trading of feelings, needs, or thoughts is called "projection" and "projective identification," unconscious collaborative processes that Maggie Scarf describes in *Intimate Partners* as a psychological barter or "deal."

Projection is when you mistakenly imagine certain traits exist in the other person when you cannot acknowledge them in yourself. This is because they are emotionally unacceptable. In other words, features that you attribute to your partner are actually disowned parts of yourself. It's like moving your "stuff" into someone else's storage space—for safekeeping. And without even being aware you are doing it, you may elicit those traits from the other person, and he or she may accept the projection and act in accordance with it. This is *projective identification.*

Here's an example of how it works: Betty has never been able to acknowledge or express her sadness, saying, "I might get a little upset, but I never, ever get depressed." Howeever, Betty sees her partner Danny as a "real sad sack." This is projection, seeing her own disavowed characteristics in the other person. It's how Betty deals with her own, unacknowledged feelings of sadness—she somehow, without conscious awareness, encourages Danny to be depressed *for* her. This is projective identification. Betty gets to identify with the emotion, experience it vicariously, and doesn't have to feel any anxiety about the not-okay feeling—because she isn't taking any responsibility for it.

People deal with all kinds of unacknowledged feeling including anger, fears, insecurities, aggressiveness, independence, badness, vulnerablilities, competence, or dependency. Here is an example of how anger gets bartered in realationships. If your partner has a deep-seated conviction that getting angry is wrong, you may find yourself flying into a rage *for* them, as you unconsciously accept the projection they're throwing your way.

Because it is important to understand the process of projection, let's take a look at how certain traits come to be "unacceptable" and submerged. How do we learn to reject certain parts of ourselves? If certain traits are unwelcome to family or society, we learned to stuff them. Parts of our personalities stay hidden from us because we learned at an early age that they were not acceptable to others, and, therefore, they become unacceptable to us. When we were children, we began to notice how we brought on someone's displeasure by displaying certain emotions or behaviors. We said or did "bad" things that were rejected by others—so we submerged them.

Suppose a woman grows up in a family where there is an overt or covert rule against expressing anger, and she finds her own angry feelings unacceptable. She may say to herself and whoever will listen, "I never get angry." Because she disavows her own feelings, she may project them onto the partner, cueing or even provoking that person to act aggressively. While she's calmly berating him for his anger, she doesn't have to experience her own, because he's expressing her anger for her. The anger that she can't deal with in herself is "out there" courtesy of her partner, and she can deal with it vicariously. In a similar way, the "never sad" person sees his or her own depressed moods only in the partner—who unconsciously conforms to the projection and carries the sadness and despair for them both.

Projection can also take the form of blaming others for one's own limitations. One man grew up in a family where it was always someone else's fault and no one ever took responsibility for their own actions. Everyone blamed someone or something for everything. He finds himself blaming his partner for his own limitations, much to his partner's chagrin. But a closer look illuminates how the partner complies with the projection by acting irresponsibly and impulsively.

Cultural demands mean boys and girls learn to hide different things. Primarily, boys are encouraged to be "real men," to push down their feelings—especially those soft, vulnerable ones. Girls begin to lose their ability to speak up for themselves and develop a "Perfect Girl" façade—compliant, nice, and self-sacrificing. So, in order to get approval and not risk rejection, both boys and girls learn to hide "unacceptable" behavior, denying their authentic selves. The suppressed behavior might involve showing anger, sadness, independence, sensuality, curiosity, or talent.

This submergence is what Carl Jung called "the shadow"—the dark part, the part we don't want to know about ourselves, the part we wish wasn't there. And these shadow parts don't necessarily contain emotions or traits that are commonly seen as "negative." Your shadow part may be your anger or your sadness, but it could also be your tendency toward silliness, you loquaciousness, or your desire to lead. Anything that was considered unacceptable in the past may have, long ago, been hidden away. When we hide these parts from ourselves, we end up not feeling whole. It feels as if something is missing, and we go looking for it in a partner.

The Rocks in My Head Match the Holes in Your Head

If you feel there might be something missing in yourself, you may choose a partner who represents the very part you need. In other words, you want your partner to fill in that space, complete you, and make you "whole." This is an example of complementarity, the reciprocal "fitting together" described in the introduction. If you've had to hide your loose, foolish side, you may look for a partner who's all jokes. If you have trouble speaking your mind, you may be attracted to an opinionated mate. You *think* you see that quality in your partner because you *want* to see it, and, of course, it's often not really there—at least not in the way you need it to be.

You feel very close to that person, merging with him or her, hoping to absorb those attributes you so badly want for yourself. However, that feeling of closeness ebbs once you get up close and personal enough to realize that you are not getting the package you thought you had bought. Slowly, an awful thought begins to hit: "I am not getting what I need from my partner. I am not getting what I long for in this relationship." And what happens next? You start to feel hurt, disappointed, resentful, and angry. This is surely not conducive to intimacy.

Where Oh Where Did My Rosy-Colored Glasses Go?

The quality that looked so good in your partner at first is not at all what you thought it was. And traits that seemed charming at first soon turn into quirks or irritating mannerisms—and guess what? You often end up not being able to stand the very feature you sought out in your partner. When you realize this person is falling far short of meeting your needs, you probably feel let down and get angry. You may even think that your partner fooled you, but, in fact, you were just fooling yourself.

Often you choose a partner who represents the disowned part of yourself, the part you can't acknowledge. One common dance that gets played out in this manner is, "I'll be your conscience, if you act out my impulses." For example, if you are someone who acts restrained because your spontaneity somehow got squelched, you may choose a partner who seems spontaneous and unfettered. It's appealing at first, but soon that spontaneity shows itself to be impulsiveness or even recklessness. It's not long before you find the "appealing" characteristic annoying or even offensive.

You may find yourself attracted to a seemingly quiet, grounded person and all too soon recognize he or she can be rather solitary and unsociable; or the strong silent type is, in fact, withholding and uncommunicative. Or perhaps you're drawn to someone who seems confident and "in charge of things," only to realize that he or she has a big need to control things—including you. Can you be open to the possibility that reality may be different from what you perceive it to be?

Let's look again at those rejected parts residing in the shadows of your being. Sometimes these parts hide out because you cannot tolerate them for one reason or another. As mentioned earlier, it's often because you came to see them as unacceptable to family or society.

These "blind spots" can really affect your relationships with other people. The traits you cannot tolerate in others are often your own unacceptable characteristics—the things you can't stand about yourself. These traits might include your sadness, your anger, your tendency to be manipulative or flirtatious or competitive or controlling. Or you might notice that the other person is a tease, seems angry, makes promises they don't keep, is late for appointments, is controlling, or is competitive. Might these be *your* own characteristics?

> The traits you cannot tolerate in others
> are often your own unacceptable characteristics.

Maggie Scarf notes the relationship begins to look different when one of the partners "has had the experience of *taking back a projection*—accepting that, for example, the craziness, hostility, incompetence, depression, anxiety, etc., that is being perceived in the partner may be emanating from the self. And for changes to start occurring in the relationship one partner refuses *to accept a projection*—to behave crazily, angrily, become depressed or the like . . ." (p. 173).

Scarf goes on to say that "each member of the couple must reown and take responsibility for those aspects of his or her internal world that are being put onto the partner. This means learning to experience ambivalence . . . seeing both one's goodness and one's badness, one's craziness and one's saneness, one's adequacy and inadequacy, one's depression and one's happy feelings, etc., as aspects of internal experience rather than *splitting off* one side of any of these dichotomies and being able to perceive it only as it exists in the mate" (p. 200).

What about you? What might *your* shadow side be? Where does it come from and why did you have a need to hide it away? Are you able to identify it in yourself or do you deal with it through spotting it in other people? It's pretty difficult to change something in yourself if it's a blind spot and you can't see it.

Recognizing these disavowed parts and owning your shadow side as well as your more desirable features is an important part along the road of getting to know yourself—and acquiring the capacity for intimacy. By getting to know yourself, you can identify and do something about your needs for closeness and distance and not have to be constantly refereeing that internal conflict.

Let's take a look at one of the most powerful internal conflicts we experience—a need for closeness and the fear of it.

3

Go Away a Little Closer

A Need for Closeness and the Fear of It

You probably know the feeling all too well. Someone gets too close, too demanding, too controlling, and the battle starts for more space—pushing, pulling, and tugging. But it never seems to be enough. There is either too little or too much space. Each of us has some sort of conflict between needs for closeness and needs for distance, but in most relationships the need for closeness is primarily carried by one person and the need for distance by the other. It's this conflict about too much or too little personal space that causes so many relationship problems.

"I Need My Space"

Most of us have a need for more personal space in relationships from time to time. You may start to get close, then find yourself needing to pull back. There may be times when your need for personal space can be overwhelming—you may find the closeness stifling, even suffocating. You try to take some space for yourself. Sometimes desperately. Sometimes shockingly. Sometimes disrespectfully. Sometimes suddenly. Poof, you're gone. You have a powerful need to leave the scene, and the "leaving" can be either emotional or physical.

Sometimes a partner's openness and expression of feelings can increase your level of anxiety, and you have to make some move to push or pull away. Sometimes it's just not possible to tolerate that much closeness. And the moving away takes place so fast that the other person doesn't even know what occurred. Hey, maybe you don't know either. "What happened here?" you might ask. "How did there get to be *this* much space between us?"

If you sense someone is beginning to distance, do you find yourself holding your breath for fear he or she will leave? This reaction is based on whatever your history with sudden leavings may be— especially if the good-byes were nonexistent or insufficient. Moving from place to place, illnesses, separations, and deaths all activate fear of abandonment, and you'll find yourself reacting to all the times you have felt abandoned in the past. The person at the receiving end of these overreactions usually doesn't have a clue as to why you felt so hurt. The story of Janice and Tom shows how easily this can happen.

> If you sense someone is beginning to distance, do you find yourself holding your breath for fear he or she will leave?

"I was just devastated the first time we made love and Tom got out of my bed, started putting his clothes on, and said he wanted to go home. I felt so hurt. And this routine continued for a while. He always had some excuse not to stay the night. He had to feed the dog, or he didn't have his contact lens solution, or he had an early appointment."

"I did make excuses," remembered Tom. "I guess the closer I felt toward Janice, the more my anxiety got the better of me, and the idea of my own bed seemed a lot safer. But we did work it out, and now I stay."

And what happened that Tom could allow himself to stay through the night? "I knew it was important to Janice and this relationship is important to me. Simple as that!"

Tom's relationship with Janice was important to him, and he took the time to rethink his priorities. However, dealing with personal space issues without getting feelings hurt isn't always so easy, as you'll see in this story about Sharon and Erica.

When Sharon called Erica asking to come over to her apartment, Erica found herself agreeing, but when Sharon was on her way over, Erica began to have second thoughts. In fact, when they were on the phone, had Erica taken the time to check in with her true needs, she might have known that having company didn't really feel like the right thing for her to do that evening. What she really wanted was to curl up in front of a blazing fire and read her new book.

This was another instance of Erica being a little too quick to take care of Sharon's needs and neglect her own. However, when Sharon arrived, Erica decided to tell her that what she really wanted to do was read her book. It would be perfectly okay for Sharon to hang out with her, sharing space, but she really didn't feel like interacting just then.

Sharon was stunned. "Hanging out" wasn't exactly what she had in mind. She had, in fact, imagined a romantic scenario, and Erica had just squelched it! She felt so hurt, so disappointed—it was almost as if Erica was telling Sharon that she didn't care about her and wanted to end the relationship. In fact, she might as well have said that very thing, because this is what Sharon heard.

But Erica was just trying to be true to her own feelings and needs. And it's not hard to see how Sharon's drive over to her house had been fueled by sexual fantasy. Most of us would have big-time disappointment in this situation. However, Sharon's reaction to this disappointment was way out of proportion to the situation. She "heard" Erica's need to take care of herself as a message of rejection.

Most likely, this message was left over from Sharon's childhood days, when her mother was so absorbed in her own interests. Whenever Sharon would try to talk to her or show her something, Mom would say, "I'm too busy." Young Sharon took this to mean, "I'm too busy for you," and felt her mother didn't love her. And when Erica said she wanted to read, Sharon felt as if Erica was choosing her book over her. It felt familiar. It felt like rejection. And it didn't feel good.

What would help Sharon to deal with this type of situation when it arises again? She thought for a while, then turned to Erica. "Just say the words, 'This is not about you, Sharon. It's about needing some time to myself.' That will remind me that I don't have to get my feelings hurt. That it's not about me—it's about *your* needs for some space at that moment."

As you can see from these stories, if we do allow ourselves to get close to someone, it may bring up old fears about getting hurt. This chain reaction can bring up tremendous amounts of anxiety. You may have learned to avoid the anxiety by creating distance. Picking fights, blaming, screaming, and slamming doors are all ways of pushing someone away. Or, you may retreat to another room, leave the house, or withdraw by freezing out the other person. Instead of expressing our feelings to the other person, we act them out through these distancing behaviors

We seem to desperately need to create comfortable space. And some of us have especially passionate feelings about certain kinds of space. Here is an illustration of the "sacredness" of the space we call "home."

"My Home Is the Centerpiece of My Life"

"House" or "home" is understood to be a metaphor for the soul. I often use the house as the focal point for the imagery I do in hypnosis. Walking through the house, furnishing the house, decorating the house, taking the stairs up to the attic or down to the basement or into the garden. The images can be rich and enlightening.

However, one man balked in the middle of our guided imagery when I suggested we team up to do some "interior decorating." "Sorry. I don't let anyone into my home," he insisted. Not even pretend. Not even you.

"To let someone into my home would be like letting people see who I really am, so I lean hard against the door to protect my private space. I remember when I was a little boy; I'd never play in the middle of the room. I always played behind a chair. It felt safer that way. I guess I'm still 'playing behind a chair.' In fact, if I ever find myself going out and buying furnishings and hanging things on my walls, I'll know I'm ready to be in a serious relationship."

Another man explains how difficult it is for him to invite the women he dates over to his house. "I'm a very private person," he says. "This is my private space. My house is the centerpiece of my life." At the same time, he finds he has difficulty staying the night at his lover's house. "It's true that I can nest wherever I am, but I much prefer my own space. Women have a hard time understanding why I like to spend so much time alone at home, puttering around. Sometimes they even take offense, thinking I am excluding them on purpose, but I'm not."

Protecting our privacy and our "turf" are ways in which we try to make sure we have a comfortable amount of space around us. But as you can see, "enough" space for one person is often way too much for another. How much closeness is enough? Not enough? Too much? Let's take a closer look at what "comfortable" space signifies.

Looking at Space from Every Which Way

People like to keep certain "safe" distances between themselves and other people or things. This invisible bubble of space constitutes each person's "territory." In *The Hidden Dimension* (1982), anthropologist Edward T. Hall makes some fascinating observations about ways in which both people and animals have worked out spatial dilemmas, especially around "turf."

"Let's Talk to the Animals"

An animal's territory is not only identified by a particular plot of ground, but also by a series of "bubbles" that maintain proper spacing between each animal, says Hall. If a person or other potential enemy approaches a wild animal within a given distance, the animal will flee. This is called "flight distance." A narrow zone exists that separates fight distance from "attack distance." We can see this clearly when the lion tamer steps toward the lion, and the lion begins to attack. When the lion tamer quickly steps away, out of the critical zone, the lion retreats.

Hall also points out another use of space in the animal world: some species huddle together, requiring physical contact, and others completely avoid touching. Cats, of course, are in the second group—and quite a few humans, for that matter! In the noncontact group, there are two important distances to note. "Personal distance" is the normal spacing maintained between individuals. "Social distance" refers to the need that social animals have to stay in contact with each other. But, according to Hall, it also refers to a psychological distance: the anxiety that arises when an individual exceeds the limits of safe distance and loses contact with the group. Hall suggests we think of it as a hidden band that *contains* the group.

People, too, tend to defend our own "turf" and also seem to employ invisible protective bubbles of space around ourselves to maintain distance. Hall notes that, because humans are self-domesticated, flight distance and critical distance have been more or less eliminated from our reactions.

"Not in *my* experience," you may be saying. "I can flee pretty quickly!" But Hall is quick to add that the flight reaction is resurrected if humans become fearful of each other, sometimes creating an explosive need for space. He describes how we are able to sense people as being close or distant, but we cannot always put a finger on which it is. The sensation of closeness can come from the radiation of warmth from another person, being spoken to in a whisper, or the smell of freshly washed hair. Or, your experience of closeness or distance might be from someone's tone of voice or loudness of voice. Their body language can say a lot, too—you could perceive it as the language of acceptance or of rejection.

Types of Distance

Humans create four types of distance, according to Hall: intimate, personal, social, and public. Each has a close and far phase.

Intimate distance consists of stepped-up sensory input, and its close phase includes lovemaking, comforting, and protecting. An example of its far phase would be a "get out of my face" situation.

Personal distance comprises a small, protective bubble separating people. Its close phase is from one-and-a half to two-and-a-half feet. Its far phase would be up to four feet. In other words, keeping someone at "arm's length."

Social distance involves situations where no one expects to touch each other unless a special effort is made. Its close phase, which is from four to seven feet, indicates impersonal business or a casual social gathering. Its far phase, which is up to twelve feet, signifies more formal types of business and social gatherings.

Public distance is well outside the circle of involvement, its close phase being from twelve to twenty-five feet, and its far phase being more than twenty-five feet.

Kinds of Space

According to Hall, there are many ways people experience space that affect our relationships. Our sense of space is a synthesis of these sensory inputs: visual/auditory, olfactory, thermal, tactile, and kinesthetic.

Visual/Auditory

There is a huge difference in the amount of information that can be processed by the ears vs. the eyes. According to Hall, the ears are not nearly as useful as the eyes—the eyes may be up to a thousand times as effective as the ears in gathering information.

Not only do the eyes *gather* information, but they convey information as well. Eyes can show love, caring, encouragement, and anticipation. But you know the power of "that look" as well. You know the one I mean—the raised eyebrow, furrowed brow, or narrowed eyes, signifying some kind of rejection. It could mean disappointment, impatience, indifference, judgment, criticism, disrespect, or a punishing "Look out, I'm angry.

We synthesize experience—we learn while we see, and what we learn influences what we see. But because we tend to fill in the details, it's important to recognize that perception is not always reality.

Space perception is not only about what can be perceived, but also about what can be screened out. Sometimes this is cultural. From early childhood men and women of different cultures live in different perceptual worlds and learn to orient themselves in space in different ways. They learn to screen out certain types of information while paying close attention to others.

It's also interesting to note that different cultures even have different ways of dealing with sound. For example, the Germans and Dutch use thick walls and double doors to screen out sound, while the Japanese are comfortable with paper walls and sliding doors. Talk about "heavy duty" vs. "light weight" considerations. There is much more information about culture styles in chapter 9.

Olfactory Space

As a method of communication, odor is one of the earliest and most basic. It is referred to as the "chemical sense," and is a powerful chemical message system for both animals and humans. However, according to Hall, the use of the olfactory apparatus by Americans is underdeveloped. Our use of deodorants and our general need to suppress odors results in blandness and sameness, depriving us of variety in our lives, obscuring memories.

Have you ever had the experience of walking into a new situation and smelling a scent that reminds you of childhood? It might be a comforting, cozy sort of smell, or it might be a smell that recalls apprehension or fear. But the memories suddenly come flooding back. The one that never fails to work for me is the smell of french vanilla. It conjures up memories of the Good Humor Man.

Thermal Space

By means of changes in skin temperature, we send and receive radiant heat messages about our emotional states. Perhaps you've experienced that flush of anger or blush of embarrassment, a "slow burn," sweating palms, or a "cold sweat." Or you may have heard expressions such as "hot under the collar," "a cold stare," "a heated argument," or "he warmed up to me."

And that heat can surely sizzle! Once I was waiting for my number to be called at the supermarket deli counter, and I sensed an undeniable "heat" near me. How could I ignore that kind of energy? What else was there to do but turn and say "hi" to him, and a space opened for a friendship to develop.

Tactile Space

"Touch is the most personally experienced of all sensations," says Hall. "For many people, life's most intimate moments are associated with the changing textures of the skin. The hardened armorlike resistance to the unwanted touch, or the exciting, ever-changing textures of the skin during lovemaking and the velvet quality of satisfaction afterward are messages of one body to another that have universal meanings" (p. 62).

Kinesthetic Space

This is body motion as a communicative process. Kinesthetic space addresses the language of body sensations and energy through the reading of body language—both our own and that of other people. You'll learn more about kinesthetic space in chapter 6.

Pheromones

Pheromones are airborne chemicals, and although they have no detectable odor, they act on the brain and have either a behavioral or hormonal effect on whoever perceives them. Many animals and insects use pheromones to communicate with each other about food, territory, and sex, and it is also believed that they have a role in human communication as well.

Some researchers describe the effects pheromones can have on interactions between strangers in big cities. In fact, a woman I know gleefully recalls walking down a busy Manhattan street wearing a pheromone-based perfume, and it elevated her mood so much that many people smiled at her. In New York City!

We Live in Two Different Worlds

Hall coins the word "proxemics" to describe the study of people's use of space as a cultural artifact, organizing system, and communication system. He goes on to say, ". . . people from different cultures not only speak different languages, but what is possibly more important, inhabit different sensory worlds" (p. 2). He describes a filtering system that admits some things while filtering out others, resulting in different perceived experiences from one culture to another.

"The Rhythm Method"

As we look at space issues, we note that time issues are often very connected. They, too, are influenced by different cultures. Because the Hopi nation considers time and space so inextricably bound up in each other, there is no equivalent for the English language word "time" in Hopi, according to Hall.

Because space and time are so bound up, let's make a detour here into the realms of time and its accompanying rhythms. These rhythms affect our *style* of relating, as you'll see in chapter 9. Edward Hall, in *The Dance of Life* (1983), describes how rhythm is the essence of time. "People are tied together and yet isolated from each other by invisible threads of rhythm and hidden walls of time" (p. 3).

"People are tied together and yet isolated
from each other by invisible threads of
rhythm and hidden walls of time."
—Edward T. Hall, in
The Dance of Life

In order to avoid misunderstandings between cultures, Hall says it's important to learn the language of time as well as the spoken language. And because each culture has its own time frames and unique patterns, it may necessitate reorganizing our thinking.

Complex societies organize time in two basic ways, Hall says. The Northern European cultures, including Americans, tend to schedule events as separate items—one thing at a time. This he terms "monochronic time." The Mediterranean cultures tend to schedule several things at once. You could say it is a form of "multitasking." Hall's term for this is "polychronic time."

Monochronic time is oriented to tasks, schedules, and procedures. It is much more compartmentalized than polychronic time. Rather than adhering to preset schedules, polychronic time stresses involvement of people and completion of transactions. Because appointments are not taken as seriously, they are frequently broken. Polychronic time is oriented to people, human relationships, and the family. Nothing is solid or firm—especially plans for the future. In addition, time is more circular than linear—you can always catch something the next time around. Neither pattern is right or wrong, only different.

Hall likens these two styles to oil and water—they don't mix. And as you can imagine, these time-style differences can cause hurt feelings and misunderstandings in relationships. "Loose time" folks and "specific time" folks can easily have some misunderstandings.

Monochronic	Polychronic
• One thing at a time	• Many things at once
• Good at scheduling appointments	• Frequently broken appointments
• Adherence to preset and schedules	• Involvement of people completion of transactions

Over time, cultures evolve their own rhythms. Geographical areas and even towns develop their own rhythms as well. Hall describes how we synchronize when we become engaged in each other's rhythms. This synchronicity is the dance of life. However, sometimes two people have such different rhythms that they "miss" each other. There is a clash of personalities or cultures leading to misunderstandings

Did Something Get Lost in the Translation?

There's a cartoon I like a lot where one bird is perched in a livingroom chair, looking down at a bird on the floor, saying, "It would never work out, Randy . . . we're not of a feather." Too often, however, we enter into relationships in which we're just not "of a feather"—where cultural time and space differences cause misunderstandings and inhibit feelings of closeness. Can we give each other the space to have our own rhythm? As you can see from Linda and Lloyd's story below, we often don't.

Linda and Lloyd have repeatedly encountered certain "oil and water" problems in their relationship. Linda comes from a Mediterranean background, and Lloyd's family is English. Theirs is a great example of polychronic and monochronic clashes.

A particular sore point for Lloyd is Linda's relationship with her mother. An unspoken rule of her culture is "if you value people, you cannot cut them off because of a schedule." Linda was frequently late because her mother would call up, wanting some attention or advice. Even though Mom knows Linda has plans to go out for the evening, she still expects Linda to rearrange her evening plans at the last minute and find time to listen to her problems. Linda occasionally tries to set boundaries by saying, "Mom, I'll be happy to talk with you tomorrow, but not now—I have to leave the house in a few minutes." Her mom takes this as a signal that Linda doesn't care enough about her. She feels slighted and takes it personally.

Another example of this style difference has to do with being "on time." As you might imagine, this concept of "on time" has different meanings in different cultures. And it plays havoc in the relationship between Linda and Lloyd. Here is a typical example: Linda and Lloyd made plans to go to dinner for the evening, and the agreed-upon plan was to leave the house at 6:45. He was ready and waiting, but when 7:15 rolled around, no Linda. She finally arrived at 7:30 and matter-of-factly told him that she was finishing errands. But what's the big deal—she was there, wasn't she? Why was he so upset? Why? Because once again, Lloyd felt very secondary to

Linda's other priorities. Every time it happens, it feels like a rejection—disrespect and invalidation. He describes it as "being four years old again, with a child's perception of time and the minutes seeming like hours."

Can we give each other the space
to have our own rhythm?

Keeping both time and space considerations in mind, let's look at some of the common relationship patterns that cause misunderstandings and hurt feelings.

Rejection/Intrusion

Gus Napier coined the phrase "rejection/intrusion" in 1978 to describe a common dynamic of couples. It goes like this: One partner (let's say #1), has experienced childhood rejection or abandonment and the other partner (#2) has experienced intrusion in his or her early years. So #1 wants closeness and reassurance: "I wish we could go out to dinner together more often," and #2 wants separateness, independence, and to be left alone: "You make too many demands—you're smothering me!"

Because #1 seeks "oneness" in the relationship, a primary goal may be to feel emotionally fused, emphasizing "we" and "our" experiences. But too much togetherness is threatening to #2, who strives for personal freedom and autonomy.

It's astounding how well their present relationship has become a repeat of their childhood experiences, longings, and disappointments. And, as Napier points out, each one's childhood experience seems to invariably provoke an overreaction to the partner's personality traits. As #2 feels stifled, imprisoned, and wants to flee, #1 again feels loss of support, rejection, and abandonment. #1 clings tightly to #2, who becomes more anxious and retreats even further. And guess what? #1 becomes more desperate, grasps even more, and when #2 fails to meet expectations, can become very depressed as well. You may notice how each reaction causes a stronger counterreaction in the partner.

Interestingly enough, #1 may have hooked up with #2 because of his or her *own* unacknowledged fears of intimacy. Surely #2's withdrawal allows for maintaining a safe distance. But resentments grow, along with hurt feelings and misunderstandings. Keep this rejection/

intrusion dynamic in mind as you read the following descriptions of the types of processes that get played out in relationships concerning time and space issues.

Engulfment/Abandonment

It's painfully simple. Engulfment is when one person fears being swallowed up by the other person's needs. Abandonment is when the other person fears the partner will leave and there will be a terrible void. This dual fear looms larger than life and surely can get you into relationship trouble. The anxiety that results is enormous, of course, but when you're in the middle of it, you don't always know why you're feeling so anxious.

The truth be known, many of us really do want to feel close to someone, to have our innermost essence join with that of another person. We hold out hope that this intimacy can happen. Or, at least we tell ourselves we do. But when you start feeling those tender feelings—depending on someone for companionship, advice, emotional support, reliability, errands, back rubs, or great sex—you might find yourself pulling away. In fact, you might find yourself affecting an "I don't need you" attitude.

What's happening here? One reason you pull back may be because you learned to "tough it out" as a child, developing a stance of, "I don't need anyone for anything!" When you think of yourself as so self-sufficient, you actually become defensively independent—defending against being *dependent*. You may become isolated or withdrawn or adapt a self-protective, compulsively self-reliant stance. You may even go so far as to disclaim a desire for close relationships. Yes, it's true—out of fear of repeated rejection, we become afraid to risk intimacy with another person.

This "I don't need you" stance can develop into an "I'm going to leave you before you can leave me" attitude. On some deep, dark, probably unconscious level, many of us are so afraid of being rejected or abandoned that we just won't let ourselves stay around long enough to find out if it's going to happen. The imagined pain is just too great.

> Out of fear of repeated rejection we become
> afraid to risk intimacy with another person.

So you may find yourself pulling back, fearing that if you depend on someone too much, they might leave you. And then you would feel all alone. And the scary, primitive fear here is: "If I'm left all alone, I could die."

"Oh, I've never *really* had a thought like that," you might say. "That's so, well, *archaic*." Okay, maybe it's never been a conscious, *tangible* fear. Maybe it was more like a twinge somewhere—in your throat. Or your chest. Or the small of your back. Can you give yourself room to consider the possibility? Sure, it's a primitive fear, but those are the ones we can't always put words to. And because we are unaware of them, they are the ones that hold the most influence on our lives.

This fear of dying is connected both to the fear of being abandoned and the fear of losing our identities. Where do these fears come from? As children, we depend on our caregivers for care and are inherently trusting, until something happens to break that trust. Lying alone in a crib, hungry or wet, can seem like an eternity to an infant with no sense of real time. That child might feel vulnerable to the parent's whim—will the parent *ever* return and give comfort? At times, it may seem like they'll never come back.

You may start worrying about being left, and you may come to fear the rejection of abandonment. At other times, you might become afraid your caregivers would overwhelm you with closeness, smothering out the spark of your identity—essentially, another rejection. When you are this young, you can't offer yourself an alternative explanation, so you're stuck with these primitive fears of abandonment and intrusion.

How does this happen? Parents may not encourage or allow us to show independence, creativity, assertiveness, or a sense of our own personhood. When parts of you were denied, you may have gotten the message that, without your own identity, you could easily be subsumed. Or, perhaps you concluded that showing these unacceptable parts would result in your being abandoned. These dual rejection fears— abandonment and intrusion—often accompany us throughout life, causing no end of big trouble in how much "closeness" two people can tolerate. The experience of Willa and Lou demonstrates this.

"He gets into his fears, I get into my fears. Then we start pushing each other away and feeling absolutely rotten about it." Willa described what happens when she and Lou start feeling too close. "Especially after we make love. We seem to need to scurry apart and make some distance.

Lou chimed in, "She's on her side of the island, and I'm on mine. It's awful how much distance we seem to need to create."

Willa adds, "What works for us, if we can do it, is 'getting back in touch.' And actual physical touch is the best. A hug works wonders."

Why do Willa and Lou think they need to create so much space after sexual intimacy? He was the first to answer. "I get scared. I think I'm going to get lost in the sexual power she seems to hold over me. I fear I'm going to get swallowed up."

Willa adds, " Me too. Same fear. The sex is so powerful that I sometimes think I can't catch my breath and I might get lost in it all." This fear of merging is common to many couples. The sensation of merging feels good and bad at the same time. Good is the feeling of "oneness." Bad is the fear of engulfment.

Merging during sexual passion adds an important component to the equation. Sex is often a merging of two energy forces, and the intensity of this merger is often hard to handle. In the following chapter you'll find more discussion of sex and boundaries.

Demand/Withdraw

There are a couple of ways this dynamic can play out, and, most likely, you'll recognize some form of it. One way it manifests is when something is on your mind and you finally take a deep breath and speak your piece so you can try to work things out. And we all know it isn't easy to get up that courage to ask for what you need, to lay out what you long for. But what a great feeling it is when you collect enough courage to make that effort to get your needs met—and you might even (deservedly) be feeling proud of yourself. But, unfortunately and disappointingly, you may find that asserting yourself this way doesn't always get the results you want.

Your requests may be heard as demands and the other person feels threatened, perceiving them as "nagging." They may feel that your "neediness" is impinging on their personal space, or that you want more time and attention than they can comfortably give to you. Perhaps you want to go to movies, or jazz clubs, or expensive dinners, and they don't enjoy a steady diet of these activities. As a result of these differences, this person begins to wonder what kind of a standard you have developed in your mind about what a "couple" is supposed to be. And, before you know it, he or she begins to withdraw from you, pulling back in self-protection. Somewhere it must be written in stone: "The more you ask from them, the faster they turn and run." Margie and Frank's story below is a good example.

Margie wanted Frank to meet her friends, so she invited him to several get-togethers. But he could only be vague about whether or not he would go, offering only vague answers. "Maybe," was all he would say. What she wanted was a firm reply, but if she pressured him, he really dug his heels in, refusing to go at all. Her feelings were hurt, and then he got angry when she began to withdraw from him.

Of course, she was feeling that he was withdrawing from *her* by refusing to do "couples" kinds of things.

"Is that why you 'disappeared' for several days and wouldn't return my phone calls?" she asked.

"Yes," he acknowledged. "You were making too many demands."

Margie was incredulous. "I only wanted to show you off to my friends because I think you're really special. I had no idea you saw it as making demands."

Once he called her a "social butterfly." That sure complicated matters. "You know, it really hurts my feelings that you think I flit around all over the place," she said to him.

"Margie, I had no idea that comment upset you," he responded. "I really didn't mean it the way it sounded. I didn't mean to hurt your feelings. I only meant to say you are much more of a 'social being' than I am."

She looked relieved. "I didn't know until today that you didn't mean it the way I interpreted it."

They agreed from then on that she would tell him when it was important to her that he accompany her to an event. In fact, she could rate the order of social events in her head and ask him only to the most important ones. He would say "yes" to some things and "no" to others. And he made it clear that the times he said "no" didn't mean he didn't care about her.

There would be times when she felt she could only go to a "couples only" kind of event if he would agree to accompany her. "Why even be in a relationship if you have to keep going alone to social things?" she asked. She asked him if he could give those requests special consideration. He agreed that he would, but he didn't want to feel pushed or obligated to go.

Luckily this exchange happened during a couple's session. I was able to offer an option that neither Margie nor Frank had considered. Why not take two cars to certain social events to give each of them some flexibility? That way the person who wants to leave after a short time can return home and the person who wants to stay longer can. In situations like this, where the social needs of one person are quite different from the personal space needs of the other partner, there are ways to work things out without being poles apart—without blame, guilt, or hard feelings.

Just knowing he had the option of leaving was important to Frank—it gave him the "out" he seemed to need without his having to actually disappear in order to avoid the anxiety that the situation brought. As you can see, when Frank felt pressured or manipulated by Margie, resentment took over. It was as if someone pressed the "get obstinate" button.

What else can we learn from Margie and Frank's story? Because it's often difficult to ask directly for what we want, when we actually get up the nerve, it can sound a little too much like a demand. By respectfully framing your request as being important to *you*, it takes the emphasis off of your partner as being a "bad person." This couple's story also points up the importance of options—especially if someone tends to perceive requests as demands. And, too, it's helpful to remind yourself that avoiding a situation, withdrawing, and running away are ways many people deal with anxiety. Hopefully, you won't feel so hurt if you repeat to yourself: "It's more about them than it is about me."

Pursuer/Distancer

It's a classic pattern: one person wants more closeness, and the other person wants more distance. You may recognize it. Here again, anxiety is often the culprit—too much closeness brings on a sometimes desperate need for more distance, and too much distance brings on a need for more emotional closeness. The more the distancer withdraws, the more the pursuer pursues, needing reassuring contact. The more the pursuer seeks contact, the more the other person withdraws. And on and on it goes. As Harriet Goldhor Lerner observes in her 1985 book, *The Dance of Anger*, "Emotional pursuers are persons who reduce their anxiety by sharing feelings and seeking close emotional contact. Emotional distancers are persons who reduce their anxiety by intellectualizing and withdrawing" (p. 57).

There is both a need for and allergy to emotional closeness that exists to some degree in all relationships, notes Michael Kerr summarizing Murray Bowen's Family Systems Theory. Although a closeness seeker can be of either gender, upbringing influences women to take on this role, just as it tends to influence men to be the more intellectualizing distancers.

Interestingly enough, the closeness seeker does have a need for his or her own space, but it may be a "blind spot," a trait hidden from awareness. Because it remains unacknowledged, the closeness seeker deals with this need for space or independence by relying on the other person to express the need for them. This is projection as we learned in chapter 2. The distance seeker complies by seeking more and more distance, an example of projective identification.

This distancing person may have his or her "blind spot" as well, and may depend on the other person to express any neediness or sensitivity to rejection or abandonment that they feel. Deep down, the distancer may want closeness, but because they can't acknowledge it, they can only see the need as coming from their partner. With projection and projective identification in full swing, folks don't have to look at their insecurities or dependency needs as long as their partner is doing it for them. One is in charge of the closeness, and the other is in charge of the personal space, and together they function as an integrated whole. This is another example of complementarity.

However, each one may be giving out totally different messages as to what they really need in the relationship—and the other complies! Each gets upset or hurt that the other person can't read their mind and see things his or her way. And when these hurt feelings lead to resentment and anger, as they surely will, the relationship suffers.

It is interesting to note that one person may be a pursuer in one area (for example, sexually, wanting physical comfort) and their partner may be the pursuer in another (for example, wanting emotional comfort). The process often involves an attack/defend dynamic: in general, pursuers tend to blame or criticize, and distancers, feeling personally attacked, tend to defend by mounting a counterattack.

Never Pursue a Distancer

Pursuers could benefit from the operating principal, "Never pursue a distancer," proclaims Thomas Fogarty in *Family Therapy: Theory and Practice* (1976). Perhaps pursuers could save themselves a lot of frustration if they would only commit this to memory. It does seem to be a fact of life—the more you pursue, the more distance the other person will put between you.

So why not do just the opposite? Here's a way of solving this dilemma. Because relationships are *relational*, one thing is relative to another (meaning proportional). There is only so much total space out there to consider, and if one person is taking up too much, it leaves too little for the other person. This may be physical space, emotional space, or both.

If one person takes a step or two forward, what choices does the other person have? #2 can stand there uncomfortably, feeling the hot breath of person #1. Or he or she can take a step or two backward. Maybe even three or four steps. Or more—lots more. And the first person wonders, "Whoa. What happened here? Where did they go?"

What if the first person were to wise up and consider, "There is just so much space available here, so how can I use it to my advantage? What are the possibilities here? What are my choices? What about if I did the opposite of what I've been doing? What might happen if I take a step or two backward and allow some space? What if that space includes pursuing my own interests? Not in anger or retaliation but rather in finding ways to be more independent—perhaps spending more time with friends, or taking classes. Could it be possible that it would leave some space for person #1 to move a half step toward me? Or maybe to even take a full step toward me and take up the slack. Well, what about that? It's actually happening. Yes, that feels good. Jeez. Why didn't I think of that sooner?"

It would be interesting for this couple to try another experiment as well. What if each one puts him or herself in the other person's shoes? Try imagining how it would feel for the pursuer to feel pursued or for the pursued to feel like the pursuer.

Approach/Avoidance

I saw a rather bosomy woman wearing a T-shirt recently that said in large letters, "COME CLOSER." But if you went up close enough to read the smaller print underneath, it said, "That's too close." Funny? I guess so. But it's also the kind of mixed message that so many folks give out—even to important people in their lives.

"Go away a little closer," is another name for this dynamic. Another way to say it is, "Come closer, go away." Giving these mixed messages is a form of self-preservation—a way of creating more comfortable distance. But it can be incredibly crazy-making for the other person.

Okay, so what's going on here? Well, it's a great example of *ambivalence*. An internal fight is taking place, and this uncomfortable inner conflict comes from that part that craves closeness butting up against the part that's scared to death of it, afraid of losing self-identity.

Feeling ambivalent at some time or other is natural. All it really means is that we have simultaneous, conflicting feelings. But ambivalence is much more than "love and hate," "good and bad." It has many subtle meanings as well, especially in regard to relationships. It usually has to do with wishes or feelings. It can mean wanting something, yet not wanting it, or being afraid to want it too much. It can mean liking some things about someone and not liking others.

How do you know when you are ambivalent?

- You can't make a decision. You feel immobilized, stuck, like straddling a fence.

- You want to spend time with a partner, but need time to yourself.

- You want to feel connected, but need a whole lot of separateness.

- You want a loving, nurturing relationship, but you're choosing someone who's not able to provide what you need.

- You want a romantic relationship, yet aren't quite ready to make a commitment.

It's not easy to struggle with conflicting feelings or wishes. When two internal voices are at odds with each other, this conflict causes friction, which can then cause anxiety. That's why at times ambivalence can be such a confusing concept, and these contradictions of feelings can take up a great deal of space and energy.

The best way to deal effectively with ambivalence is to give both voices some attention, a chance to be heard. Give voice to both sides of the ambivalence. In order to do this, try making two lists: a "What I have to gain" list and a "What I have to lose" list. You can also let both sides carry on a conversation with each other. Hearing yourself argue both sides out loud, in the presence of another person, is best. It helps to have someone to talk to who can guide you in discovering your two voices.

> The best way to deal effectively with ambivalence is to give both voices some attention, a chance to be heard.

By the way, sometimes you can only hear one voice, because you may have a blind spot about the other. The other side may contain thoughts or feelings that you haven't yet acknowledged about yourself, so it stays hidden from your consciousness. The problem here is that if it's hidden from you, it needs somewhere to go. That "somewhere" may be that it is projected onto your partner or friends or associates or children.

So, here's the thing about needing closeness: The person who wants so badly to feel closer to the other person is aware of this need for physical or emotional closeness because it's lacking in his or her life. However, at the same time, there may be an unacknowledged need for personal space, creating a comfortable distance. We all have this need to some degree or another.

How do you manage to create this distance for yourself when you don't even know you need it? You may find yourself pushing for more and more closeness, until you end up pushing the other person away. It's easy for that person to oblige, because he or she feels intruded upon. So, before you know it, the person is distancing from you. You get the space you didn't even know you craved, but you end up with more space than you know what to do with!

How do you manage to accomplish this maneuver? These things are guaranteed to push people away at one time or another: try demanding more time from them, or initiating unwelcome public displays of affection, or asking lots of questions. What are *your* techniques? Are you aware that you're doing them? Wouldn't it be nice to be aware enough to give yourself the choice of whether you want to continue to use them or not?

I Push, You Pull

When ambivalence surfaces, you might find yourself doing "the approach/avoidance dance," which Lillian Rubin describes so well in *Intimate Strangers*. Here, the pursuer becomes the distancer in the blink of an eye. One woman describes it this way: "I want a whole lot of closeness at first—I want to know someone really loves me. But once I feel secure in that knowledge, I begin to want a lot of space. I find some way of distancing. It confuses my lovers, but I can't help it. I once heard a woman comic say, 'The perfect boyfriend is someone who is madly in love with me and leaves me alone!'"

If someone seems to be saying, "Go away a little closer," it's as if they are holding up one hand in a "come closer" beckoning gesture, while the other hand is signaling, "Stop—don't come any closer!" Yes, it's maddening, but it's hard to say who's more confused, the sender of the message or the receiver.

The messages can change so quickly, it's mindboggling. One week, day, moment, someone can't get enough of your company, your laughter, your attention, and your body. Then, all of a sudden, the "push away" messages begin. At times they're subtle, but other times you get whacked with a hurtful "get away and stay away" comment. Each time it happens it feels like another rejection. But chances are this person will switch gears and approach you once again, seeking closeness. Once the necessary distance has been created, it feels safe to take a step forward and, of course, the challenge of the "chase" is there once again.

"We used to do just about everything together," one woman remembers.

"Yeah," her partner says, "I guess you could say we were fused at the hip. But then one day I realized I couldn't breathe. And I needed to get away.

"Whenever I start feeling closer to her, I need more time to myself," he admits. We start to get close, and I start to pull back. She hates it, I know, and her feelings get hurt."

"Sure my feelings get hurt," she injects. "I think he doesn't want to be around me when he disappears like that. It's really hard to feel connected to the system when all I get is a 'dial tone.' And then I end up disappearing on *him*, because I'm so hurt. I get so silent—it's as if there's nobody home.

"And that reminds me of my childhood," he realizes. "'The Disappearing Father Act,' I used to call it—when my dad would come home from work and disappear behind the newspaper or behind a couple of bottles of beer.

"Let's do something to stop this vicious cycle that we've created here," he ventured.

"Let's not do this anymore," she agreed.

Can these two really agree to make every attempt not to disappear on each other? Well, they agreed to try, and something important happened. From that day on, they were able to be objective observers of their process together and make some adjustments to it.

Inflate/Deflate

Another version of "approach-avoidance" is the inflate-deflate caper. This is when person #1 offers suggestions for plans that hold out the promise of closeness or commitment. Examples would be taking a trip together, an invitation for Thanksgiving dinner with parents or siblings, mention of a special gift, or even plans for the future.

Person #2 feels elated because this feels like a real validation of the relationship. Then, poof. Person #1 changes his or her mind or sabotages the situation. It's as if they've stuck a pin in the buoyancy, deflating the anticipation. It could take the wind right out of you, couldn't it?

When you get right down to it, repetitions of these kinds of behavior are crazy-making and may even feel emotionally abusive. Most especially if person #2 grew up in a family where promises were not kept, leading to one disappointment after another. As an adult, it's hard not to expect disappointment when a partner repeatedly makes empty promises. And trust gets hurt as well, damaging the relationship.

Overfunctioner/Underfunctioner

This is another example of reciprocity—also referred to as overadequate/underadequate functioning. Here, again, is another "only so much space in the world" concept. When underfunctioning exists in one partner, the other partner will compensate. In some situations, this kind of flexibility is advantageous, especially when one partner becomes ill and the other temporarily steps in and takes over responsibilities.

However, in quite a few situations, there is no flexibility. When one person tends to overfunction on a regular basis, he or she infantilizes the other one, leaving no room for day-to-day adequate functioning. Overfunctioners may be constantly giving advice or initiating plans, but this "I'm always having to think for you" message also translates into, "What's wrong with you, can't you think for yourself?" Overfunctioners may be constantly worrying about their partner, who, as a result, feels smothered. But the most common form of overfunctioning is to say things such as, "Did you remember to take the theater tickets?" "Let me sew that button on for you," "Do you know it's already eleven o'clock? You'll be late for your appointment." This is a "Doll's House" relationship, much like Henrik Ibsen described through the characters of Nora and Torvald. In the play, Torvald took care of everything, reducing Nora to the status of a child. Needless to say, this arrangement failed when she felt the need to "grow up" and take responsibility for herself.

Borrowed Functioning

The overfunctioner/underfunctioner pattern points up a vital concept for understanding interactions between couples. This is the idea of borrowed functioning, a kind of fitting together, where couples borrow, lend, or trade the ability to function within the relationship. The characteristics of one person may be complementary to the characteristics of the other, but differentiation suffers. For example, one person props up the other person, one may be dominant and the other submissive, or one may be seemingly self-assured and the other insecure.

There are many and varied examples of borrowed functioning throughout Schnarch's *Passionate Marriage*, describing how functioning is artificially inflated or deflated. But for our purposes here, let's stick with the overadequate/underadequate dynamics. In order to feel needed and more useful, the overadequate partner may need the partner to feel less than competent. This desire is frequently related to a need to control things, to feel effective adequate and worthwhile. Yes, it fills up space that would otherwise feel too empty and incomplete. It's most likely similar to the old childhood job description: "the responsible one," or "the capable one," or the "good boy or girl." Did you grow up being the one everyone depended on? Did you prop people up? Were you sure things would fall apart if you didn't take charge and accomplish what your parents were not able to do? You assembled an identity back then. It was the way you defined yourself and bestowed a measure of self-worth. And it still is—you would probably feel lost without it.

> To feel more useful, the overadequate partner
> may need the partner to feel less than competent.

Or maybe you were the one on the inadequate end—the one who feels inept, incapacitated, incapable, inconsequential, incompetent, ineffective, inadequate, invalidated, invisible, inferior, indebted, or perhaps even intimidated. What you *don't* feel is independent. Often a kind of learned helplessness develops, and the underfunctioning becomes more pronounced. If no one expects you to remember things or to take care of business, you probably won't.

You may carry this identity card with you into your adult years, finding a partner who needs you to "take over." You most likely became proficient at trading and borrowing functioning at a very early age, and carry this proficiency with you into your adult relationships.

When couples borrow functioning, both the overfunctioner and the underfunctioner feel resentful. The overfunctioner feels stressed because he or she feels way too depended on. The underfunctioner resents feeling so dependent. This has been a big problem for Jim and Nancy.

"I'm the pivotal person in the family," Nancy likes to say. "Everyone depends on me. Nothing would happen unless I took charge. But Jim gets so mad at me when I try to get him to take charge of something. He's always afraid he'll screw up, and guess what—he does!

"Recently we were going to the opera. So I asked him to be sure and take the tickets. Well, I made myself just trust that he would take care of it. I didn't say anything until after we were in the car and on our way. I asked if he had the tickets. He didn't. They were still on the dining room table, where I had left them. Then Jim got furious at me for not reminding him before we got into the car! Shit, if I hadn't reminded him at all, we would have arrived at the theater with no tickets!"

But Jim adds, "But you shrieked at me, 'What's wrong with you? Why can't you remember something as simple as the tickets?' You didn't have to yell like that."

When Nancy decides to step back and give Jim the space to take some responsibility, he isn't able to do that. Again, she has to take over, and she gets angry about that and mad that he forgot the tickets. And he gets angry that she didn't remind him earlier. What a setup for the repetition of this destructive dynamic! What a setup for the repetition of the old negative messages that each one experiences as well: Nancy's belief that no one can step in and take care of things as well as she can, and Jim's belief that he just keeps messing up.

Okay, so what can they do? They can start by making some rules, the most important being "no judgments." This means no set-ups for failure by asking the other person to do something they don't do well. This also means that there is no right way or wrong way of doing things—it's important to honor style differences here.

Each person has strong points that they bring to the relationship. For example, how do couples decide who cooks, or does the dishes, cleans the toilet bowl, vacuums, or takes out the trash? Some couples decide who does what chores by stating preferences. For example, "I like this one, and I don't like to do that one."

Why can't things like remembering theater tickets be one of the "chores"? Why shouldn't the one who does it most easily get to have that "job"? In this case, it can be Nancy. Jim can have some other job he chooses. Perhaps Jim's job can be to order the tickets, or arrange for a sitter, or make sure the car is cleaned out beforehand. Nancy's job is to bring the tickets for operas or plays or plane flights.

By the way, there is a very good reason that one of Jim's jobs is to take out the trash every Tuesday. It's because he remembers, without fail, to do it. In fact, when he was out of town on business for a week recently, Nancy forgot to take it out. Jim didn't remind her how badly she screwed up, though!

As you can see from these examples, the way we manage closeness and distance plays an important role in our ability and our *willingness* to be intimate with another person. And, more specifically, creating and maintaining comfortable space in intimate relationships is influenced by our ability to respect one another's personal space. Let's take a look at what that means for you and your partner.

4

"Gimme Land, Lots of Land ..."

What Is Personal Space?

Personal space is the respectful distance dance that we do with the people in our lives. It includes both physical and emotional space. As you may recall from the beginning of this book, "space" includes personal boundaries, privacy, and safe distances. The concept of personal space signifies something different to each of us because our needs and our tolerances are individual. We are all unique, so our personal needs for space depend not only on the present situation, but on our experiences of growing up as well.

I once saw Bruce Springsteen interviewed on the TV show 20/20. He was describing how psychotherapy taught him how to exercise options and choices. When he was asked if he could say more about that, Springsteen firmly replied, "No, I don't want to talk about that." Obviously, he was making a choice in that moment to honor his privacy. It's a hard lesson to learn and Springsteen didn't say how long it took him to develop respect for his needs. Many of us don't know how to take such good care of ourselves in relationships.

Many years ago, when I was a graduate student taking clinical psychology classes, the students would sometimes pair up and practice psychotherapy skills on other class members. Sitting cross-legged, facing each other, we'd alternate between being the "therapist" and the "client." I especially remember once when I was the "client." I must have been looking pretty uneasy, because the "therapist" asked me if I felt comfortable with the distance between us. Reflecting back, I actually did feel that that the foot or so between us was too close—another six or seven inches away would have been much better. But I wasn't able to tell her that. I didn't know how to put words to it.

In the years since, there have been times I feel someone is too close to me, physically, emotionally, or both. I recall that classroom experience, and in the remembering, I can check in with myself to see whether or not I'm comfortable. I ask myself, "On a scale of one to ten, where am I?" If I'm not comfortable enough, I let myself take a step backward. Sometimes it is an emotional step; sometimes a physical one. Either way, it gives me some necessary breathing room.

I'm acquainted with a fifteen-year-old who was struggling to work things out in a high school romance. She asked, "How do you explain to someone that you need personal space? How do you get them to understand that you care about them? How do you not hurt their feelings if you're trying to take care of yourself?" At fifteen years of age, she recognized the problem and was honing the skills to deal with it. She'll have those skills the rest of her life.

The issue of not enough closeness or not enough space is a problem for most of us. It causes no end of frustration when a partner's needs for space are so different from our own. "I just don't understand him," lamented Vivian. "There we are sitting on the sofa, watching a video, and I wanted to snuggle up to him. He didn't want me to. He said he 'needs some space.' Needs some space! What the hell is that supposed to mean? I don't get it—there we were, sitting together, so why not sit close and touch? But no, he needs his space. It drives me absolutely crazy. I just don't get it. Is there any hope?"

I guess I'm asked that hope question by couples more than any other. But hope is relative and depends on what can be negotiated. For example, what kind of contact can he tolerate? If cuddling is too much, then what about holding hands? Or even touching fingers? Can she make some contact with him by holding on to his sleeve? How much is too much? And what about her? What is the minimum amount of contact she is willing to settle for? How little is too little? Can they work something out so they don't have to go to that place of hurt feelings or resentment?

By Invitation Only

Personal space is the safe distance that we create between ourselves and others. It has a lot to do with respect. However, some of us grew up in families or communities without the benefit of anyone teaching respect for the personal space of others. Although some of us did learn a version of it on the streets if we crossed the line and "dissed" someone. Talk about personal safety!

Once I heard sports consultant and sociologist Harry Edwards describe how sparks fly if athletes get into each other's personal spaces. This is especially true if one or both of them grew up on the streets where getting inside of a respectful eighteen inches means, "You're in my face, man." Several years later, I had the opportunity to talk more with Professor Edwards about this issue of personal space. Private space is more than just physical space, according to Edwards. It can also include staring at someone too long, making them feel that you are intruding. Unless you enter someone's private space by personal invitation, you have crossed a line. Don't be surprised if someone feels "disrespected" and takes it personally.

This is also true in potentially romantic situations. If you notice someone staring, you can make a choice about whether to give out the message, "It's okay if you enter my space—I'm inviting you in." But if someone is staring, and it's not okay with you, it feels like disrespect, points out Dr. Edwards.

Our feelings of personal safety can be affected by the amount of personal space around us. Sometimes there's not enough; sometimes there's too much. And this perception of space varies from culture to culture, gender to gender, situation to situation. If, for some reason, you don't feel safe, it's helpful to look at reasons why that might be. What are you thinking might happen to you? Has it happened before? Did your ancestors live in "unsafe" environments? Might that fear have been passed down from generation to generation in your family? This familial "inheritance" can really affect the way you react to space issues.

It's All Relative

As you take a look at the personal space in your relationships, keep in mind that these interactions are *relational*. By this I mean that if you take up less space, it leaves more space for the other person to fill. And, if that person tends to be a caretaker or a controlling person, he or she just might fill it up pretty quickly.

Learning to caretake or take control are roles you most likely learned in childhood. Often the reason for this is a gaping hole of incompetence and insecurity in your family as you were growing up. Maybe a parent wasn't fully functioning. Perhaps a parent inappropriately treated you as a confidante, or looked to you for emotional support or for help with a younger sibling. Some of us figured out that, in order for our families to function better, *someone* had to fill up that empty space. And you may have been that someone.

But remember how these things are relational. As you begin to take up more space, the space between you and the other person decreases. It doesn't leave as much room for the other person, and he or she may feel diminished in the relationship. Most of us know that feeling diminished doesn't feel good. It can quickly leapfrog into those "dis" words—feeling disrespected, dismissed, discounted, dispensable—as if you had disappeared from sight.

I Am You and You Are Me: Exploring Boundaries

Many of us did not learn crisp, clean, personal boundaries in our childhoods. Family members would often slip and slide in and out of each other's physical and emotional space. Good boundaries involve knowing where you stop and the other person begins, but family members may have trouble separating their own ideas, needs, and feelings from those of others.

A good place to begin to work on boundaries is to keep reminding yourself that you do, indeed, exist separately and distinctly from other people. You do not have to think their thoughts or feel their pain. Nor do you have to speak for someone else. Your experience of life can be uniquely your own. Your needs can be different from their needs. Yet you can be empathic to their needs or experience. You can put yourself in their shoes for the moment, but you don't have to stay there. Having good boundaries means you can choose to move in or out at will. The trick is to disentangle your feelings from those of others. This makes it possible for you to be close enough to feel connected, yet distant enough to be objective and more effective.

Learning to say "yes" and "no" defines who you are in the moment—and what you stand for. In fact, these words are great personal boundary setters. The trouble is many of us did not have very good modeling of boundaries in childhood. We had no idea how to define what we stood for or what we needed. In fact, in many families, defining things was discouraged or even forbidden. Instead, things had to be vague, cloudy, and amorphous. It's as if people were speaking with mouths full of mush.

Family members would play guessing games with each other because being specific was simply not okay. And what could be more specific than learning to say "yes" and "no" loudly and clearly? Too often we learned to say "yes" when we really meant "no," and we never learned to say "no."

Sex and Boundaries

Boundaries play a big role in sexual experiences. It is often said that making love is a temporary blending of boundaries, a merging of two people, two spirits, and two energy forces. Some people find that experience scary, so they hold back. Even those who are able to let go find themselves wanting to return to their own space and reestablish their personal boundaries when sex is finished. So they roll over and fall asleep.

How can you transition from this temporary loss of self during passion, and return to yourself? One way is to make sure that you have a few moments of contact with your partner after making love. Holding, touching, or cuddling with each other works for some couples. Even holding hands could work. And if your partner says, "Please hold me a few more minutes," that's okay, too. Then you can both get comfortable (whatever that takes) and go to sleep.

For some people, sex interacts with boundaries in another way—it provides a container for anxiety so it doesn't spill over and make a big mess. For example, one day Amelia realized why she jumps into sex so early in new relationships. "I get so anxious, trying to figure out the relationship, and sex defines the relationship right away for me. Sex is a known quality for me, so I initiate it because the unknown is so unsettling. The trouble is, when I define a relationship right away through sex, I have a hard time seeing it in any other way."

Navigating Through Boundary Confusion

Keeping these points in mind will help you navigate through boundary confusion.

- Figure out where you stop and the other person begins.

- Know that you exist separately and distinctly from other people, with different feelings and different needs.

- Remind yourself that another person's words or actions are often about that person and that person's history, and not about you.

- Learn to say "yes" and "no" loudly and clearly.

When you have good boundaries, you begin to have a more defined sense of who you are and can work on communicating your needs clearly. Having boundaries is like having a fence around your house. Pia Mellody and A. W. Miller in, *In Facing Codependence* (1989) asserts that these symbolic fences serve three purposes:

- To keep people from coming into our spaces

- To keep us from going into the spaces of others

- To give us a sense of wholeness (p. 11)

What are the best ways to navigate personal-space issues? It is helpful to have a framework regarding what space is yours and what belongs to other people. Psychologists John and Linda Friel, in *Adult Child's Guide to What's "Normal"* (1990), offer seven categories of personal boundaries. I've used their descriptions as a foundation and added some of my own impressions.

Physical boundaries mean that other people respect your physical space. These boundaries are violated when someone goes into your room without permission, uses your stuff without asking, or reads your diary. They're also violated when someone touches or tickles you inappropriately, or hits you.

Intellectual boundaries mean that others respect your ideas or thoughts. These boundaries are violated when someone tries to discount your thoughts, saying things like, "You're imagining it," or "You don't really think that, do you?"

Emotional boundaries involve respect for your feelings. These boundaries are violated when someone tries to invalidate or ignore your feelings, takes you for granted, or psychologically abuses you by criticizing, belittling, or shaming.

Social boundaries mean a respect for your choices of social contact. They're violated when someone criticizes where you go or whom you choose to be with, for example: "Why on earth would you want to go out with her?" or "I can't believe you would drive thirty miles just to go to that movie."

Sexual boundaries are about the right to privacy and choosing who can touch you, where, and how they should touch you. In other words, no one can touch you without your permission. Some sexual boundary transgressions, such as stranger or acquaintance rape, are obvious. But others, such as tickling, staring, and leering, can be confusing because they are not so obvious.

Money boundaries involve how you earn it, spend it, save it, and how much you need to feel a sense of security. There's no question that different attitudes about money can cause relationship problems, especially if you don't respect the other person's style. Asking someone personal questions about how much things cost crosses bourndaries, as well.

Time boundaries mean having respect for your own and others' ways of getting things done. Some of us are on time or even early for meetings or getting projects done. Others of us are "under the wire" people and thrive on the excitement of deadlines.

Poor personal boundaries are often mistaken for personal affronts. Roles and rules should be clearly defined so there does not have to be guessing and mind reading. When there is a clear pattern of roles and rules in families, then there are clear boundaries.

Privacy

When I think about "privacy," I link it to "respect for privacy." But definitions of these terms often differ from individual to individual. Some people are more private and need more privacy than others. Some people easily overreact when they feel their privacy is being compromised.

Perhaps this is because someone didn't respect their privacy. Personal boundaries may have been transgressed when someone walked in on them in the bathroom or the bedroom, or insisted the bedroom door always be open. I've even heard stories about parents removing their kid's bedroom door from its hinges.

Joan's experience may help to illustrate how this invasion of privacy works. She is a very private person who found herself feeling violated by Jerry's tendency to intrude on her private time.

"I just hate it when you come into the bedroom when I've closed the door," Joan complained. "You knock lightly and open the door without waiting for me to say, 'Come in' or 'Don't come in.' You just walk in on me."

"But it's my bedroom, too," Jerry counters.

"But the door is closed," Joan insists. "I have the door closed for a reason. Can't you understand that?"

"Maybe it would help if you told me the reason so I could try to understand," he suggests.

She hesitates. "I've never said this to anyone before. Sometimes I feel so totally ugly, I just can't bear for anyone to see me before I put on makeup."

And when did Joan feel like that in the past? She didn't have to think for very long before answering. "My mom never respected my privacy. She felt she was 'privy' to everything in my life. She read my diaries, too. I felt I had nowhere to go back then, just as I feel I have nowhere to go now. I should be able to have private time in the bedroom if I want it. I need to be able to have time to myself."

As you can see, experiences in childhood can make long-lasting imprints and affect our sense of safety in our adult relationships. You'll read more about the sacredness of private spaces in chapter 14.

Quiet Time/Transitional Time — a Time to Recharge

What are some ways you can choose the best "context" for both of you to get what you want and need from each other, and at the same time, respect each other's needs for "alone" time? What set of conditions is necessary here? Who among us doesn't have a need for quiet, reflective time? Recovery time? Recharge time? Room to breathe? Often this need is for transitional time, a space for making a transition from one role to another, from one environment to another. It's a way to alleviate stress and oversaturation.

An example would be coming home from work and not being expected to immediately plunge into the caretaker role, or the cook role, or the nurturing spouse role. It's helpful to be able to retreat to a quiet place and read the paper, meditate, listen to music, or just simply sit and stare into space for a few minutes. The point is, to have enough time to smoothly make the switch from one context of your life to another.

Making the transition from waking to sleep is another problem area for many couples. It often happens when that someone gets a thought that doesn't want to go away and just *has* to talk to the partner right away. But what if the partner is just about to fall asleep? What if they can hardly keep their eyes open? What if they have no earthly idea that the person who needs to talk is really hurting and really does need to talk? So, instead of listening, they grunt, turn away, and go to sleep. Instead of being heard, the other partner feels dismissed, "blown off," and frustrated.

This is where context is important. There are two existing conditions to consider here: The first is the timing. Eleven at night is not the very best time to start a "heavy" conversation about something that has been bothering you for six weeks or six months or a year.

But there is also another matter of context to consider. What place are you really coming from? Is it from a space of complaining or criticism? Or is it really from a space of concern or hurting? If you approach your partner with a blunt, accusatory attitude instead of from a sincere, authentic place, you probably won't get a great reception. In fact, if you scratch the surface of the hard edge of complaining or criticism, you will most likely find the softness of yearning underneath. Yearning for needs that aren't getting met.

If you can allow yourself to be soft instead of tough, it can open the door to the possibility of an intimate moment between the two of you. At the very least, you can make contact, let your partner know something important is on your mind, and arrange for a time to talk the next day, when the context might be more amenable to getting the attention you need. At least it gives your partner the option of how best he or she can respond to you, and when. If your partner feels they can better give you full attention the following day, it doesn't mean they are dismissing your needs (or you) as unimportant. They are simply suggesting a more workable context.

Children and Space — an Oxymoron?

Space juggling becomes all-important and often incredibly difficult when there are children in the picture. Our lives can be so incredibly busy with career and community concerns that there is little or no space for children. Sometimes we bring children into a family to fill a vacuum—perhaps some emptiness in our own lives. In these situations, children can become a focus for our unrealized achievement. Or perhaps the child becomes a replacement for a dead or absent family member—especially true if we have cut ourselves off from our family of origin. Unless we are true to ourselves, balancing our personal and relationship needs with those of our children, we are in danger of becoming real resentful, real fast.

Susan Jeffers (2000) addresses this problem honestly in her book, *I'm Okay . . . You're a Brat*, pointing out that it cannot be denied that an enormous chasm is created when a couple brings a child into the relationship. The nature of children is that they demand attention—they don't always like it when you relate to your partner or other people. What ever happened to privacy? Sleep? Sex? Jeffers notes how nothing stays the same in the parent's relationship—there are changes in the couple's way of relating to each other, their perceptions, their lifestyle. In other words, the "package" they bought in the early days of their relationship changes considerably.

Resentment can take up a huge amount of space when there are children in the picture. Sometimes we find ourselves putting our hearts and souls into taking care of our children, ignoring our own needs. A twenty-seven-year-old woman recently said, "I want to discover who I am first, to know my self well enough so that I can let others know me. Then I will be ready to have children. I don't want to feel I'm having a child to complete myself. I'd rather get a good start on doing that on my own." Sometimes we look to our kids for things that we would be better off getting from ourselves. This is especially true if we expect them to be skilled in the things we never were good at or smart in ways we never were. If they're not, then we get disappointed and hurt. Sometimes we get resentful, perhaps even thinking or saying, "Look at all I did for you. . . ."

There are so many situations where children might take space in your relationship with your partner. Take a look at the list of "space fillers" in chapter 5, and see which of these might also apply to the presence of children.

Here are one woman's impressions: "I've never been a great extrovert, but it was not until after the birth of my daughter that I started actually craving time alone. I had absolutely no idea what true solitude was until I became a mother. I have learned the value of my own company, and I've learned to protect it by making time alone for myself.

"Having a child has helped me realize that it was time to drop the caretaking of my husband. It gave me a different perspective on my mothering responsibilities. I am my child's mother—no one else's. When a child is born, there's an uncharted territory born as well, which sometimes stands between the parents. How do you fill this expanse? With what does your mate fill it? Do you decide together or separately how to fill it?"

Taking time for yourself is, of course, important, but so is making time and space for your relationship with your partner. A regular "date" is something to look forward to, and some couples try to work out preplanned, prescheduled child care from the time they feel comfortable leaving the baby in the care of another person. Then the couple knows that they have that date every two weeks, or so—at least once a month, if possible. No matter how much you love your child, resentments do grow unless you have some "couple time."

Turf

In an earlier chapter on the qualities of "space," I used a definition of "turf" from Edward T. Hall's *The Hidden Dimension.* People like to keep certain distances between themselves and other people or things. This invisible bubble of space constitutes each person's "territory." This woman's thoughts about "turf" are useful:

"It's a fascinating thing," she declared. "The way people guard and preserve their space. At the moment, I maintain the kitchen, the patio, and the little alcove I call my 'office.' Nothing else. I always feel I need to clean up after my husband and child in the kitchen, but I no longer maintain the rest of the house.

"In fact, I can hardly stand being in the living room these days. It seems to always be awash with papers, telephone books, odd bits of hardware, masses of newspapers, books, and toys. I don't expect everyone to be as orderly as I am, but I also refuse to do maintenance for the whole house. So, I stick to my comfort spaces: the kitchen, foyer, patio, and my little alcove where everything is clean and orderly and smells good. I have my pieces of turf and try my best to ignore the rest—to not waste my emotional or mental energy on it. Sometimes I succeed, sometimes not."

And, speaking of turf, isn't it incredible how some people will go to extremes to defend their space, even if it means injuring or destroying that space? Do you remember the film *The War of the Roses*, in which Oliver and Barbara Rose decide to divorce, but neither will move out of their showplace home? They battle over possessions— the Stratfordshire figurines, the cars, the gourmet kitchen range, and the chandelier. I think of this movie as "The Turf Wars," where household objects and territory become more important than people and life itself.

Misjudging Space

There are two realities—each of you has a point of view, seeing life from a different but equally valid vantage point. Your perceptions are important and you want them to be respected, but they may not be the same as your partner's perceptions. And if an objective third person were by chance in the room, they might have yet a different perception. The operating word here is "different." Not right, not wrong, only different. This way of looking at situations can prevent lots of misunderstandings.

It's Not the Intention, It's the Interpretation

We use our perceptions to make assumptions. Any time you make assumptions, you are filling up the space of "not knowing" with your own interpretations. It's so easy to misread someone's meaning because of inflections, tones of voice, cadence, or loudness. You might even misread the spacing between someone's words, putting the emphasis in the wrong place, misunderstanding their intent. Or your own past experiences might jump in, filling up the spaces, ascribing meanings that aren't really there. Perhaps then you respond with your own meanings from your own history.

> Your perceptions may not be the same as your partner's—not right, not wrong, just different.

For example, if you sense that someone is distancing, you might fear that he or she will leave you. Based on all the past times you may have felt abandoned as I described in the previous chapter.

The Child Default Position

Here is an important point: Your reaction does not come totally from the adult part of you. The child's fears and questions and worries are in there, too. Your adult part might say, "He really isn't angry enough at me to leave me," or "She really isn't rejecting me, just my suggestion." But the child part of you doesn't know any of this. The child isn't able to reason it out quite so well, and the panic in the child's voice often drowns out the rational adult.

If this child reaction happens often enough in your relationship, it becomes hard to repair the damage that is done. Resentments build, frustrations mount, anger seeps in and spews out. Ruth and Bob provide a good example of how couples fill in the spaces with their own interpretations.

"I feel we don't spend enough time together when we get home from work," said Ruth as she turned to face Bob in their couple's session.

He stared at her in disbelief. "What do you mean? We're together all the time. In fact, there's times I'd like to have more time to myself."

She, of course, heard his comment as, "I don't want to be around you." She was mistaking her fears for his intentions, and she took it personally. She was filling in the spaces, attributing meaning to his words without checking them out. This was, of course, based on her childhood experiences with a father who never seemed to have time for her. Look how easily she went to that child default position. See how easily she jumped to conclusions about her partner's meaning? But Bob reminded her that's not what he said. He was talking about *his* need for space—it wasn't a judgment about *her*.

And isn't it interesting how Bob and Ruth each have such a different impression about the amount of time they spend together? Too much for him, too little for her. So what can they do? We worked on some possible solutions. A transitional time might be in order. Maybe reconnecting briefly (a warm hug might be just the ticket—just as long as it's not a perfunctory one), and then each one can take some time and space alone to unwind from their respective workdays, coming together again later in the evening.

When Is Too Much Togetherness Too Much?

One day I received a call from a woman who was very dismayed. Her husband had suddenly taken off to go camping over the weekend—without her. He told her he needed his "freedom." And she jumped to what she saw as an obvious conclusion, translating his actions to mean, "I don't love you," "I don't want to be with you," "I want out," or even "I don't want to be married to you anymore." But when he returned from his camping trip, he readily agreed to come into a session with her. She was surprised that he agreed, because she was sure the marriage was over.

And by the way, what *did* he mean by "freedom"? Well, it turns out he just needed some breathing room. He explained how he realized he has a need to go off occasionally on his own to get some space for himself. It was definitely *not* about her; it was about *his* needs for alone time. Their life together was sometimes just too much togetherness for him to handle.

So how could they work this out? How could he have his freedom and still stay connected to her? How could she be supportive of his need for freedom, not take offense, and still feel connected to him? He came up with a super idea. He often goes sailing. He said he would love for her to take lessons and join him some of the time. However, he wanted to make a deal. He wanted to go on an occasional solo weekend camping trip to "clear his head"—and he wanted that to be okay with her.

She was thrilled that he had invited her into his sailing world, a pastime he had enjoyed long before he met her. She was just fine about agreeing to the camping part when she understood that it had nothing to do with her personally. All of a sudden she went from feeling left out of his life to feeling very included and very cherished.

However, it doesn't always work out quite this well. Another couple I know were going through a hard time about how much time they spend together on the weekends. It was usually not enough for her, but he felt it was a fine amount. She started giving him a hard time about how much golf he was playing with friends, feeling as though he should be staying home with her.

"Okay," he thought. "Why don't I offer her golf lessons and she can join me on the links." After a few lessons, she started joining him every weekend. It was fine at first, but, after a while, he began to notice he was beginning to missed just being with "the guys" for a game. Somehow it was different when it was just he and she.

So, he told her how much he really liked doing other things with her. Cooking together, planning parties, even going grocery shopping. But he did need some time with the guys to "chill out." However, he'd still like to play golf with her once a month or so, and definitely when they took vacations.

He had been concerned about telling her this—afraid she might feel he didn't want to be with her, didn't love her as much as he used to, or something like that. In fact, she was relieved. She had been loyally going to the greens with him every weekend even though, many times, she would rather have been home reading or having lunch with a friend. But she was afraid to tell him for fear his feelings would be hurt; he was so considerate in giving her those golf lessons and all. After they both "confessed" to their true feelings, they were able to work out a schedule that suited them both.

Guerrilla Tactics for Getting Space

There are times when you may feel desperate for more space, and you don't know how to ask for it from your partner. Because you are not putting your needs into words, you may act them out in various ways. One way of manipulating for more space is to create diversions. For example, picking a fight is guaranteed to get you some space every time. And another "picking" technique might be finding fault with the other person by criticizing, nagging, complaining, or whining. Take your choice, they are all great space-makers.

Doing a "disappearing act" works, too—spacing out, reading the paper, daydreaming, not phoning for a while, walking around with headphones while you listen to your CD player, or walking out of the room while your partner is talking. Any one of these diversions can force the issue of securing more space for you and is almost guaranteed to push your partner away. But keep in mind that your partner may interpret this "push" as abandonment.

"Abandonment? Not my partner," you might protest. "I can't imagine my partner having fears of abandonment." But the fact is, you may not know. Some experiences of rejection and abandonment can be obvious and some can be subtle, but if they repeat over time, they leave an imprint that often translates into the fear of being left. One woman I know was married to her partner for over fifteen years before she heard his abandonment stories. He was a pretty macho guy and always spoke of having a "regular" kind of childhood. But, one day in their couple's session, he suddenly remembered how his mother would get angry and threaten to leave him in department stores if he didn't behave. She'd pull this in supermarkets and in movie theaters as well. Once she did "disappear" for a while, and it seemed like an eternity to him. So now this man would gets very anxious if his wife gets angry at him. He tries to stop her anger by lashing out at her. This is his way of trying to quell his own anxiety.

As you can see, intimacy is affected when actions are misinterpreted by your partner, causing hurt and anger. When intimacy gets pushed aside, the space gets filled with damaging debris. But read on to see all the other ways space gets filled.

5

Fill 'er Up

Filling Space

"I hate Sundays when I'm not in love," a friend once told author Marianne Williamson. "They seem so empty." In *Illuminata* (1994), Williamson reminds us that "empty spaces can be unbearable before we discover the power of silence.... Most people are addicted to stress-producing stimuli.... We are deeply afraid of the silence, the void, the emptiness" (p. 103–4).

Psychiatrist Thomas Fogerty writes in *Family Therapy: Theory and Practice* (1976) that feelings of emptiness exist for all of us. Only the degree and details vary. This "emptiness" is made up of feelings of being uncared for, of not belonging, of insignificance, sadness, failure, and shame. It is a feeling of loneliness as well. Fogarty suggests that the best way to deal with emptiness is to stop running from it. But, instead of stopping and facing our feelings of emptiness, we continue distracting ourselves away from them. Empty space makes us feel so alone and lonely that we have to fill it up with something, anything. And what do we fill it with?

- Words
- Music
- Clutter
- Overeating
- The rush of adrenaline

- Work/Activities/Television
- Perfectionism
- Ambivalence
- Money issues/Consumerism
- Alcohol, cigarettes, and other substances

- Anger/Arguments/
  Provocations

- Jealousy

- Projections

- Secrets

- Possessiveness

- Obsessions/Compulsions

- Anxieties

- Stress

- Hurt/Blame/Annoyances/
  Resentments

- Complaining

- Drama

- Mistrust/Doubt/Suspicions

- Competitiveness

- Triangles

- Worries/Fears

- Illnesses

Horror Vacui—the Fear of Empty Space

What if you find yourself with some space around you, facing some time alone? Do you have to fill it with words, sounds, thoughts, things, or people? Take a moment to think about this. Is the empty space uncomfortable? What is it about empty space that it makes us feel so uneasy?

This fear of emptiness and open space has been with us throughout the ages. There is even a term for it: *horror vacui*, the fear of the void. For example, consider Early Minoan art (from 1600 B.C.) or Greek art (from 500 B.C.), which exhibited great attention to detail. Vase painters started with simple designs and filled in more and more decoration, until all available space was used up—even to the point of saturation. There was a kind of superstition connected to it, a way of keeping the unknown out.

There are other examples of this fear of empty space. Stylistically complex and overly elaborate baroque art is an example of this fear of bare surfaces and empty spaces. Cuban novelist Alejo Carpentier describes baroque as an art that moves from the center to the outskirts, transgressing its own margins in the process, leaving no open spaces. And Cuban poet and essayist José Lezama Lima describes baroque as the desperate overflow of the dispossessed,

And, too, the idea of *horror vacui* is associated with Aristotle's contributions to physics, giving rise to the theory that nature abhors a vacuum and prevents the production of a void at any cost. This was used to explain various phenomena, such as the workings of the pump and the siphon.

And what about our tendencies to fill up space? Might we suffer from *horror vacui* as well? Let's take a look at the ways we manage to fill space. This is a brief overview to be sure, but my purpose here is to be helpful in opening up some new ways for you to look at the distractions that may fill up the frightening space around you.

Many of the space fillers in these next two chapters also serve as distance regulators—affecting how close we allow ourselves to get to a partner and providing us with much-needed personal space. All too often we employ anger, depression, affairs, or jealousy to get space from our partner, although we don't know we're doing it.

Sometimes we fill space simply because we need to fill space. And we fill it with whatever is readily available. Of course, it's easier to utilize something we know well from our early experiences, perhaps from childhood.

Words

Some of us use words to fill space, because we are uncomfortable with the quiet. We chatter on and on, heaping on piles of words. Have you had the experience of not being able to stop talking? Sometimes you can even feel the other person pulling back and losing interest. You may even notice that their eyes glaze over—yet you continue to talk.

What would happen if you experiment with sitting alone, taking a deep breath, or two or three, and sitting in your own silence for a short while. Try sitting for a minute or two to start. Yes, those are long minutes. What happens for you? How uncomfortable are you? Where in your body do you feel the discomfort? What about trying to sit in silence for ten or fifteen minutes? It surely is hard to do—many of us can't tolerate the anxiety that arises.

What happens if you give it a try? Can you just sit quietly for ten minutes and listen to your breathing Can you allow the space to let your thoughts come and go, but not let any one thought take up the space for too long? What is it like for you to just sit? To just be with your breath—and with the silence?

Perhaps this thought about silences will help put it in perspective: Musicians will tell you that you can't have music without silence. It's the spaces between notes that make music. You may not know how long the silence will last, but you do know another note will come.

But, for many of us, words are easier than silences. And words are often erected as barriers—keeping us from being genuine or vulnerable or sincere, and preventing us from connecting. Words are used to protect us from authentic communication and to inhibit intimacy. They come in lots of shapes and sizes: walls, smoke screens, gates, and roadblocks. Why are we so quick to throw them up? What might these barriers be protecting?

No Strings Attached

Words are often used as a means of control—keeping people at a distance, not letting them get too close. The combination of that "tone" and "that look" can be very distancing indeed. You'll find more about control in chapter 7.

Sometimes you may find yourself using words to cut your partner off. That is to say, cutting off their words by inserting your own. You may not even wait for a space in a conversation—you may just jump right in. You might do this when you don't like what you are hearing, when you're feeling defensive, or when you disagree with your partner's point of view. Can you leave space for both the positive and the negative, the light and the dark? As with the yin and the yang, they may seem to be opposites, but there is continual movement and interaction between these two energies. What would it take to leave space in your relationship for them both—and for both of you as well

Words can also get in the way of growth and change. For example, one person in a couple may have had some exposure to psychology, pop psychology, or even groups such as est, The Forum, etc., acting as if they are more aware of psychological issues than their partner. It's a false perception: all it means is that they can talk the talk. Because they *think* they know so much, they stunt their personal growth and their partner may, in fact, come to surpass them in that area.

Work/Activities/TV

It's very acceptable in our society to put energy into work and projects and hobbies. These are ways of creating a safe and comfortable space for yourself. But you may find you don't leave enough room to have a relationship with another person.

Working long hours, or rehearsing that play, or writing that novel are all ways of diverting energy from a one-to-one, intimate relationship. Television works this way, too. You can even be sharing the same bedroom, the same bed, and the same TV, and one person will regularly "zone" out in front of it—losing "real" time and "real" space. "It's as if I'm brain-dead. Watching TV this way seems to be a way I self-medicate—a way of not dealing with things," says one woman.

"I find myself just doing this mindless clicking," she continues. Yes, channel surfing is another great diversion. It can cause rifts between couples when one wants to watch a program and the other one wants to skip through them. And these rifts are also perfect ways of filling empty space.

Music

We all have different styles of being alone. Some of us do it with music as a companion. We turn on the CD player, radio, or TV as soon as we get up in the morning or as soon as we come home in the evening. We don't even think about it—we just switch it on and fill up the space.

Others of us hardly ever turn on sound in our living space or in our cars. Our alone time is in silence. Some of us may prefer quiet time at home, but we like to have the company of music or talk radio in the car. One woman I know insists how comfortable she is with being alone. But, in fact, since she was a child, her "alone" time was never without the companionship of music. Alone, yes. Silent, no.

Perfectionism

If you make sure you do things perfectly, you don't leave any room for someone to tell you, "It's not good enough." Perfectionism doesn't allow for anyone to see whatever imperfections you imagine about yourself. It doesn't allow for mistakes or questions. It's a way to protect yourself from rejection, allowing no room for comment or criticism.

You may have had lots of practice learning to be "perfect" in childhood. You may have been designated as the one who steps in and fills up any empty spaces in your family. Your job was to fill up the existing void, especially if other family members thought of themselves as inadequate or if they *were* inadequate. Sometimes there is just no space to be a child; you were just too busy trying to fill up the space that your parents left empty.

Now, as an adult, you may keep on trying to do a perfect job of filling the space around you. After all, that was where you received your childhood validation. One man says, "My role in my family was filling up space. Now, as soon as I see a place where I can fill a space, I'm home free. When I can give and give and give, I can fill myself up."

But perfectionism gets even more complicated when it gets mixed up with having unrealistic expectations of our partners. We often don't leave room for someone to be less than the perfect person we need them to be. As one woman says, "Sometimes I think I'll never find the right person for me. I get my hopes up, but then guys repeatedly disappoint me. I guess I don't allow people the space to be human."

Clutter

Okay, here's a great research topic. Do people who have a tendency to clutter their living spaces also clutter their lives with too many people, projects, or distractions? With all those balls in the air at the same time, we feel pressured not to drop any of them. In fact, if we didn't have to do a juggling act with our time, wouldn't we then have more time for intimacy with the people with whom we *want* to spend time? It's all too easy to dilute relationships by spreading ourselves way too thin—perhaps similar to the way we tend to spread out clutter.

Clutter is a pretty effective way to throw up barriers. For instance, for some of us, piles of papers might symbolize protective walls or small, cozy, secure spaces. And clutter surely can get in the way of relationships. There is no question that people have different styles: some folks are museum quality tidy, some are down- right messy. Some folks prefer complexity, others like simplicity.

However, excessive clutter can be connected to great anxiety as well. For example, the "pack rat" may be holding on to stuff to avoid the anxiety of deciding which things to throw away, just in case a need for it should arise sometime. And do you suppose that pack rats have a *horror vacui*—a dread of empty spaces?

But, at the same time, some people are just the opposite, craving neat, tidy, wide-open spaces. In relationships, both clutter and orderliness can easily become a battle for space.

Making Room

What's comfortable for one person can be stifling for another. Rachel and Ted fight about Ted's takeover of Rachel's space. He likes his minimalist space, and only if it is totally uncluttered does it feel like *his*. The trouble is that Ted's need for open spaces is taking up way too much space, and Rachel feels there is no room for her to be herself in the house. In fact, Rachel is really pushed out of shape about Ted's need for clean surfaces. "It doesn't feel like there is any room for me at all," says Rachel. "My dresser top is the only place I can be myself—I feel I'm being relegated to a two-by-three foot space. I wish I had someplace else I could call my own in the house, a place to stack my mail in the kitchen or my magazines in the living room. I hold my piles sacred. They're a sign of life, proclaiming, 'Rachel lives here!'"

What's cozy for one can be smothering for the other. A couple I know has been dating for three years, but still live separately. They like to cook together, but she always prefers that he come to her house. She is just too uncomfortable at his, because the kitchen counters are piled high with all sorts of stuff. "There's no room for me in this space," she says. She often asks him to clear off some of the piles of papers, and he always says he will, but doesn't come through. In fact, she is starting to question if there is really room for her in the relationship. It's a good question.

Juanita, too, was in a relationship where her papers and things seemed to be multiplying during the night. And, to make matters worse, she started taking over the dining room table during a work project by piling up papers and notes and phone message slips. Her partner developed the conviction that she was driving him out on purpose by not leaving any room and he started threatening to leave. Well, at this point, Juanita started paying attention to the situation. "I always put off picking up the piles of stuff because I never could find the energy to do it perfectly," explains Juanita. "But I had to do something about it or before I knew it, I'd be living alone in the middle of the stacks. So I created a strategy. I decided to pick up things, starting from the center of each room and moving outward. This created a larger and larger space, and I soon could see I was making room for both of us."

Sometimes clutter is more than the piles or stacks or jumbles. It can also be tangles of obligations. For example, when your professional life takes away from your personal or family life. This is how Angela feels when Andrew is always taking on new projects at work and in the community. He can't seem to say "no" to requests for his time, and Angela has taken to making "appointments" to spend time with him. "I want him to make room for me in his life, but instead I feel as if he's barely squeezing me in."

One man tells this story: "I have a friend who has a lot of free time. Once she told me about a tree in her neighborhood that blooms only one week out of the year, producing lustrous purple blossoms. She suggested that I try to stop by to see it, and you know what? I felt my life was so cluttered with work at the time that I didn't have the energy to stop by. Because I was resentful that she has so much free time, I told myself I didn't have the time to experience it the way she could, so I didn't even try to visit the tree. I didn't even make an attempt to make the space to enjoy it and take it in. Since then, I've made an effort to simplify my life, to become less and less entangled. I'm trying to open up to new experiences, rather than shutting them out. I guess you could say I'm trying to become more intimate with life."

Ambivalence

Although ambivalence is discussed in chapter 3, I'm listing it here as a major player in the list of "space fillers." Simultaneous, conflicting feelings or wishes can take up a great deal of space and energy. Two internal voices that are at odds with each other can cause lots of anxiety, and anxiety is surely capable of filling up every nook and cranny, as we'll see in the following chapter.

Overeating

Food is a way many of us elect to fill space—especially lonely space or painful space or anxious space. It feels so good in the moment to fill up our stomachs—oatmeal, baked potatoes, chocolate—take your pick. We all have our comfort foods, don't we? Most of us have noticed how that space inside of us seems larger at certain times, especially when we are sad or unsure of ourselves, anxious or fearful. So we try to fill it by shoveling more and more food into our mouths. And it's true that, for some of us, the only relationship we have is with food.

Gena recalls, "I didn't get emotionally fed enough in childhood, and now I'm hungry all the time." She goes on to describe a "gnawing pain," a huge, empty space inside of her. "I look to other people to fill it up. I pick a partner from whom I try to extract what I need. But I wish I could take it from inside myself instead." In *Don't Take It Personally!*, I described an imagery exercise Gena and I did regarding this empty space. I think it's worth repeating here.

Gena visualized a big, brass wine goblet with a wide base and substantial rim. As the wine flowed in, it seemed to stop near the bottom. "I want the cup to fill up faster and faster," she explained, "but then I do something to stop it before it gets half full. There seems to be a membrane inside the goblet, a barrier. I think it means that other people have to fight to get past my barrier."

Gena came into the next session all excited and told me, "I decided to visualize pouring the wine from the metal goblet into a smaller, delicate crystal wine glass. It's much easier to fill. The same amount of wine appears to be more because the glass is smaller. Now the glass is over half full." We realized that, in fact, wine is usually poured half full, leaving room for it to breathe. Gena brightened. "Yes, of course. If the cup were all the way filled with wine, I couldn't breathe! Yes, indeed. It needs air and light to intensify its potential. There's more than just the wine; there's the light and the bouquet. Yes, I think I could learn to appreciate the unfilled parts of me. After all, emptiness is just space—it doesn't *have* to be painful."

Alcohol, Cigarettes, and Other Substances

Addictions cover a lot of territory, and there are scores of books available about any aspect you might want to explore. I touch on the subject here because addictions are a popular way to fill space. If you want to read more about how these issues affect relationships, I've listed some titles in the Suggested Readings list.

"I was so lonely," one woman says. "So I began a relationship with alcohol. It became my lover and my best friend." Sometimes that empty space becomes so unbearable, and the need to fill it up with something, *anything*, becomes so great, that we keep pouring or inhaling or shooting or swallowing more and more stuff to fill up.

Any addiction serves to insulate, cover up, protect, and blot out. You may realize one day how you have filled up all those crevices of your heart and soul with this addictive need, leaving no space for feeling or thinking or experiencing. And you've also severely shrunk the space that you can make available to the important people in our life.

Pick a Substitute

Okay, so there seems to be a space that needs filling, but you realize that your ways of filling it aren't working too well anymore. Perhaps a substitute "space filler" is in order here. Let's look at the substitution theory regarding alcohol or substances.

One of the most popular times to use substances is during transition times from work to home. When Lois realized that she seemed to need that beer or two (or three or four) to "unwind" after work, she began noticing how she experienced opening each bottle. She began to realize that this process constituted a kind of ritual that marked the end of her work day and the beginning of her home time. Then she had another thought. Maybe one or two was all she really needed to unwind. The third and fourth were more a matter of a habit than a need. Some days, she got down to one beer after work. She decided to try an experiment. What if she substituted some other unwinding activity for the beer? She experimented with solitaire and embroidery, then settled on one of those designer coloring books. You know the kind I mean, the ones with those intricate patterns. This way, she had a methodical and meditative ritual to take her through her work-to-home transition, and she no longer needed that ritualistic opening of beer bottles.

The Rush of Adrenaline

Many of us love the "rush" of living on the edge, thriving on crises. It's as if we crave the high of anticipation—a new relationship or a new job will do it. We get a thrill from the feeling of anxiety that comes from pulse-racing activities. These can include procrastination, tight deadlines, or the stress of chronically arriving late for work or appointments. We might thrive on high-risk sports, such as sky diving, hang gliding, rock climbing, mountaineering, bungee jumping, or whitewater rafting. Or we love the excitement of risky sex, wild parties, intense music, and fast driving.

This compulsive need for excitement also spawns thrill-seeking activities such as gaming, horses, lotto, and other forms of compulsive gambling. In addition, there is the "high" of compulsive Internet use, which will be discussed in chapter 11. And, yes, margin trading on the stock market is another way many people live on the edge.

Courting physical or psychological "danger" brings on a rush of adrenaline, which leads to faster heart rate, pulse rate, and respiration rate. This "high" is often referred to as adrenaline addiction, but it is also related to the trait of sensation seeking, the tendency to seek intense sensations and experiences. In *Behavioral Expressions and Biosocial Bases of Sensation Seeking* (1994), Marvin Zuckerman states that sensation seekers are genetically predisposed for the need to experience varied, novel, complex, and intense sensations and are willing to take physical, social, legal, and financial risks in order to achieve these sensations.

Many of you may have lived with this "rush" for lots of years, without even being aware of your need for it. Often it has existed since childhood, especially if danger or unpredictability characterized your life. You may be so used to it hanging around, you might even be lonely without it. What an empty space would exist if it wasn't there.

Money Issues/Consumerism

Both spending money and not spending money can fill space in the relationship. Buying lots of stuff can work in the same way as overeating or overdrinking, especially around loneliness or anxiety. Sometimes you may find yourself shopping for expensive clothes or electronics. But often you may not even go for the big-ticket items— small, useful things will do just fine. The next time you notice a flurry of activity in the buying department, ask yourself if, just maybe, you might be filling up some space. And if it's true, do you know why this might be? Is there a need that's not getting met? Can you find a way to meet it? Too much spending can be a sore spot in the relationship and resentment builds because "things" seem to take on a bigger priority than the partner.

But not spending causes hurt feelings as well. Amy expected her live-in boyfriend to contribute his share of groceries and other household expenses. She thought he should pay half of her mortgage as well. Sometimes he did, but not consistently, and she found herself becoming more and more resentful. She had never talked with him about her concerns, and she had no idea what his income was.

Finally, she got up the courage to have this long-overdue talk with him. She found out that his income was much less than she presumed. And his way of contributing was to give her his services. He did "handy" kinds of things, and, being a professional gardener, he had redesigned her yard, planting some exotic foliage. He saw this work as his contribution to the household, but didn't tell her that. She saw it as a gift and had no idea it was in lieu of money for expenses. It turns out that he thought he was bartering services, something he was used to doing in his business. Having the talk with him made a huge difference in her attitude. Rather than being angry at him for "holding back," she found out he was doing all he could do financially. We acquire attitudes about money from our families or origin. What messages did you receive from your parents? Did your parents struggle over money? How did it affect you? How is it affecting your relationship with your partner?

Jealousy

Feelings of jealousy can be normal when you feel threatened. If you've ever felt the pain of rejection in the past, it's easy to start worrying that your partner will leave you for someone else. Jealousy can take up lots of space and energy, especially if it gets obsessive.

Jealousy can puff up like a balloon and take on a life of it's own. J. Ruth Gendler, in her 1988 *The Book of Qualities*, gives personality to jealousy as she describes how it "sometimes stands by the blue flame of the gas stove stirring obsession stew . . . He certainly has a flair for drama. After a while, though, the roles Jealousy takes begin to seem shallow, dishonest, repetitive" (p. 44). In fact, you might ask yourself if your jealousy might serve a space-filling purpose that isn't even related to your partner's actions.

Jealousy is also a way of feeling connected to someone, but it tends to be an overconnectedness—a form of emotional fusion with the other person. If you remember from chapter 1, emotional fusion is the opposite of differentiation.

Once Chris was able to step back from her jealousy, she came to this realization: "I'm not as jealous of my partner's friendships now, but I also notice I don't feel as close, either. My jealousy was so intense, it brought passion to the relationship, and I actually felt more connected. Now that I'm not so jealous, I feel more detached."

Jealousy leads to hurt and anger and is a primary cause of domestic violence. Early experiences of rejection intensify the fear that someone we care deeply for might leave. Watching your partner flirt with someone at a party or finding old love letters can be unsettling, leading to intense jealousy. Usually the best way to deal with it is directly—describe what you have observed and ask your partner about it. Most likely the answer will be no worse than the worst-case scenario you've conjured up in your mind. And look at the energy you will have saved! By talking with your partner directly, you will most likely avoid building up resentment.

Hurt/Blame/Annoyances/Resentments

Sometimes, when there is a large, empty space and not enough love and acceptance, we tend to fill that space with hurt. The hurt expands as fast as Wonder Bread dipped into milk, and in no time at all, every nook and cranny of the space is filled. And, as you may know, sometimes it's hard to give up the hurt because there's a kind of soggy comfort from it.

Blaming ourselves or blaming others is another surefire way to fill up space. When we blame others without considering our own roles in these relationship dynamics, we feel victimized. When we blame ourselves, we are victimizing ourselves. Neither situation is very proactive. Not very productive, either.

Blaming yourself is not the same as taking responsibility for your own actions, but all too often we confuse the two. Taking responsibility is standing on your own two feet. Blaming is leaning on the other person to take responsibility.

> Blaming yourself is not the same as
> taking responsibility for your own actions

Another blaming behavior is more subtle, where one person will convince the other to make a decision that ideally they should be making together. These decisions include things like where to go for vacation, or what movie or restaurant to go to. This can even include big decisions involving the children, such as schools or medical determinations. Then, if things don't go right, the ambivalent, "uninvolved" partner can say, "It's your fault. I didn't make the decision, you did."

It's Your Problem, Not Mine

Little annoyances can fill lots of space and can be, well, so annoying. You know the kinds of things I mean—if your partner repeatedly jingles the car keys, it can jangle your nerves. And there are other annoying habits as well, such as throat clearing, noisy eating, belching or farting, picking their cuticles, drumming fingers on the table, cracking their knuckles, or fidgeting. Those of us who are highly sensitive to our environments will most likely be more annoyed than someone with a different temperament would be. Sometimes we are even bothered by the smells that our partner gives off. In *The Highly Sensitive Person in Love* (2000), psychologist Elaine Aron describes how being in a close relationship creates a quandary for highly sensitive people. In order to tolerate closeness, it's practical to be "lovingly tolerant—and turned off. But that's not a close relationship, and so we decide there's something wrong with us. We may just not be able to love anyone." Aron goes on to say "Once a partner understands and appreciates your sensitivity, you really will be able to love someone and express your being bothered by these 'little things' that seem so big," (pp. 87–8).

But, all too often, we hold back on expressing our feelings to our partners. When we stuff these feelings of hurt, blame, and annoyance, resentment appears. And you'll see how it ripens in chapter 12. Resentment has a "half-life," like some medications that linger in the system quite a while after you stop taking them. And resentments have a way of expanding into something else—anger.

Anger/Arguments/Provocations

Many of us grew up being very confused about expressing anger. Anger was often dealt with in an either/or manner—we swallowed it or exploded in it. There was no space for inbetween. Anger meant someone might withdraw into stony silence, or threaten to leave, or explode into uncontrollable rage. So we grew up thinking anger isn't okay. But as Harriet Goldhor Lerner notes, "Anger is neither legitimate nor illegitimate, meaningful nor pointless. Anger simply is" (p. 3). She goes on to say that anger is a feeling, existing for a reason, deserving our respect and attention. She emphasizes that we have a right to our feelings and anger is no exception.

If, however, we learned in our families that anger was not okay to express, we may have cut it off, pushed it down, and stifled it. As adults, we must find a way to make space for anger and express it in ways that work.

Anger serves an important function for most of us. It is an excellent distance regulator, because it serves both as a distancer ("I can't stand to be near you when we fight") and as a connector ("We're not talking if we're not fighting").

Picking a fight works—sometimes—and anger is a guaranteed space filler when we need a little distance from someone. But, of course, sometimes we get more space than we bargained for. If we really take a good look at it, there may even be times when we find ourselves creating the anger by provoking a reaction from someone. As I discussed in chapter 1, we fill up space with anger and resentment, and we often project anger onto another person.

Anger is so powerful that we often get in more deeply than we planned on. It's hard to know that anger is not forever, and once it surfaces, it can bring up fears of withdrawn love or abandonment in either you or your partner.

But anger can bring people closer together, too. The best part of a good fight for some people is the making-up part. Wouldn't it be useful to be able to have the closeness of that "making up" experience without having to have the anger. (See chapter 15 for ways to make these kinds of substitutions.)

Let's talk about provocations. One reason we provoke is because it helps us to feel more in control of the situation, because we are setting the time and place. This is especially true of anyone who experienced emotional, physical, or sexual abuse in childhood. There is never a question in an abused child's mind "if" the abuse will happen again. It will. The only question is "When?" So the child often learns to manipulate the time and place it will occur, thus having an illusion of some sort of control. This tendency to provoke continues right into adult relationships.

Another form of provocation is throwing out a line that is sure to get a rise when your partner bites the bait. Couples can develop an exquisite macabre dance, baiting and biting, biting and baiting, alternating between the two. I've heard this dynamic referred to as "the fish and the fisherman."

Complaining

Some of us are the "glass half empty" type, pessimistic and discontented about life. A half-empty glass leaves lots of space for us to be disappointed and complain about all the things that are missing. Perhaps it's a cultural kind of thing as well—passing the art of complaining down through the generations! I grew up hearing expressions such as, "What else are you going to find to complain about?" or, "One more complaint out of you and you'll be sorry." Complaining, like nagging or anger, is a way some of us learned in our families of origin to stay connected to each other. We learned this so well, we bring this "skill" into our couple's relationships. As the saying goes, "It ain't much, but it's home."

Complaining has another function in relationships. It is often a sign that you are disappointed in something your partner did or didn't do, and you may find yourself getting on their case about seemingly insignificant things. Complaining might sound like fussing, nagging, scolding, grumbling, or whining. These behaviors all have something in common—they are a way to get attention from your partner. Very possibly it will be negative attention, but, as the saying goes, "any attention is better than none"—especially if you have been feeling ignored or neglected lately.

But what might be under that hard edge of complaining? If you scratch the surface, you may find the softness of yearning. Maybe it was a hope or expectation that didn't get met or a need that didn't get fulfilled. Sometimes finding a direct way to ask for it will get you the results you need.

Lois' story illustrates this so well. She used to complain about work at the dinner table just about every evening. At first, her partner tried to be helpful, but every time he offered a suggestion she'd "yes, but" it. He soon tired of trying to rescue her from her "poor me" situation, and he grew more and more frustrated and irritable. Finally one evening, he yelled, "All you do is complain, and I don't want to hear it anymore."

Yes, it would have been helpful if he could have listened to her express her feelings, and let her know he heard her. But he didn't know how to do that—he thought that to "help" meant to "fix it," so he tried to rescue her.

It would have been helpful if she could have found a way to let him in on what she needed from him. What did she really want? Well, it took her a while to figure that out, but with some thought, she did. She wanted to be held and comforted. She wanted a safe space.

Once Lois was able to take the space to put into words what she wanted from her partner, it was so much easier for him to know what to do. Once he didn't have to spend so much energy guessing, he could try to give that energy to her.

The Karpman Drama Triangle

You may have noticed how it becomes a quick trip from feeling victimized to provoking a "rise" out of your partner, or from feeling blamed to blaming. This is a good place to make a little side trip into the wondrous world of the Karpman Drama Triangle. This concept was developed by San Francisco psychiatrist Steve Karpman, and I consider it an invaluable tool for sorting out complex couple interactions. You'll notice stories throughout this book of couples who are engaged in pushy, nagging, complaining, bullying conduct or caretaking, infantalizing, rescuing behaviors, or who experience resentful or victimized feelings. As you read these descriptions, it may occur to you that even though a person sees him or herself one way, their partner may see them from a different perspective.

In the Karpman Drama Triangle, the three points are represented by the roles of Persecutor, Rescuer, and Victim. The roles are interchangeable, with each player trading positions at any given time. Sometimes a person may switch from Victim to Persecutor to Rescuer in a flash; other times, it's more gradual.

First of all, I want to point out how easy it is to become a victim if we tend to take things personally—especially if we feel singled out. But we take on other roles as well. The classic martyr mother or mother-in-law offers a good example of the triangle in action. She usually complains of doing so much for other family members (Rescuer) that she feels unappreciated (Victim). She may frequently be heard to say, "You never write, you never call. Look at all I do for you and look what I get in return—nothing."

But this poor, unfortunate martyr happens to be the most powerful person in the family. Other family members keep trying to please her (Rescue)—until they get resentful, that is. Then they begin to feel victimized by her (Victim). If they retaliate by acting rebelliously or procrastinating or making empty promises, they take on the role of "bad and uncaring" in her eyes (Persecutor), because she is feeling victimized by them. For more in-law stories, see chapter 13 about "outlaw in-laws."

Can you see how the martyr moves from role to role on the triangle? This occurs in a similar fashion for other "rescuing" kinds of behavior—codependence, overfunctioning, infantalizing. When one partner "takes over" for the other (Rescuer), the dependent one feels infantalized (Victim) by the pushy one (Persecutor). Anger and resentment build up (Victim/Persecutor), leaving the "rescuer"

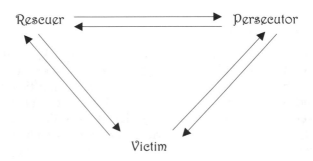

The Karpman Drama Triangle

feeling hurt (Victim) that these caring behaviors are not appreciated by their partner.

The Victim spot is on the bottom of the triangle, but because of the power the victim holds in the family, it might as well be on the top. Isn't it fascinating how one person may see him- or herself in the role of Victim (or Rescuer), and another person may see that person as a Persecutor And we wonder why people get so upset with us!

Awareness of how this process works between family members can help stop interactions that lead to hurt feelings, misunderstandings, and resentment. Most especially, it can help curb that destructive cycle of feeling personally attacked and needing to defend by mounting a counterattack.

So often we get stuck in an intractable position, seeing ourselves in primarily one role—ususally the rescuer or the victim. However, once we recognize that these positions are fluid, we can understand that others see us quite differently than we see ourselves. Then we can more easily see problematic situations from a wider lens, perhaps even from the other person's point of view.

Projections

As you read in chpater 2, we sometimes have "blind spots" about ourselves that affect our relationships with others. It's often the very same traits we can't stand about ourselves that we have the most trouble tolerating in others. Projection is when we mistakenly imagine that those characteristics exist in the other person when we cannot acknowledge them in ourselves. Blaming others is also a form of projection. Look to chapter 2 for more about how much space is taken up in relationships by projection and projective identification.

Competitiveness

Some couples can't seem to resist getting competitive with each other. For one couple, it was okay as long as they both had the same education. But the minute she received her doctorate degree and added "Dr." to her voicemail message, he began to have a hard time. In fact, he even asked her if she'd mind removing it from her outgoing message, because whenever he called to leave her a message he just hated listening to it. She refused, of course.

Feelings of competition can be even worse for couples who are in the same field of work. I've seen instances where one holds back so as not to overtake the other. Then, too, there are situations where one flaunts promotions or accolades. Not only are couples competitive around successes but in the amount of money each earns as well.

Envy can also be a problem in relationships. One partner may feel threatened by the other's successes, or feels threatened that school or work takes away from time that could be spent together. The energy that it takes to fight about, skirt, or dwell on these issues takes up a whole lot of space in the relationship.

Drama

Recently I saw a small, black velvet pillow in a gift boutique that stopped me in my tracks. The words embroidered in white on the black cover called out to me: "DRAMA QUEEN." "Hey, that's me," I blurted out. "I recognize that one!" And everyone in the shop stopped to stare.

Some of us do tend to use drama to fill up space. Maybe it gives us a sense of identity or self–importance. Maybe we can't stand things to be quiet for too long because we are used to some drama in our lives—perhaps from childhood. So we stir up a little drama here and there. Well, perhaps we don't do it totally from scratch. The basic ingredients are usually already there. Ingredients such as someone being too intrusive or too elusive; someone being condescending or patronizing; someone being too . . . well, you get the idea. If any (or all) of these things are hot buttons, then we just make a super big deal of it. Very dramatically.

Secrets

For some of us, secrets were woven into the fabric of our lives from an early age, leaving little room for honesty or authenticity. All kinds of things are kept secret. Parents may feel they are protecting the child by not answering questions truthfully. These questions might be about an illness or death, an uncomfortable situation in the family, or even about frightening world events. At other times, it is an adult child who is protecting the parent by not divulging medical information about that parent. Someone may be dying, but no one will tell them the truth about their situation in order to "protect" them.

A common secret is making up a story about a family member's cause of death. This is especially true when there is a suicide. A man I know lost his father in his early teens and a few years later a classmate teased him about his father committing suicide. When this man asked his mother about it, she denied it. When he was in his forties, he finally learned the truth. The family had been living a secret all those years. And he had been living with the secretiveness.

If someone didn't trust you with the
truth when you were growing up, it's hard
to trust others when you are a grown-up.

Often, on some level, children sense what the secret is, but because of the family rules about secretiveness, they feel that they can't say anything. So they remain very lonely in their isolation.

When people grow up in secretive families, they often continue be secretive in their adult relationships. Trust becomes an issue because they will also be expecting secretiveness from others. If someone didn't trust you with the truth when you were growing up, it's hard to trust others when you are a grown-up.

Because it's hard to "open up" when you've been raised in a secretive family, it's bound to affect your level of intimacy with another person. In chapter 1, I described intimacy as "sharing your secret thoughts and feelings, allowing yourself to expand, opening your heart, so your truest essence is revealed. It means inviting another person into this sacred space and understanding that the other person is willing to allow you in, as well." Just be aware that this is a really hard thing to do if you grew up in a family that put secrets first. Take a breath, be aware, notice, observe—and you will find yourself opening up, a little at a time.

Mistrust/Doubt/Suspicions

Mistrust and suspicions can take up so much space, time, and energy. And once the seeds get planted, this mistrust becomes an overgrown weed patch that gets out of hand. It's usually a good thing to remind yourself that if you become suspicious of someone, it's possible that you are attributing something to them that you have concerns about in yourself. One woman I know began to suspect that her husband was having an affair with an associate at work. She began imagining that the object of his affections was another guy, but, in fact, she had no real indications or evidence. It was just her imagination. As it turns out, this was a projection from her own unacknowledged attraction to women. She had no conscious idea it was going on at the time and only realized it in retrospect, when she became aware of her interest in women several years later.

It's such a fine line between trusting our intuition and mistrusting the important people in our lives. One of the best ways to get a reality check is to ask an objective third party. But better yet, if you are wondering about a situation, why not directly ask the person involved? Usually the answer is not as bad as the dire expectations that you repeatedly play out in your mind. And, even if it is, you'll get a jump start in dealing with it.

Possessiveness

Another fine line is the one we step over as soon as we get too attached. What happens when we think we own the other person, when we get so possessive? "Having sex with someone does it every time," one woman said. "I get so damned possessive. I hate that word, but I don't know what else to call it. Actually, to tell the truth, it's worse than possessive. I feel almost crazed when things don't go the way I think they should, or when I feel I'm not getting enough attention, or the phone calls aren't frequent enough, or we don't go out as much as I think we ought to. When I get so invested in a relationship, I seem to lose my objectivity. I'm so sensitive and get hurt so easily. Way too easily." Along with possessiveness comes jealousy, mistrust, and many of the other elements listed here. No wonder it takes up so much space! And it can lead to obsessing.

Obsessions/Compulsions

It takes a lot of energy to be compulsively obsessive. This goes along with possessiveness, competition, and mistrust. You know— those thoughts that just keep on coming and won't stop.

We've talked about how much time, space, and energy worry can take up in relationships. Well, worry can be a form of obsessing as well. You know the kind of worry I mean here—if your partner is late arriving home, or something feels suspicious to you, or there is something in the air and you can't quite put your finger on what it is. That's when it becomes all too easy to start obsessing. And if you happen to be involved in a relatively new relationship or one that feels a little shaky, how often do you compulsively check your phone messages just in case they called to suggest meeting after work for a romantic dinner or something? If you live in separate abodes it's so hard not to drive by the street where they live and see if their car is there. Well, maybe you stop just short of doing that, but you may very badly want to.

Triangles

As Murray Bowen (1978) asserts, when anxiety develops because there is too much closeness or too much distance in the relationship, emotional triangles often occur. Even from early childhood, when the relationship between two friends gets too intense, they usually pull in a third person to help defuse it. Well, we do the same as adults when the tension between partners gets too intense, we pull in a third person, problematic behavior, or even an object. That person may be a child to depend on (parentified) or to turn on (scapegoat, problem child). It might be a lover or it could be in-laws. Often it's someone in whom one of the partners confides, perhaps a best friend, Internet buddy, teacher, mentor, or even a therapist. The problematic behavior may be gambling, alcoholism or other substance abuse, and this behavior may lead to further triangulation if it becomes a heated topic for discussion. The object may be a journal or diary that one partner confides in, leaving the other person on the "outside." Any of these "third points" functions to diffuse the tension and lower the intensity of the real problem, which is usually one related to issues of intimacy between the couple.

The space fillers I've touched on here can take over relationships if we let them—pushing out the positives. You may notice how there seems to be a need to hold on to them, a way of filling space. You may also notice how many of these space fillers spring from or lead to anxiety or stress. In order to give ample space to the very important topic of anxiety and its frequent companions—stress, fear, and illness—I'm giving them a chapter all their own.

6

Reaching the Saturation Point

Anxieties, Fears, Stress, and Illness

Anxiety can stand alone as a way to fill up lots of space. It's very effective and doesn't need any help. However, in combination with fear, stress, or illness, it can become overwhelming, spilling over and leaving little room for relationships.

Anxieties

When I hear the word "anxiety" it calls up the image of how my cat's skin "crawls" if I approach her too energetically. When Elizabeth gets nervous her lower back seems to go into a kind of spasm. Perhaps it has something to do with the fact that she was three years old when I adopted her from the Humane Society. Apparently, she and her sister came in together, but sis was adopted two weeks before Elizabeth. Who knows what Elizabeth's life was like before and during the three weeks she spent in the small space of that cage. Who knows how many people may have taken her home, tried her out, and returned her. At any rate, the cat has lots of trouble being in a relationship. Her anxiety gets in the way.

That happens for many of us, too. Perhaps the best way to understand how anxiety affects intimacy is to describe and diagram the anxiety cycle. Anxiety leads to the need to control and stop the anxiety, which leads to an attempt to control the environment.

Unfortunately, people are part of the environment, and they can feel that you're attempting to control them as well.

Think about the things that make you nervous, uneasy, apprehensive, fearful, or anxious. Usually it's when someone says or does something that upsets you or neglects to say or do something you really long for. Perhaps it's when you have mixed feelings about a commitment you've made—for example, agreeing to attend a dinner or a party or a wedding and realizing that you don't really want to go. It can be especially nerve-wracking if you know it's important to your partner.

So, you may become uneasy or anxious or fearful. And it doesn't feel good to feel this way. It's uncomfortable and sometimes reminds you of some old feelings you had as a child—maybe dreading something or feeling afraid. These are uncomfortable feelings, to be sure. You didn't like those feelings when you were a kid, and you don't want them around now, either. So you try to stop them. You try to control the environment to make your anxious feelings go away. But because people are part of the environment, you may run into some resistance. Below is a sort of flow chart to give you a visual idea of the anxiety/control cycle.

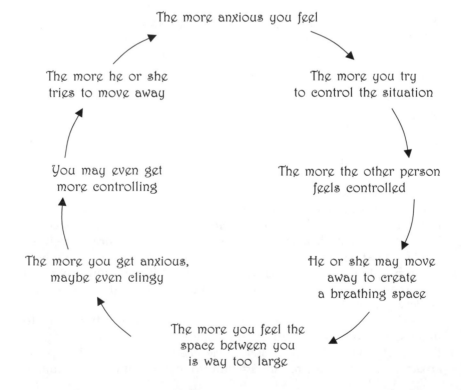

The more anxious you feel

The more he or she
tries to move away

The more you try
to control the situation

You may even get
more controlling

The more the other person
feels controlled

The more you get anxious,
maybe even clingy

He or she may move
away to create
a breathing space

The more you feel the
space between you
is way too large

Whew. You can see that the more anxious you get, the more you try to control, leading to results that make you even *more* anxious. It's a no-win situation.

Expecting to Be Judged

One couple had a terrible fight right before they were to leave for a fancy family wedding out of state—*her* family's event. The husband had already made arrangements to rent a tuxedo, and the plane tickets had already been purchased. Then the day before they were to leave, he started fighting with her. He began making some crude remarks about some members of her family who would be at the wedding, and she got defensive. It escalated into a really nasty fight, ending when he shouted, "Well, then I'm not going to the wedding, so there!" And he didn't.

As it turns out, he had been so nervous about going to an event where he felt he would be judged, his anxiety took over. To get some control, and stop his discomfort, he initiated a fight. And because he had not wanted to go to the wedding anyway, he fixed it so he didn't have to. It worked to calm his anxiety, but it surely didn't help his marriage.

Feeling Panicky

Anxiety can also arise in everyday situations, and the partner who experiences it is often too ashamed tell the other person about it. Some of these anxieties show up in the form of fears and even panic attacks. Being in crowded public places or small, constricted spaces can bring up tremendous anxiety. Some people with mild phobias may not recognize that they avoid these situations. Imagine the trouble this can cause, when the fearful partner, who hasn't told their mate anything about their fears, tries to change plans to control their panic. The other person would be understandably confused, and maybe even irate, as their partner repeatedly backs out of plans.

Let's look in on what happens when Joanie and her partner go out to the movies or a play. Joanie always wants to sit on the end of the aisle, whereas her partner much prefers the very middle and gets irritated by Joanie's constant insistence on the aisle seat. It was years before Joanie even had a glimmer about why she preferred her "spot." She would get really hot and uncomfortable with people on both sides of her and no "escape route." She eventually figured out that she was mildly claustrophobic. Once she understood this and could explain it to her partner, the tension that had been between them on these outings disappeared. Unacknowledged or unexplained fears can lead to hurt feelings and cause big-time relationship damage.

Anxiety about waiting can also lead to relationship misunderstandings. Let's take a look at how the anxiety cycle plays out while waiting for someone's arrival or phone call.

The Angst of Waiting

For some people, the act of waiting for that arrival or phone call leads to catastrophizing and subsequent protective pulling back from the "late" person.

"I freak out waiting," says Connie. "The uncertainty drives me crazy. I wait and worry, whenever James is late. Where is he? Why doesn't he call? Whatever could have happened to him? There must have been an accident. As the minutes turn into hours, I pace the room, beside myself with worry. Not knowing feels so terrible. I feel so vulnerable to my imagination. I just hate how this feeling of helplessness comes over me. I hate it when I expend so much energy by being dramatic."

No question, this is a lot of anxiety. And, it's a good guess that it's not just about worrying about James. Where might all this anxiety and drama come from? Did Connie worry as a child as well?

"My dad was a fireman," she relates. "If he was late coming home, it might have meant he was injured or dead. My mom and I spent many hours waiting up for him—who could sleep?"

"I've tried many times to get James to understand how important it is for him to phone me if he runs late. I guess I wasn't able to make it clear enough, or he was being dense, or something. Maybe he doesn't want to feel controlled. But I'm really not trying to control him. I just want him to respect my difficulty with this problem. Whatever it is, we have been together five years, and he is just now beginning to call me some of the time when he is late. Can you imagine the amount of energy I have put into all that worrying in our first five years?"

For many of us, waiting can be pure torture. Waiting for a phone call. Waiting for a phone call to be returned. Waiting for an arrival. Waiting for an explanation. Waiting for an e-mail. Waiting for an invitation. Waiting for someone to remember a birthday or important "anniversary" date. Waiting for a confirmation. What kinds of waiting torments do you go through? Where did they come from? What kind of messages did you give yourself then? What kinds of messages do you give yourself now?

And Another Waiting Torture

"I just hate it when I do this," states Eddie. "I hate becoming unglued like this just because she hasn't phoned. I know in my *head* how silly it is to jump ahead to my worst fears. I feel so helpless waiting for that phone call. I hate it when I do this to myself, but I can't stop. Something seems to take over. I want to trust that she still cares for me, that she's not going anywhere. But I can't. I'm so afraid of being hurt again.

"I just can't stand how much this fear hurts. I have to do something with it. So I manage to turn it into anger. Maybe if I get angry enough, I can create some space and talk myself out of staying involved with her. So I start building a case against her: What an inconsiderate jerk she is. How can she do this to me? And I think, 'There's no way in the world I'll ever put myself through this torture again.' And then, just as I'm thinking I'm going to lose my mind, she calls. And it's all okay until the next time it happens."

Where does this anxiety come from? "Well, I sure was a worrier as a kid. Especially when I was in my bed at night. My dad worked late, and I'd lie there and worry that he wasn't coming home. I couldn't let myself go to sleep until I knew he was home safely. Sometimes I'd doze off and wake up and he still wasn't home. That's when I'd really worry. Did something happen to him? Was there an accident? Why wasn't he home yet? I would feel so alone in that bed all by myself. I felt so helpless. I remember worrying that people I loved might be sucked into outer space and disappear, leaving me all alone. Who would take care of me?"

Then came that flash of recognition: "Oh, wow. I can see how it affects my relationships now. To this day, I keep worrying that the people I love and depend on will disappear."

Yes, even though we're all grown up, child fears seem to spill over, under certain circumstances. And that's the point. We can't help some of these anxieties and overreactions in relationships. They exist in a deeply ingrained way, not easy to erase, not easy to blot out. They are always staining, always coloring our interactions. And they take up so much energy.

Uncertainty—Another Kind of Waiting

When your partner is sulking, pouting, or freezing you out and isn't forthcoming about the reason, it can really drive you crazy with anxiety. You may ask yourself, "Did I do or say something to cause this upset? Was I annoying or irritating?" This feeling is often described as walking on eggshells or waiting for the other shoe to drop, as you ponder what it is you might have done and wait with that sickening feeling in your stomach.

Worry Takes Up So Much Energy and Space

With all the worrying some of us do, it's a wonder we get anything accomplished. There just doesn't seem to be any space left for taking care of business. The anxiety seems to take over.

But worry can be useful in some strange ways. Worry, like so many of these space fillers, can be an alternative to loneliness, filling up that void that otherwise would seem so empty and desolate. Another way worry can be useful is when it functions as a kind of preparation for things that can go wrong, which I discuss in the section on catastrophizing.

Okay, so it might have a virtue or two, but who needs it? Often you may find yourself taking a worry and compartmentalizing it, sticking it in into a separate space for safekeeping—to deal with later. But putting things into one small space compresses them and gives them a lot of power. It's not always a case of "out of sight, out of mind," because stuff seeps out, intruding into your daily activities. This intrusion may stick its worrisome head into your business meeting and you lose your focus. Or you may notice how you seem to be misplacing or losing lots of things. Perhaps you become a little absentminded while driving and almost didn't stop for that light. Or it found it's way into your thoughts when you are slicing onions— and oops, you just sliced your finger!

Here is one of my favorite ways to put worry in its place, especially at those times when you're worrying about what might happen—what the results of a test might show, how someone will react, and so on. Just remind yourself: "Why worry twice?"

Just remind yourself: "Why worry twice?"

You might give a thought to how much worry displaces your concentration and how much energy and space is taken up. You can choose to give worry less importance in your mind and in your life. Here's an experiment to try for defusing worry.

Start assigning a number to each worry. How much actual weight does it carry on a scale of one to ten? Does it deserve all that weight? What if you assign an eight to that particular worry? What would have to happen for it to become a seven, or perhaps a six and a half? How much space would it take up if it went back up to an eight? Or even up to a nine? Then back to a svelte six and one half?

Here's one of the most powerful things about anxiety: It's contagious. One person will catch it from another, like a bad cold or mean flu. When we were children, little sponges that we were, we often absorbed our parents' anxiety. And because we couldn't put words to it and describe our feelings, we "acted it out" as a way of releasing the tension it caused. And as adults, we act out feelings if we can't talk them out. It's one way of relieving the anxiety.

The term "acting out" describes inappropriate or excessive behaviors, such as flying into a rage, antagonizing, slamming doors. It also includes excessive spending, gambling, extramarital affairs, destruction of property, and self-destructive behaviors, including abuse of substances such as tobacco, alcohol, drugs, and food. Many couples deal with their uncomfortable feelings of anxiety by starting fights, and before they know it, this kind of quarreling can get down and dirty, becoming a dumping ground for unresolved feelings.

> We act out feelings if we can't talk them out.
> It's one way of relieving the anxiety.

But acting out is not always active. It can be passive as well, such as foot-dragging, "yes, butting," sulking, and giving the silent treatment to your partner. All of these behaviors are ways we deal with the anxiety that builds up when we're not able to put words to our feelings and worries. This can be true of our fears as well.

Fears

Our fears take up increasing amounts of space in our minds the longer we fail to deal with them. Some of the biggest space-takers are the fear of rejection, fear of abandonment, fear of change, and imagining the worst.

Fear of Rejection

This fear seems to be everywhere, doesn't it? When you get right down to it, this is the basic fear that dominates so many of our interactions. It can take many forms: fear of being judged, fear of being disrespected, fear of being criticized, fear of being not good enough, fear of being "found out," fear of being manipulated, fear of being betrayed, fear of being cast off.

Don't Take It Personally! addresses the fear of rejection in detail, but here are some high points of how to deal with rejection:

- Remind yourself that it's usually more about the other person than about you.

- Remember, "not thinking" doesn't mean "not caring"—everyone has their own style of doing things.

- Don't presume—check things out.

- Don't try to read minds.

- Put yourself in the other person's shoes.

- Remember that you have choices and can take action.

- Ask directly for what you need.

- Take a "time-out." Try counting to ten.

- Don't take it personally!

Fear of Abandonment

What about the fear of being abandoned! For many of us, this is the most profound rejection fear of all, as we saw in chapter 3. One woman has such a strong reaction when a relationship ends that she sometimes finds herself hyperventilating. It doesn't seem to make any difference which person ends the relationship. "I feel as if I can't get enough air into my lungs, as if I can't breathe," she relates. "Sometimes I even think I might die. Yes, I know it's not just about the breakup. I know that it's related to my father dying when I was a child. I just don't do well at all when people leave me. Every new 'leaving' feels like another death. I guess a part of me dies, too."

Abandonment fears are scary; sometimes they seem to spring out of nowhere and take over. These fears color our relationships in profound ways, influencing how we interact with others and how they interact with us. We sometimes end up scaring people away—or perhaps we scare ourselves away. There's no question that fear of loss influences how we love.

Millie experienced such fears, but she didn't know it. She only knew how anxious she got whenever she and her partner fought. So she dealt with her fear by frequently threatening to leave her partner.

It was very controlling, to be sure—but what it really controlled was her own anxiety about being left.

Abandonment fears are not easy to tame. They are feisty little devils with wills of their own. Sometimes it helps to use some type of a "mantra," reminding yourself that someone is returning. Sometimes it helps to ask that person to cooperate by sticking to the agreed-upon schedule, or phoning if there will be a change or if they're going to be late. But, then again, they have to be willing to cooperate—often they just don't "get" the depth of your fear. Sometimes it helps to actually speak to and calm the fears of that part of you that is the most upset—that child part of you. You can do this by visualizing yourself as a child and speaking to that child in a comforting, loving way, reassuring him or her that they won't be abandoned.

> Fear of loss influences how we love.

Fear of Change

The fear of change can also deeply affect a romantic relationship. So much space is taken up worrying about a change in circumstances that may be on the horizon. The possibility of changing jobs, moving to another location, or a partner suggesting an extended vacation can be scary. Some of us don't do well at all with change. We like consistency and predictability, and the prospect of change produces uncertainty. Our world as we know it threatens to come tumbling down around us if someone suggests change. It's important to try to take things one step at a time and not jump to overwhelming thoughts of "I can't do this." You most likely can, if you work on it in manageable chunks. And, as Susan Jeffers suggests in *Feel the Fear and Do It Anyway* (1987), security is being able to handle things. By telling yourself, "I can handle this," you can begin to move past your fears.

Imagining the Worst

Another fear that intrudes is imagining the worst. This is also called "catastrophizing," "awfulizing," or "overgeneralizing." If you don't know the whole story, you might find yourself blowing things out of proportion, making up details to fill in the spaces. In other words, connecting lines where there aren't any dots.

Catastrophizing is a dress rehearsal for dealing with difficult predicaments. By worrying enough about something and expecting the worst, then whatever happens won't seem so bad. This behavior becomes automatic, operating without conscious awareness. By playing out our worst fears, looking at all the awful things that can go wrong and preparing ourselves, perhaps we may fool ourselves into feeling safer.

Let's take a look at what happened when Don's wife told him she wanted to take a week-long trip to a spa with her best girlfriend. He freaked out, imagining that she didn't love him anymore. He tried every way he could think of to get her to change her mind. It turns out they had just begun couple's therapy to work on some stuck places in their fourteen-year relationship. "I know we have some problems," he ventured, "but has our relationship deteriorated so much that you want to get away from me? Your wanting to go off to the spa means to me that you want out of the relationship." Of course, none of this was true, she assured him. She simply wanted "girlfriend" time. And Don was jumping to conclusions, filling in what he didn't know with his own imaginings.

> Catastrophizing is a dress rehearsal for dealing with difficult predicaments.

Has this ever happened to you? How can you keep problems manageable, avoiding treating them as catastrophes? One effective way to do this is to use a continuum, a powerful tool for keeping things in perspective. The poles usually represent "good/bad," "right/wrong," "either/or." Because you're often unable to recognize other possible choices, placing options along your continuum is a nifty way of considering the space in between the poles.

Try visualizing some points along the continuum—points A, B, C, D, and E, for example. Then recreate how you may be jumping from A to E, skipping over B, C, and D. Try backing up to B, consider it an option, and give it a descriptive name. Try again, moving along to C. It's another option with a name. Remind yourself that you don't have to be in a rush to get to E. In fact, perhaps you'll decide that you don't want to get to E at all. You may find you don't even need to go past C.

I'll be the first to agree that it's not easy to break the awfulizing habit. After all, many of us became experts at it in childhood as a way of protecting ourselves from the unknown—we just filled in the blanks. But look at all the energy it takes to be always on the lookout, always prepared. Look at the energy it takes to deal with the worry and anxiety involved in catastrophizing. It surely does magnify the drama of it all.

All of the fears described above can threaten our self-esteem, security, or way of life and lead to stress.

Stress—Reaching the Saturation Point

Some stress is great for us—it acts as a motivator, stimulator, and activator, presenting opportunities to show that you can handle problems that arise. But when you reach a stress saturation point, the stress factor becomes negative instead of positive.

You've probably heard at least one of these pronouncements from family members or teachers as you were growing up. Maybe you've even heard them all in some form or other:

- "I've reached my limit."

- "I've had it up to here."

- "I can't take anymore."

- "One more peep out of you, and you're going to get it."

Each of us has a limit somewhere, a saturation point. We have only so much space to hold information, feelings, and concerns. Once this space starts filling up, a certain density level is reached. When you reach the boundaries of available space, something has to give. Something has to be compromised. The simple fact is, no more "stuff" can be absorbed, and the result is stress.

Reaching this saturation point stresses the system. Because it triggers the mind-body connection, it can lead to both emotional and physical problems. You may feel exhausted or depressed, listless, worried, or fearful. You may find yourself eating too little or too much, or drinking too much. You may have headaches or tense muscles or aching neck or shoulders. You may experience fatigue, sleeplessness, trembling, sweaty palms, stomach upset, itching, or even heart palpitations

Illness

Just as a reciprocal relationship exists in couple dynamics where each partner's behavior affects and is affected by the other person's behavior, so are stress, fear, and anxiety intimately connected with illness. When anxieties, fear, and stress reach the saturation point, the body runs out of room, and emotional and physical illnesses can develop. This, in turn, can lead to more stress

There are lots of physical problems that can affect relationships. The most obvious would be the life-threatening or chronic illnesses, which can take their toll for sure. Chronic bronchitis, asthma, or lung difficulties are very clear examples of "can't breathe" illnesses. But there are other, more insidious physical problems that can lead to relationship difficulties. When you think about it, hormones are out of whack for most women many years of their lives because of PMS, pregnancy, and menopause. And for many couples, the resulting stress can take up a great deal of space in their relationship.

Another highly stressful situation is when one partner has symptoms of ADD or ADHD. If he or she has difficulty focusing or concentrating, instructions or comments can get "missed." And enormous amounts of energy can go into accusations and hurt feelings. One couple has learned to work with written lists and a system of priorities. Because he has an attention deficit disorder, he gets overwhelmed when she gives verbal instructions, especially if she changes her mind about something. She used to only make verbal requests and would be afraid to ask him to repeat it back to her—afraid he'd think she was patronizing. So she ended up spending a lot of time being angry at him. Now she writes things down, but if by chance she does make a verbal request, she has him repeat it. He's so relieved to be able to know that he really did understand what she said. His anxiety has dropped dramatically.

But what happens when the anxiety is not relieved so readily? Too much pressure needs to be depressurized, and depression may serve this purpose. In other words, depression may counterbalance too much anxiety. Depression serves a function in many relationships. Sometimes it is the "glue" that holds relationships together, and some couples actually compete for who is the most depressed. And, too, some couples rotate their depressions—first one, then the other takes their turn. That works until both are depressed at the same time—then who takes care of whom? Sometimes, however, one partner's depression leads to the other person feeling left out. But the nondepressed partner contributes to the depressive system in two basic ways: by either being punishing (angry), as in "Cut the crap, already," or by being solicitous (nurturing), as in "What can I do for you?" What *are* the benefits for this partner? And what is the price paid? It is often more stress. Just getting through the day takes up so much energy, causing disconnection from the partner, and leaving little room for intimacy.

How can we prevent becoming oversaturated? How do we make enough space? Making "enough" space begins with developing an awareness of the energy within our bodies. This is kinesthetic space—recognizing the language of body sensations. Reading both our own and the body language and energy of other people. This means honing in on what our bodies are telling us about our needs— including when we need to take space from our partner. This also means sensing when our partner's body language is saying, "I need more space." Once we develop this awareness, we can create "permission" to take or give space, to take or give closeness.

But the taking and giving of space is not easy for those of us who have a need to control our environments so we don't feel so out of control. Sometimes we enter into a tug-or-war with our partners for control.

7

It Feels Like a
Tug-of-War

Controlling Space

When you get right down to it, many space issues between people reflect some kind of battle for control of that space. Life becomes a struggle about taking space and giving space—or about taking up space and giving up space. When we're feeling stressed, pressured, overwhelmed, anxious, nervous, scared, or inadequate, we may feel we lack control. So we try to find ways to micromanage our environment. We just want to feel more in control of our situation. Unfortunately, this control spreads to all parts of our environment and the people in our environment also feel controlled by us. And they don't like it one bit!

It's not unusual for struggles for control to take place in the bedroom and the bed becomes the zone of battle. Here is Caroline's story:

"I guess I was trying to snuggle up to him in bed—I think I was more or less asleep." 'You're taking up the whole bed,' he roared. I just wanted more physical contact with him, to share that space with him, but he says that I'm trying to control him. He especially wants his own space in bed. He complains that I move too close to him in my sleep, taking his share of the bed. His voice even becomes indignant, treating it as if it were an awful transgression, as if I were doing it deliberately. I find myself indignant right back, because I don't see how the hell I can control what I do in my sleep!"

After a pause, "I'm also hurt, of course. I used to regard sharing a bed with him as one of the great pleasures of my life, and if I moved closer to him it was out of affection and not because of any conscious desire to take over his space. I feel jerked around by him. It was as if he were saying, 'Be warm and affectionate when I need you to be, but get the hell out of my space when I want it—whether you're conscious or not.'"

Another couple has a different sort of space problem in bed. Manny wants to sleep with his arms around Lois, but she feels she needs more space to breathe freely. Manny needs more touching in bed than Lois does, but how much contact does he need to feel close to her? Would it work for them to touch feet or legs, or to hold hands? Could this be enough contact for Manny to feel secure, yet allow Lois the space she needs? It's important to take a look at what each person in the relationship needs to feel secure. Each may have a different idea of what constitutes closeness and what constitutes comfortable space.

Here is a story about controlling space that takes it out of the bedroom—it even transcends walls. One woman explains, "The only way I feel in control of the situation with him is when I'm carrying him in my purse!" She was referring to the beeper he gave her to carry so that he could reach her whenever he wanted. He expected her to keep it turned on at all times. But she resented what she saw as his way of controlling her. She resented his intrusion in her life. So guess what? "I keep the damned beeper turned off."

Jockeying for Position— Power and Control

For many of us, it becomes critical to our sense of well-being to be "in control." And we end up doing some rather unusual things to give ourselves this sense of control. One of the ways we manipulate our sense of power is to second-guess ourselves. We start fussing about that old "checklist." You know the one I mean—the "shoulda, woulda, coulda" inventory. We just keep going over the checklist, item by item. Who of us hasn't asked these questions of ourselves at one time or other?

- "What did I do wrong?"

- "Did I say something inappropriate?"

- "Did I forget to say something?"

Isn't it fascinating how easily we blame ourselves when we're confused or disappointed about a situation with someone? "I should have done it differently." We forget that, just maybe, it may be a limitation of the other person and not about you or your ability to control the situation at all.

The fact that it's so often utterly beyond our power is exactly why we have this need for the checklist. The list gives us a sense of structure and helps us feel back in control when things seem so crazy-making and overwhelming. Somehow, if we take responsibility for something, it seems we feel we can influence the situation. Then we don't feel so helpless.

Taking responsibility for things that are actually beyond our control is also a way to feel connected—perhaps keeping a connection that no longer exists. So don't be so hard on yourself if you find yourself retracing those interactions before a person suddenly didn't call again or unexpectedly ended the relationship. Just notice that you are doing this. By noticing, it presents the opportunity for choices. You might ask yourself:

- Do I really want to be connected to this person?

- Do I want to *continue* to stay connected?

- If so, do I want to try to find another way to feel connected?

Micromanaging Your Environment

One woman I know kept replaying those vivid last scenes of the melodrama she had been living with her boyfriend. "I guess I was pushing him," she'd recall. "Maybe I shouldn't have insisted he call me more often. Maybe I shouldn't have called him so often. Or talked so much. Or been so quiet. Or _____ . Or _____ . Or _____ ." (You know how to fill in the blanks.)

I bet that checklist you pull out at moments like these is familiar to you from childhood days. You probably used it lots of times when you were young. How often did you use it? What questions did you ask yourself? How hard were you on yourself back then? Are you as hard on yourself now? What would it take for you to cut yourself a little slack and realize that the situation you're obsessing about may actually have very little to do with you?

If You Win, Do I Lose?

Conflicts sometimes arise that boil down to the need to be right, leaving no space to be wrong. Issues become "right" or "wrong." People become polarized, "I'm right, you're wrong," or "If you're

right, that might make me wrong—and I can't stand to be wrong."
Sometimes it can get to out-and-out warfare, as we can see in Cathy
and Erin's story below. (Take special notice of the italicized words in
the story.)

Cathy is speaking calmly, but her eyes flash. "Erin is always telling me what I should do. She thinks her way is the only way, and I
begin to feel that what I want or think doesn't count. Finally, I
stopped buying into her *insistence* that she was always right, and I
started asking questions. She hates it. Now she accuses me of using
delay tactics. She takes it as a *personal affront* and thinks I'm doing it
to make her angry. It's not about *her* at all. I can't always think on my
feet, so I ask questions to *get my bearings*." Cathy is quiet for a few
moments. "Well, I guess sometimes I do use *delay tactics*, but it's only
when I feel *pushed*.

"Come to think of it, I've been doing that since I was a little girl.
I learned that if I asked questions, I could delay things I didn't want
to face. It gave me the space to think things out. This was how I took
care of myself. So, even now, asking questions is a protection for me.
Somehow it gives me the illusion of having some kind of *control*."

Her ability to delay, catch her breath, and get her bearings is a
useful skill that has served her well. "The trouble is, around Erin, I
feel it's not okay if I ask a question," Cathy laments. "I know I
shouldn't, but I feel bad about myself for doing it.

"My reaction seems to fluctuate. Sometimes I feel *bushwhacked*,
held hostage by Erin's demands and her anger. When she lashes out, I
feel *diminished*. She doesn't leave me any place to go," Cathy says. "I
feel *trapped*, as if I'm *slipping into bondage*. At these times, I have a
need to protect myself and I go *head-to-head* with her. At other times,
when she's really rough on me, I feel *squelched*. I resent her comments
and become sullen and passive. When I feel boxed in like this, I tend
to disappear.

"When I was a child there was never any space to be 'me.' I
always felt I had to be what my parents wanted me to be. It just
wasn't okay if my desires or wishes happened to be different from
those of my parents. They didn't appreciate that 'different' part of me
at all. And I lost my spontaneity and my creativity. It got *squashed*. It's
like they felt I was rejecting them personally if I thought differently
or had a different way of doing things. It seemed it was a *struggle* to
be myself."

And what about Erin? "I guess I do have to be right a lot of the
time," she admits. "Somehow it seems if I *give up* my opinion that I'm
giving up part of myself. I always felt afraid as a child that I couldn't
have my own needs or wants or fears. My mother would always tell
me that I was imagining things—I wasn't really having a nightmare, I

wasn't really afraid, I didn't really see my father *hit* my mother. The list of 'imaginings' goes on and on. My perceptions were *diminished*. I felt *squashed* and *ganged-up on*. It seems as if I didn't count. So I puffed myself up. I became *combative*."

Erin recalls, "I guess I was always *fighting* as a kid. It was always a *struggle* to get my mother to love me. Everything seemed like a struggle. My mother and I *fought with passion*—the only way she could hear me was when I showed my anger. I guess I'm replaying this same scenario with Cathy."

Them's Fightin' Words

Cathy, in the unconscious way one partner often accommodates the other, joins Erin on her battlefield. Notice how both sprinkle their descriptions with war like over tones:

CATHY'S BATTLE CRIES	ERIN'S BATTLE CRIES
• *get my bearings*	• *give up*
• *delay tactics*	• *hit*
• *pushed*	• *diminished*
• *control*	• *squashed*
• *bushwhacked*	• *ganged-up on*
• *held hostage*	• *combative*
• *diminished*	• *fighting*
• *trapped*	• *struggle*
• *slipping into bondage*	• *fought with passion*
• *head-to-head*	
• *squelched*	
• *boxed in*	
• *squashed*	
• *struggle*	
• *insistence*	
• *personal affront*	

If we were to do a word count of those fighting words, Cathy would win the contest. Maybe Cathy is more of a five-star general than she imagines herself to be! What a power struggle these two are engaged in. What a war! Why does this couple have to cancel each other out? Why can't there be room for two valid experiences of the same thing? Why is it that in order for one person's perception to be validated the other person's perception has to be squashed? It's as if when someone rejects your way of doing things, they are rejecting *you*. What would it take for one person to say to the other, "That may not be my way of seeing it, but I recognize it as your way." What would it take for each of them to learn to choose their battles? Some things are just not worth fighting over.

> Some things are just not worth fighting over.

Inflating and Diminishing

When we puff ourselves up or push someone around, it doesn't leave much room for the other person, and they end up feeling diminished. In reaction to someone puffing up, many of us quickly get intimidated, wilt, and disappear. It just doesn't feel good to be on the receiving end of puffing *or* pushing.

In Patrick's family, if you were going to make a statement, you had to make it *big*, or you wouldn't be heard. "Big" meant loud or angry. In his partner Rosy's family, you were calm and reasonable. His bigness is scary for her. Her calmness is confusing for him.

What about you? Do you take your full space? Do you make yourself smaller? Or do you puff yourself up?

Puffing Up Fills Space

"When I don't know where I stand," says one woman, "I take a stand. If I don't speak emphatically, I won't be heard." Another says, "When I feel backed into a corner, I start to disappear and pull back. So I puff myself up, getting overly harsh and delivering ultimatums. But I hate it when I see myself doing that. I wish there were some sort of a middle ground." And a man I know describes, "When I'm hurt, I want to hurt back. And I do it in a desperate sort of way."

Who among us hasn't at some time felt unsure, small, and insignificant? When you feel that way, you may tend to puff yourself up in order to feel bigger, stronger, more important, or more adequate. People do this in different ways—sometimes bragging or boasting, giving orders or instructions, or sometimes bullying. The end result is that we take up a lot of space and don't leave room for the other person to breathe or be themselves.

One way of inflating ourselves is to be self-absorbed and filled with a sense of self-importance. This doesn't leave much space at all for your partner. As one man put it so well, "This is the only relationship I've ever been in that consisted of the needs of only one person—there just wasn't room for me."

Sometimes we exert our influence in very subtle ways: surprising someone with restaurant reservations, buying new clothes, making vacation arrangements without discussing it first with our partner. Sometimes when we're feeling vulnerable or unsure, we tend to puff ourselves up and bully the people around us. But that wouldn't feel very good, would it? And do you imagine bullies feel very good about themselves during the act of bullying?

"Don't Dress Me, Change Me, or Try to Control Me!"

"I yam what I yam!" proclaims Popeye. And there are quite a few people who might add, "And don't even *think* of making me your project. I'm not going to change. That means don't buy me clothing, jewelry, or accessories. I will resent the hell out of it, because it means you are trying to control me."

> "I yam what I yam!"
>
> —Popeye

But if you are one of the people who resents it so much, why do you react so intensely? Why do you immediately think someone wants to *control* you? Why do you automatically reject the action instead of just saying "thank you" and moving on? When in the past did you feel so controlled? By whom? Under what conditions? What did you tell yourself at the time? Did it feel as if someone was robbing you of your personhood? Were they stepping on your toes? Were they in your face? Did you feel stifled?

Your childhood experiences affect your adult needs for respect for privacy and space. One man describes how it is for him. "My partner is always looking for an excuse to dress me," he complains. "My birthday, Christmas, Valentine's Day. Always buying me sweaters, ties, shirts. It's getting so I'm beginning to hate the holidays. This mean fights about how she pushes all these clothes on me."

Of course, his partner doesn't see it that way at all and entreats, "I enjoy searching out things for you. Please don't take the joy of shopping for you away from me!" But he can only answer, "I feel as though you're leading me around by the nose—trying to make me into exactly what you want me to be. I am who I am. Please don't try to change me. You give with gifts, but you take away when you try to control me. Take me or leave me. Better yet, just leave me alone!"

A woman I know couldn't bring herself to speak up about her distress when her husband insisted on going shopping with her for her new clothes. He always managed to talk her out of her choices of clothing: "Why would you want to wear that color? It makes you look all washed out." He insisted on his choices. There was no space for her preferences; they just didn't count. Before long, she had begun to doubt her own taste. Then one day (yes, it was very suddenly) she moved out of their house, rented an apartment, furnished it the way she liked, and went on a huge shopping spree for new clothes—her way.

Another man remembers how a woman friend wanted to "tidy up" his apartment. In fact, she even brought her *own* vacuum cleaner! "I was so offended—even my vacuum cleaner wasn't good enough for her!" And just look at the metaphor: "It felt as though she was sucking up my soul," he recalls. Is it any wonder he has been a little skittish ever since about inviting women over? "A strange vision keeps reappearing in my head," he says. "What if I come home one day and all my furniture is rearranged?"

This is exactly what happened to another man I know. When his girlfriend moved in, he came home from work one day to find several pieces of his furniture missing, replaced by new furniture of her choosing. And, wouldn't you know, those were his favorite pieces. He kept thanking his lucky stars that he was able to retrieve some of it from the Goodwill!

"I'll Never Get Involved with 'Potential' Again"

Redecorating houses is only part of the problem. What about the times you may have wanted to "redo" your partner. Perhaps a little reupholstering here or there, or a new paint job. You may find yourself thinking, "Oh, if only they would dress a certain way, or be more social, or not belch so often. Yes, this could be a grand-scale makeover project."

"I used to call him my 'fixer-upper,' Megan joked, "but time went by and he wasn't changing a bit. I began telling myself that he'd change if he loved me, but he saw it differently—why should he change if he wasn't broken? I'll never get involved with 'potential' again!"

Everything Is Relational

Change *is* possible, but the most effective way to bring about change in your partner is to change your way of relating to him or her. If *you* change, the other person will usually change in relationship to you. Here's how it works: visualize a set of scales, like the ones used in the olden days to weigh gold bars. As you change the weight on one side by adding an additional gold bar, that side goes down while the other scale goes up. If you add the weight to the other side, the same thing happens. The bars move in relationship to each other. And it's the same with people. If one person changes, so does the other.

> If you change, the other person will
> usually change in relationship to you.

There's no question that pushing and prodding, nagging, manipulating, and demanding that someone change can cause resentment and anger to build up, causing alienation in relationships. The distance grows wider and wider, until there is little space left for tender, loving feelings. How do these misunderstandings come to be? In the next chapter, we will take a look at the many ways feelings get hurt in relationships.

8

"I Feel Shut Out When You Shut Down"

Hurt Feelings and Misunderstandings

Misunderstandings take up so much space in relationships that they can crowd good feelings right out. They come in many shapes and sizes—miscues, miscommunications, mistakes, missteps, misgivings, miscalculations, and even mischief. One of the biggest sources of misunderstanding is feeling hurt and "shut out" because your partner "shuts down."

Feeling shut out is one of the most frequent complaints I hear from the couples I see. Shut out, left out, devalued, discarded. The list of descriptors goes on and on. And, of course, intimacy is greatly affected: when you are feeling hurt by your partner's distancing, it's hard to maintain closeness. Lynn and John talk about how misunderstanding each other's behavior pulls them apart.

> Misunderstandings come in the form of miscues, miscommunications, mistakes, missteps, misgivings, miscalculations, and even mischief.

"I get this awful, sickening feeling when he withdraws," Lynn said. "I know this sounds extreme, but I tell myself: 'If he doesn't want to be around me, I must be a worthless person.' Then I retreat into my own shell. Then this stony silence settles between us. God, it feels so awful. I get such a terrible feeling in the pit of my stomach. I remember that exact same feeling from childhood. My mom would get into one of her 'moods,' go into her room, slam the door, and sit alone for hours. I felt frozen out of her life every time she'd do that."

John jumped in. "Yeah, I guess I learned this stuff from childhood, too. 'Go to your room,' my father would say. 'You're talking too much. You can't sit at the dinner table with the rest of us.' I guess I became an expert at 'going to my room,' and I'm still doing it. In fact, it's as if I'm sending myself to my room! Whoosh—I'm gone." So John keeps on "going to his room" in his head, and Lynn still feels as if a door has been "slammed in her face."

Another man complains how his wife walks around much of the weekend wearing headphones, listening to her portable CD player. "I feel so shut out," he says. 'It's as if I don't exist, as if I'm not important to her. It seems as though she'd much rather be with her music than with me. And then she tells me sometimes that I'm not attentive enough!"

"When I Give You More Space, You Think I Don't Love You as Much"

Another way of feeling shut out is when the partner who has been the closeness seeker all of a sudden switches and creates more distance. The other partner gets confused and sometimes even hurt.

Polly was finding herself becoming suspicious all the time. Her partner, Shawn, is a musician who travels a lot, and, of course, there are all these "groupies" to be suspicious about. There they would be, just waiting to get some attention from "the star" and willing to do just about anything to feel special. And Shawn, the entertainer, just loved that they were focused on him.

Polly found herself asking Shawn a lot of questions. "Where did you go? Who did you see? What did you do after the performance? Who went along? Who did you screw?"

Shawn's answer was always a resounding denial of any wrongdoing, but Polly persisted anyway. The more Polly intruded, the more Shawn withdrew. Soon there was an ocean of space between them. And hurt. And resentment. And anger. And soon there was no space left for caring.

Polly knew something had to change if the relationship was going to survive. *She* had to change something. So she experimented with taking steps backward and allowing Shawn more space, more room to breathe.

Then a funny thing happened. Shawn wasn't used to so much respectful distance, and became a little nervous. In fact, he became a lot nervous. He began to believe that Polly didn't care as much because she wasn't doing her usual "in your face" number with him.

"I'm Not Nagging, I'm Showing I Care About Us"

Another "in your face" scenario develops when one person feels intruded upon by the other person's overattention. A situation developed between Gary and Grace that illustrates how this dynamic can interfere with intimacy. Grace grew up in a family that nagged over every little thing. Nagging was how they connected and showed they cared about each other. And, as you may have guessed, Grace's mom was constantly picking lint off her clothes. Intrusive, perhaps, but Mom would always say, "It's just an act of caring." It was certainly a way of filling space!

Gary hated it. He had an "in-your-face mom who didn't know when to stop," and was put off by so much attention. So Grace's little acts of caring seemed intrusive to him, even smothering. But an interesting thing happened when Grace made an effort to stop the nagging. All of a sudden a huge space opened up in their relationship, and Gary didn't know how to fill it. It felt a little lonely and it almost felt as if Grace didn't care about him.

"You Let Me Down"—Dealing with Betrayal

Feeling "let down" by people we care about can be a recurrent source of hurt. I'm talking about betrayal here, and I have to admit, this is one of my own big issues in relationships. I guess I expect others will be as loyal, considerate, and understanding as I perceive myself to be. It doesn't take much for me to feel let down by someone.

Some of you may have some issues around betrayal as well. If you react strongly to perceived betrayal, you can probably trace the intensity of your reaction to childhood experiences. Perhaps someone wasn't fair to you, didn't stand up for you, failed to protect you, manipulated you, exploited you, was disloyal, disappointed you, or shamed you. Maybe it happened more than once—maybe lots of times. Even though many years have passed, you may find yourself in a situation where it seems as though someone is mistreating you again. You may find yourself feeling let down by that person, because you trust them and their behavior seems to betray that trust.

When betrayal feelings pop up they can be overwhelming. It's as if all the old gut reactions come flooding back again. It hurts. It can feel as if you are seven years old or twelve years old or sixteen again. And you react from that child place, that raw, hurting, child place. It's as if you are frozen in time. If betrayal is your issue, you'll most likely find yourself overreacting and wondering, "Where on earth did that feeling come from?"

The best way to try to deal with feelings of betrayal is to make some distance between you and the incident. Step back, take a breath, and remind yourself that even though it feels as if you are very young and defenseless, you are really an adult. With a little distance from the feelings, you can actually respond in an adult manner. Yes, you can. But you have to be able to catch your breath and get some distance.

It also helps to try to determine the context that created these feelings of betrayal early on. Perhaps it was feeling shunned or slighted by peers, or that a teacher treated you unfairly, or the betrayal of trust by an adult's inappropriate behavior. Any of these experiences in your early years can knock you for a loop.

Unfortunately, when you feel betrayed, you may also go back to that child place of blaming and berating yourself. It may help to regain your composure by reminding yourself that you are the same okay person you were before the betrayal occurred, and that it's not always possible to control the thinking or motivations of others.

"I Calibrate Myself to Your Emotions"

There may be times when you're feeling hurt by something your partner did or said, but you end up not bringing it up because you're so concerned about upsetting your partner. You tell yourself (because most likely you heard this growing up), "Wait 'til he's in a better mood," "This isn't the right time." Well, it's never going to be the right time if you keep waiting. As one woman says, "I keep waiting for the perfect moment, but it never seems to present itself. I guess I want someone to step up and offer me the opportunity to say what's on my mind. I must need permission, or something. Maybe I could practice giving permission to myself. If I keep depending on someone else's moods, I'll always hold back, just as my mom did. She used to always tell me, 'Let's not talk to your father about this now, it's not the right time. You'll only upset him.' And I've been tip-toeing around people ever since." This is the dance we learn to do early on. It continues into our adult relationships, holding us back from being "present" and making intimacy difficult.

Randolph is so "in tune" to his partner's moods that he has difficulty keeping his own equilibrium. "It's just too easy to merge with her," he concedes. "My partner's moods seem to rule my life. When she's up, I'm up. When she's sad, I'm lonely without her emotional company. I try so hard to get her to cheer up, but I feel like a failure when my efforts don't work.

"I used to try to cheer up my mother, too. I'd find reasons to stay home from school when she was sad. In fact, I would pretend to be sick a lot of the time so I could stay home and make sure she was okay. When I was away from home, I'd worry that something terrible would happen to her and I wouldn't be able to help her. In fact, whenever I'd hear a siren outside the school building, I'd sneak away from class and run home. I just had to make sure my mother was all right."

Randolph has difficulty in his relationship because he is too "tuned in." But as you will see in the following chapter, sometimes the problem is that you may be "tuned out" to the fact that your partner may have a different style than you do.

9

You Say Tomayto and I Say Tomahto

Style Differences

It's as simple and complex as this: because we grew up in different families, we grew up with different ways of doing things. Our families learned their "ways" via cultural influences going back many generations, affecting beliefs and values, comfortable closeness and distance. Our frame of reference is our cultural upbringing. Let's look at "culture" as meaning gender attitudes, ethnicity, country, area of the country, and even our city and neighborhood. All of these factors can influence how we think about time and space and how we learn to balance closeness and distance. Let's classify these variations as "style differences."

> Because we grew up in different families,
> we grew up with different ways of doing things.

Grandma Passes Down More Than Just Her China

Back when I was married and in graduate school, I would comment to (nag?) my then-husband about how he'd never close the kitchen cabinet door after getting a plate or glass out. The door would be hanging there wide open, and it seemed to me that I'd always be going around and closing up after him. One day, after I commented on it for the umpteenth time, he turned to me and made this incredibly astute remark: "This just proves that I'm from an 'open family system' and you're from a 'closed family system'!" Well, he was certainly absorbing my family therapy studies by osmosis, picking up information about open systems, where families are open to new information and amenable to change versus closed systems where change and conflict cannot be tolerated.

His observation can be carried a step further. When people are from different types of families or different cultures, styles of doing things can be very different—whether it's about opening and closing cabinet doors, squeezing toothpaste, celebrating holidays, taking vacations, talking quietly or loudly, buying gifts, or calibrating time and space. And these differences of style are attributable to the voices of our ancestors. Yep, grandma passes down more than just her china.

Besides differences of culture we also inherit:

• Different values

• Different rituals

• Different beliefs

• Different rules

• Different rhythms

• Different ways of dealing with space, time, sex, money, and household chores.

These inherited values have a lot to do with the fact that we have different styles of doing things. Sometimes it's as simple as the fact that you grew up in your own unique family—different from your friends' families and different from your partner's family. Some families take vacations together and some take them separately. Some families celebrate holidays with expensive gifts, some with small practical kinds of things. Some families are generous with money and some are pretty tight-fisted. Some families make a big deal about birthdays, in some it's not a big deal at all. None of these are "right" or "wrong," but the tension these style differences can bring up in a relationship can make you feel like you need to judge them.

My Way Is Better Than Your Way

So what happens if you choose a partner who comes from a family with different ways from your own? What happens if you always had a big deal made of your birthday and your partner treats it as if it were just another day? Do you feel hurt? Probably. Do you get resentful? Perhaps. Do you take it personally? Most likely.

One woman remembers, "In my family, birthdays were always treated as special. I love to do extra special things for birthdays, and I get so disappointed if my friends or my husband treat my birthday as just another day. My feelings really get hurt. I guess I expect other people to do the same for me that I would do for them."

Her partner remembers what it was like growing up in his own family: "We kids maybe got an extra slice of bacon on our birthdays. Birthdays are no big deal to me and I have to tell you, in the early years of our marriage it was a real effort for me to do something special for her. I just didn't see the need. She already knows I love her." She chimes in, "Lately he has made a real effort—he says he knows it's important to me."

Cleaning the apartment was a big problem for another couple. After all, they each grew up in different families, right? And cleaning techniques and standards just aren't the same at all. Each had a "right" way of scrubbing the bathtub, but it never seemed to meet the other one's standards. The tension built, until it became a real hot-button issue for them. "I feel when you do just a cursory job, that you don't care about me." He responded, "When you criticize me, I feel I'm not doing my part, and it feels shaming." They often had misunderstandings about housework in general. She felt that she generally did more then he, and she resented it. He had no idea she was upset, and felt that he kept up his end by doing all kinds of heavy-duty jobs like rearranging furniture or moving heavy boxes. "I feel I am taking care of things," he reminded her. "I guess I didn't realize you were doing all of that," she said. "I thought you didn't care about me the same way I care about you." And why was it so important to her that he immerse himself in chores? She recalled, "My dad did a lot around the house. It felt so nurturing."

Talking about these feelings in couple's therapy allowed both of them to begin to let go of the resentments that were building up. They began to see that the problem was simple style differences from childhood, not reflections of disrespect.

Cultural Differences Can Be Confusing

Cultural experiences can also create different styles that lead to couples taking things personally. For example, families of various ethnic backgrounds may show caring and connection to others by gift-giving, by raising their voices, by nagging, through offering food, and sometimes these ways come into direct conflict with another person's ways.

> Cultural experiences create different styles
> that lead to couples taking things personally.

Let's take a look at issues of privacy and intrusiveness, and how they can lead to misunderstandings in both personal and business relationships. Hans' parents were born in Germany. He grew up in a household that placed a high value on privacy; they were all very sensitive to intrusions. Having their own space was essential, and family members often retreated behind closed doors. Involvement with others was kept to a minimum.

Because the German culture tends to handle time in a monochronic way, Hans' family scheduled things one at a time and planned carefully. There was orderliness and a tendency to compartmentalize. And, as Edward Hall points out in *The Dance of Life* (1983), in keeping with the typical German communication style, communications were precise, with an emphasis on *words* to convey meaning. Hans' family believed if information was not explicitly stated, the meaning could be distorted.

Denise was born in France, coming to the U.S. as a teenager. Her family's style was very different from Hans'. First of all, because France is a Mediterranean culture, time is generally organized in polychronic style. Order is not that important, and lots of things go on at once. This overlapping extends into personal space as well. Denise is used to being around people who not only are very involved with each other, but who are packed together as well—on public transportation, in cafés, and at home. Well, you can imagine the misunderstandings that must happen with this couple! If Denise stands in the doorway of Hans' study and sticks her head in to ask a question, Hans feels she has crossed a boundary. He perceives this act as intrusive. And for the life of her, Denise doesn't understand why he gets so upset. After all, she did not enter into his space. But to his way of thinking, she did.

Hans has been trained to pay close attention to words, but Denise tends to communicate with facial expressions and gestures more than words. As a result, Hans and Denise often misunderstand each other's meanings. And conversely, because Hans takes pains to use specific words and gives precise descriptions, Denise sometimes feels he is talking down to her by overexplaining. And this she takes personally.

But it gets even more complicated. Hans sees Denise as disorderly and spontaneous, and this makes him nervous. On the other hand, Denise gets anxious around Hans' formality and rigidity. This couple would actually be a good balance for each other, if they could only let go of their tendencies to polarize—each thinking their own way is the "right" way.

Gender Differences

Let's face it: There are differences in how men and women think, feel, and react, and these differences affect closeness and distance in relationships. Heaven knows there has been more than enough written about the topic, and most likely you are as acquainted with the material as I am. I want to stay away from generalizing about the subject, but this story is worth telling.

Ellie starts thinking out loud in the car: "Do you know, we've been seeing each other for exactly six months?" Dennis remains silent.

His silence makes Ellie wonder: "Maybe I shouldn't have said anything. Maybe he thinks I'm trying to get him to marry me, or something."

At the same time, Dennis is thinking: "Gosh. Six months. That was about the same time I had the car in for servicing. I'm way overdue for an oil change here. Six months? That's when I got into that fight with the dealer about the warranty. Those people made me so angry."

Ellie continues worrying: "Oh, now he's upset that I said something. Well, maybe I don't want to commit either. He's upset. I can see it on his face. Maybe I'm reading this wrong. Maybe he wants more from our relationship. Maybe he has sensed I was feeling some reservations. Yes, I bet that's it. He's afraid of being rejected. Maybe I'm just too idealistic, waiting for a knight to come riding up on his white horse, when I'm sitting right next to a perfectly good person, a person I enjoy being with, a person I truly do care about, a person who seems to truly care about me. A person who is in pain because of my self-centered, schoolgirl romantic fantasy."

"Dennis," Ellie says aloud.

"What?" says Dennis, startled.

"Please don't torture yourself like this," she says, her eyes beginning to brim with tears. "Maybe I should never have . . . Oh God, I feel so . . ." She breaks down, sobbing.

"What?" says Dennis, alarmed.

"I mean, I know there's no knight. I really know that. It's silly. There's no knight, and there's no horse."

"There's no horse?" says Roger.

"You think I'm a fool, don't you?" Ellie says.

"No!" says Dennis, glad to finally know the correct answer.

"It's just that ... it's that I ... I need some time," Ellie says.

There is a fifteen-second pause while Dennis, thinking as fast as he can, tries to come up with a safe response. Finally he comes up with one that he thinks might work. "Yes," he says.

Ellie, deeply moved, touches his hand. "Oh, Dennis, do you really feel that way?" she says.

"What way?" says Dennis.

"That way about time," says Ellie.

"Oh," says Dennis. "Yes."

Ellie turns to face him and gazes deeply into his eyes, causing him to become very nervous about what she might say next. At last she speaks.

"Thank you, Dennis," she says.

"Thank you," says Dennis.

Then he takes her home, and she lies on her bed, a conflicted, tortured soul, and weeps until dawn. When Dennis gets back to his place, he opens a bag of Doritos, turns on the TV, and immediately becomes deeply involved in a rerun of a tennis match. A tiny voice in the far recesses of his mind tells him that something major was going on back there in the car, but he's pretty sure there is no way he would ever understand what, and so he figures it's better if he doesn't think about it.

The next day, Ellie will call her closest friend, or perhaps two of them, and they will talk about this situation for six straight hours. In painstaking detail, they will analyze everything she said and everything he said, going over it time and time again, exploring every word, expression, and gesture for nuances of meaning, considering every possible ramification. They will continue to discuss this subject, off and on, for weeks, maybe months, never reaching any definite conclusions, but never getting bored with it, either.

Meanwhile, Dennis, while playing racquetball one day with a mutual friend of his and Ellie's, will pause just before serving, frown, and say:

"Norm, did Ellie ever own a horse?"

Ellie is talking about their relationship while Dennis is talking about his car, and how do they manage to carry on a conversation? It's a wonder they've lasted six months, isn't it? Some conversations between men and women are so confusing that it's a miracle that relationships can make headway. But, then again, some of us are much more comfortable with vagueness than with clarity and definition. Maybe this is because we grew up in families that tolerated ambiguity. So, lets now take a look at what happens when one person needs definition, and the other is more at ease with being unclear.

Definition vs. Vagueness

When one of you craves definition, and the other is more comfortable being vague, it can lead to big-time problems. This is how it often plays out. Maybe you like to have a plan. In fact, you *have* to have a plan, or you become very anxious. You need to know when that next phone call is coming. You need to know when that next rendezvous is going to happen. You need to know what the plan is going to be for the weekend. This need for definition provides you with a sense of security.

But your partner likes to "free-float" through life. Maybe he or she has a need to be obscure, or indefinite. Maybe even a little flaky? The vague person hides in vagueness, "If you don't stick your neck out, you can't get hurt." But this vagueness can leave far too much unknown space to deal with for folks with a proclivity for definition. It's just too easy to fill in the space with worries, fears, or worst-case scenarios. Can you image the hurt feelings that come from this pairing? Maybe some of you don't have to imagine it—you may be living it. If so, you know how it can drive you nuts!

One woman was trying to make weekend plans two weeks in advance with someone she was romantically involved with. Her birthday was coming up, and she was pushing for his agreement to go ahead and rent a house near the ocean. If they didn't send in a deposit right away, they'd lose the rental. He felt pushed to agree to cooperate and found himself resisting making actual plans.

Could he see that this was an important weekend for her? Yes, he could. Could he see that, because it was so important, she might want to make plans to celebrate her birthday? Yes, he could. "But I don't like to be pushed, and it feels as if she is pushing me into things. If she keeps it up, she'll end up pushing me away."

So how *did* he want her to propose a weekend trip? "I wanted her to say, 'What do you think about going to the ocean for the weekend of my birthday?' I wanted to be *consulted* about the plan, not just told that she wanted to go there."

Definition vs. vagueness is an example of style differences. Maybe your style is to feel more comfortable with defined agreements, with a beginning and end. Or, maybe your style is to be casual, unplanned, noncommittal. Knowing the perimeters from early on could be a big help.

Predictability vs. Unpredictability

This need for definition is connected to a need for predictability—knowing what to expect. Some of us just feel way too much discomfort with the unknown. For example, one woman was involved in a new relationship in which her boyfriend wouldn't agree to go out once every weekend or even once every two weekends. She was disappointed, because that wasn't her idea of what a relationship was supposed to be.

"I know what you want," he said. "You want a commitment."

"No," she tried to explain. "I want predictability. I need to have some idea of what to expect."

He didn't understand what she was talking about. "What's the difference," he countered. "You're still saying you want a commitment."

I guess it did seem like a commitment to him. He just couldn't let himself make those plans. "It just makes me uncomfortable to plan things in advance." Why? "Well," he explained, " I might not feel like going when the time comes, or something else might come up and then I'd be stuck. It feels too much like an appointment."

The relationship didn't last for long. They continued to trip over their different styles—he couldn't get past his resistance to making even simple "commitments," and she couldn't get past her disappointment that she couldn't have predictability. Neither was able to give a little and work it out.

Giving vs. Withholding

And what about giving? What if one person is a "giver" and the other person is a "withholder"? Someone who is generous with time and energy more or less expects their partner to show they care by being generous also. Janet was always quick to offer to pick up Herb's dry cleaning or to drive him to an appointment if his car was in the shop. She pretty much expected him to reciprocate when she needed some help. But Herb often didn't think to offer—it didn't really cross his mind. Janet would tell herself that he didn't care about her as much as she cared about him. This style difference can obviously be extended to money issues. In this instance, let's call it "generosity vs. frugality." Not thinking doesn't mean not caring, and not spending doesn't mean not loving. It's just a different style.

Defensive Independence vs. Neediness

Sometimes we are so afraid of others seeing us as needy that we cover our needs with the veneer of defensiveness. As a counterreaction to our fear that we may be too needy, we sometimes develop a defensive independence, and the message we give out is "I don't need anything from you." This, by the way, is not autonomy. This is merely a defense against feeling dependent on someone. When people profess to be *that* self-sufficient, is there any space for another person to be in their lives? And, in fact, where is the space for intimacy?

If you say "I don't need anything from you," the other person may hear it as, "I don't need you." You can imagine how damaging this attitude could be to the couple. This is another style difference that can get in the way of a smooth relationship.

There are many more areas of style differences we could address here. For example, there is romantc/pragmatic, soft-hearted/hardnosed, trusting/wary, cautious/adventurous, and outgoing/private. The list could go on and on, but you probably have some of your own ideas about style differences affect intimacy.

Are You My Type?

When we can't quite get a handle on our relationship, we may find ourselves trying to "look it up"—turning to various typologies in an effort to figure him or her out. There are lots of ways to go about this; the Myers-Briggs Type Indicator is one way and synastry, which assesses the interplay of significant planets between a couples' individual horoscopes, is another. The Enneagram seems to be popular with my clients and workshop participants these days, so I'll use it here to illustrate how typologies are used to understand other people.

According to psychiatrist David Daniels and psychologist Virginia Price, authors of *The Essential Enneagram* (2000), the Enneagram describes nine fundamentally different patterns of thinking, feeling, and acting. Each is based on an explicit perceptual filter that determines what you pay attention to and how you direct you energy. This typology dates back to ancient teachings of the Sufis and the Kabbalah, but the psychological descriptions of these types were developed in the last one hundred years. Most importantly, the Enneagram allows the space in relationships for understanding individual style differences, because each type has a different value system, point of view, and set of instincts for living. Couples begin to recognize that they were born with a style or developed it at an early age, so they don't have to take a partner's actions so personally. In other words, there are no judgments here. This style of yours is neither good nor bad—it's just how you are. You may, in fact, see the world differently from your partner, but both points of view are equally valid. I was first introduced to this typology by Audrey Fain in her groundbreaking 1989 couple's study that demonstrated how differences in basic personality types affect couple's relationships.

> There are no judgments here. This style of yours
> is neither good nor bad—it's just how you are.

Are You My Type, Am I Yours? Relationships Made Easy Through the Enneagram by Renee Baron and Elizabeth Wagele (1995) describes how each personality type affects and is affected by every other type: The Perfectionist, The Helper, The Achiever, The Romantic, The Observer, The Questioner, The Adventurer, The Asserter, and The Peacemaker.

The Enneagram symbol is a nine-pointed star within a circle. Each point is influenced by the types on either side of it, and two lines radiate from each point to other personalities that can help it grow. Several of the Enneagram points reflect issues regarding personal space—comfortable closeness and distance. For example, when a Two gives, it may be a "giving to get." There may also be a "go away a little closer" message when the Two believes "if you love me, you'll want to be with me," while at the same time needing personal space. And the Fives who "felt intruded upon as children" tend to "do whatever they can to create distance," says Helen Palmer in her 1988 book, *The Enneagram*. They are "very private people . . . often at home with the phone unplugged. They watch the action from the edge of a crowd, making tentative effort to join" (p. 204). You can see how this need to protect private space could lead to the kinds of couple's dynamics described earlier: Rejection/Intrusion, Engulfment/Abandonment, Demand/Withdraw, Pursuer/Distancer, or Approach/Avoidance.

Let's take a look at one couple with different Enneagram points. Randy is a One, The Perfectionist, wanting to do things well, no matter how long it takes. Arnie is a Three, The Achiever, who wants to accomplish a lot fast. Before they were aware of this basic conflict, each tried to push and pull the other into their own rhythm. For example, during conversation over dinner, Arnie gives an overview of his whole day, briefly recapping the highpoints, while Randy elaborates on one aspect of his day. Arnie often finds himself wondering what Randy did with the rest of his day—thinking that perhaps Randy was not telling him everything. But now he reminds himself of their differences in style.

The Enneagram, like other typologies, is useful for helping people understand one another. The more you learn about how you and your partner might differ, the more you can accept and respect each other.

So We're Different; Now What?

Let's summarize some ways to handle style differences. First of all, neither style is right or wrong—it just *is*. If you can practice some tolerance for differences, some flexibility, and compromise, you can be more accepting. Instead of poarizing, seek out some common ground. If you can "agree to disagree" and use these differences as enrichment, you will complement and balance each other, enhance the intimacy in your relationship, and create space to grow.

All too often, however, because the other person is not like us, we begin to think the problem is with them. If only they would change, it would solve everything. Having unrealistic expectations about changing our partner and failing to accept their differences can lead to resentment, as we will see in the following chapter.

10

Getting Pushed Out of Shape

How Resentments Grow

They just seem to creep up, those resentments, taking up more and more space in the relationship. Before you know it, there isn't room for the good feelings and intimacy that used to exist. Where did those feelings go? How did resentment build up so fast? What happened?

Do you remember how it used to be? It's quite a wondrous thing to watch yourself opening up to someone you care about. You can almost see that space around your heart filling with confidence, expectancy, anticipation, high hopes, and security. What a fabulous feeling it is to be so open and accepting, without those usual barriers and inhibitions. But as incredible as it can feel, it also can be a little scary. Okay—a lot scary. Well, it's a vulnerable position, isn't it? Opening up like that leaves an opportunity for possible rejection. And then something happens to throw things off-kilter for you. This "something" can take the form of misunderstandings, misreadings, and miscues—and resentments begin to grow.

Unrealistic Expectations Lead to a Heap of Disappointments

Having unrealistic expectations or living in a fantasy world of anticipation or illusion takes its toll on relationships. For example, do you remember how fabulous it was when you first got together? The sex was really great, and you started thinking to yourself, "This is wonderful—this person can anticipate all my needs—I don't even have to ask." Wrong! Sexual needs don't equal *all* your needs, and the great sex may not last all that long, either. As the relationship moves into second or third gear, and your partner isn't reading your mind the way you're expecting them to, you may find yourself getting disillusioned.

Disappointments can take myriad forms. I came up with seven, but you can probably add a few of your own. You'll find examples of them throughout this book.

Seven Surefire Ways to Get Disappointed

- Having unrealistic expectations/anticipations

- Putting someone on a pedestal, making them your icon

- Getting involved with "potential," hoping to change them

- Looking for "proof" of love and hoping the person will read your mind

- Fooling yourself into believing exaggerated promises

- Having hidden agendas and secret contracts

- Not checking things out with the other person

Disappointments can cause a relationship to slide off its tracks. And, as you'll see in the following illustrations, usually this slide is connected to unrealistic expectations.

Relation-slips

Maybe it was that phone call that didn't come, the broken date, the broken promise, the forgetfulness, or the thoughtlessness. And then it happens again. And again. You find yourself closing up, little by little. That space for intimacy had softly and gently unfolded to someone begins filling up with hurt. Something terrible happens to the trust. It erodes, and resentment starts to grow in its place. Before you know it, there's no room for hope and anticipation. And often the resentment turns into anger, and the anger into alienation.

One woman recognizes that her anger is in response to thinking that someone broke a promise or agreement. "'I'm able to work through my anger by figuring out what agreement I believe was broken. Often the 'agreements' are kind of silly or not known by anyone but me. A lot of the time I realize that it may have been wishful thinking, and that realization takes most of the anger away."

Dueling Dual Relationships

Resentments can build up at double speed if complicated dual relationships exist. Getting a romantic relationship to work is no easy task, but what if the couple is in a business partnership as well? Feelings from one context can so easily spill over into the other.

Emily and Bruce not only live together, they also run a business. Well, actually it's her business, but he functions as her "right-hand man." Trouble here is the right hand (Bruce) doesn't always know what the left hand (Emily) is thinking or wanting or expecting. It's the "expecting" part that causes the biggest problems.

This business is a fast-paced, cutting-edge venture, with lots of management things to look after. She gives the orders and he carries them out. Sometimes that means he oversees two or three part-time employees.

"I really feel pissed off at you. I feel like you're taking advantage of me," fumes Emily to Bruce. "You don't take any responsibility and the burden is all on me. I told you to make those phone calls from the list I gave you. Why didn't you?" Then Emily shifts gears and accuses, "And you make decisions without consulting me." Whoops. Bruce appears to be wrong no matter what he does. Then, clearly taking both his inaction and his action as a personal affront, she adds, "How could you possibly treat me like this?"

Bruce seems to shrink in his seat. He looks as if he might be close to tears. In a small voice he says, "But I'm unsure of myself in a new situation. I'm supposed to know all the questions to ask and I don't. I really need your help."

He has to make judgment calls about things in which he has little experience. And Emily changes her mind quick as a wink. So his "calls" are frequently wrong. And she gets very upset.

"I'm so afraid I'll screw up, so I try to hold off on even making phone calls," he explains. "I worry that if I screw up, she'll leave me." Emily looks a little sheepish. "Yes, I do threaten to leave him," she acknowledges.

What would help here? Bruce would like Emily to be crystal cleare about what she wants him to do. Emily would like Bruce to tell her which tasks he doesn't feel comfortable doing instead of saying "yes" and not doing them.

By the next session, some important changes had taken place. Bruce was asking himself which tasks he felt comfortable with and was telling Emily, "This is what I can do. This is what I cannot do." He was also trying to explain how he gets easily frustrated, which makes planning difficult for him. Emily was trying to accept this. "But in all honesty, I get a twinge of resentment that he can't do this stuff, especially that he gets distracted so easily."

I needed at that point to check out if Bruce might have Adult Attention Deficit Disorder. The distractions were a clue, but along with that were his easy frustration, hypersensitivity, and pronounced anxiety. I lent him a book to read and he recognized many of the symptoms generally associated with this diagnosis. And what a relief it was for him to have a framework to identify with. "Since child-hood, I always thought I was weird—different from other kids. Now I can see many people have the same difficulties that I do. I feel as if a weight is lifted."

We talked about everyday stressors and how Bruce and Emily each handles the anxiety that arises. "I panic," says Bruce. "What happens to the time? I fear there won't be enough time to get things done. I seem to lose track of time." And what happens when Bruce panics? "I get paralyzed. I feel stuck."

And Emily? How does she deal with *her* anxiety? "I move full-steam ahead. I *do* something—anything. In fact, I start doing things that don't really have to be done. I can see now how that helps to control my anxiety." Clearly Bruce and Emily have different styles of dealing with time stresses: he freezes; she mobilizes.

Bruce decided to ask Emily for daily lists of what she wanted him to do, and he agreed to try to ask her if he didn't understand something, instead of trying to muddle his way through it.

The trouble is, because of their complicated business demands, the priorities seem to change from day to day, and sometimes several times a day. So they decided to spend time every morning going over what she expected from him during the day.

Because Emily knows how distracted Bruce can get, she worries that, while she's out, he's not taking care of business at home. The moment she arrives home, she checks on him. "I can't stand not hav-ing control over my living space," declares Emily. Bruce answers, "But the phrase 'what have you been doing' is really loaded for me. It reminds me of my childhood, when it seemed I could never do any-thing right." And if, in fact, Bruce did have some form of learning disability in childhood, he most likely would have come to think of himself as inadequate.

What about Emily's childhood messages? Where did this des-perate need to control her living space come from? What other forms does it take? One way Emily feels she loses control over her living space is when someone attempts to surprise her. "My mom used to surprise me by cleaning my room and giving away all my clothes," she remembers.

Once Bruce tried to surprise her on her birthday weekend by flying in when he was living in another state. She wasn't pleased—in fact, she hated it. She had already made plans, thinking he wouldn't be able to join her.

"I don't think these things out," Bruce said. "It never occurred to me that she would be upset. I love surprises, and I thought Emily would be so happy. It turned out very badly for both of us."

What would have been another way for Bruce to handle the situation? How could he have done it differently, respecting her dread of surprises and honoring his flair for creating happenings? He might have phoned in advance and asked her to save the day, letting her know that he wanted to plan something special for her, but that part would be a surprise.

"I Hate It When You Do That!"

I'll bet these words conjure up all sorts of images for many of you. Take a moment and think of some examples of things your partner does that you "hate" (or that *really* bug you). You may have so many examples that you're not quite sure where to start. Here are some common ones:

- "I hate it when you say you'll call and don't."
- "I hate it when you're late."
- "I hate it when you make promises you don't keep."
- "I hate it when you _____."

I suspect you won't have problems filling in the blank. But here's a good general plan to deal with all of these examples and more: Now that you're pretty clear about what you don't like, practice rephrasing these to say what you *want* from your partner, rather than what you don't want.

With that in mind, here are some strategies for communicating the changes you'd like to see happen in the relationship.

Misreadings and Miscues

It's so easy to send confusing messages to your partner. And it's even easier for them to misread you. You can be on two different wavelengths and may never discover the confusion.

One of the biggest areas of misunderstandings is when you think you're giving a clear message to your partner, but you put it out with one hand and take it away with the other. We often give hints or indirect requests, or we may just resort to wishful thinking. Jennie and Jordan offer a good illustration of the kinds of trouble that incomplete communication can cause.

Instead of telling Jordan how much she needed his help with an errand she couldn't fit in, Jennie said, "Could you pick up a color cartridge for me at the office supply store, if you get the chance?" Jordan took her "if you get the chance" to mean it was no big deal whether he was able to get it for her or not, so he didn't. Jennie was upset when he didn't get the cartridge, feeling that he was dismissing her request, that she wasn't important to him. She felt that, if he loved her, he would have done this little favor for her—after all, she didn't ask for much from him. Jennie didn't realize how she had dismissed her own request as not crucial, even though it actually was important. Jennie does this in other ways as well. She leaves phone messages for Jordan saying, "Call me, if you get a moment," or "If you feel like going with me, there's a movie at the Rialto." Then, if Jordan fails to meet her unstated expectations, Jennie feels rejected and resentful.

Many of us don't let on that certain things matter, and then we wonder why our partners don't comply with our requests. Our relationships would go more smoothly if we could find a way to say what we want and need instead of expecting our partner to read between the lines.

> We don't let on that things matter to us, and then wonder why our partners don't comply with our requests.

Another source of confusion in relationships concerns feeling shut out of someone's activities. Joe and Marsha have had a series of miscues that lead to misunderstandings.

Marsha and Joe usually prepare and eat their dinners separately, because Marsha is on a medically prescribed special diet. Even though they are not eating the same food, Joe would love to sit together at the table and share dinnertime with her. Joe's wanting to connect with Marsha was not always the case, however. In the past, he used to read the evening paper while they were at dinner. Somewhere along the line, Marsha started wandering off into the living room and turning on the TV while she ate. Joe needs some help clearly communicating to Marsha that he'd like to share dinnertime with her.

In addition, Joe's newspaper reading has created on-going difficulty. Marsha's problem with it is that, when she wants to talk, she wants Joe's attention right away. She complains bitterly if he is absorbed in reading the paper or a book while she's trying to talk to him. Joe doesn't understand why she gets so upset. "If I'm reading, just ask me if we can talk. I'll put down the paper." But she doesn't ask, she just presumes. Yes, presuming can cause relationship difficulties, but as you can see from the following story, a little extra effort can clear up misunderstandings.

Catherine says to Pat on their way home from a concert, "Oh, there's that new cute, cozy-looking bar. Would you like to stop in for a nightcap?" Pat thinks about it for a minute and says, "No, I really don't." Catherine is hurt. She wanted to talk and wind down from the performance. She wanted to have some quiet time with Pat.

She almost pouted all the way home, but she thought, "Maybe I didn't make myself clear." Then she turned to Pat and said, "I really don't quite want the evening to end. I'd like it if we could talk for a while."

"Oh! Thanks for saying so. I don't want a drink, but I can have a mineral water. Sure, let's stop at the bar and talk. I'd like that."

It's amazing how we allow ourselves to miss out on intimate moments by jumping to conclusions, as was the case with the couple in the first story. However, the second couple was able to have enjoyable late-night time together by making the effort to remedy their misunderstanding. It really only takes a moment to clear things up. Try asking yourself: "Did I jump to conclusions? Can I backtrack just a bit to clear things up?"

Sexual Misconceptions

Sexual misunderstandings can conjure up hurt feelings in an instant. This is certainly an area where many of us are hypersensitive to rejection. What if you make advances and your partner turns away? What if your partner "turns off" in the middle of making love or doesn't have an orgasm? When these things happen, do you tell yourself you're not attractive enough or sexy enough? Do your feelings get hurt?

Mark and Julie certainly have their share of sexual miscommunications. Mark turned to Julie in the couple's session and said, "I'd really like it if you would initiate sexual contact some of the time. It would reassure me that you want to make love to me. Sometimes I think you don't desire me because you don't initiate."

Julie looked puzzled. "But Mark, the other night I initiated sex, and you said you were too tired. I was so proud of myself for getting my nerve up to proposition you, and, to be honest, I felt hurt when you turned me down."

Then what did Julie do? "I withdrew—and haven't been able to approach you since. I'd be opening myself up for another rejection."

Mark was surprised at her words "I didn't mean to hurt your feelings, Julie. I was so exhausted that I was afraid I wouldn't be able to 'perform.' Now I wish I had just let you in on how I was afraid of disappointing you. Maybe I could have suggested that we substitute other kinds of lovemaking that night."

If the disinclined partner can be clear about their physical situation or state of mind, even offering an alternative, it surely would save a lot of hurt feelings and misunderstandings. In other words, saying something like: "I love it when you tell me you want to make love with me, but I just can't manage having intercourse tonight. I wish I could, but I'm open to finding other ways to show how much we care about each other." Or, if any kind of lovemaking is out of the question at the moment, try touching your partner's arm and saying this: "I love making love to you, but not tonight, thanks." The following story about Carla and Art also illustrates how quickly feelings can get hurt when one person feels sexually rejected by their partner.

Something woke Carla up. She got out of bed, walked into the living room, and found Art on the sofa, masturbating. She was devastated. She felt totally rejected by him. It was not easy for her to talk about this incident, but this is not the first time I've heard this story. This situation comes up every so often during couples' sessions. I was used to it. But Carla wasn't. Hurt and anger spilled out, but as we looked under the surface, we discovered that there was more to it than the experience of walking in on Art.

Carla was overwhelmed by feelings of rejection with a touch of betrayal. This wasn't the first time she had felt unappreciated. "What's wrong with me?" she wondered. "How can he prefer to do that when he has me right here, waiting for him in bed?" This reaction comes from losing perspective and taking things personally. It's not really a case of Art "preferring" masturbation over Carla. The choice between the two probably did not cross his mind. He simply was doing what felt right in the moment, and besides, as he said, he "didn't want to wake her up."

Can Carla try to put this experience into perspective? Yes, it is hard to get past those hurt feelings. But if she can step back, there may be some options. What might she say or do? What about approaching Art and offering to join in? Getting past the initial hurt is the tough part, but it couldn't feel too good to withdraw and disappear. Reaching out just might feel better. So if it should happen again, Carla has an option to fall back on—and Art thought it was a pretty sexy idea.

But Carla had yet another thought. "Now that we've talked about what happened, I realize Art's masturbation didn't have anything to do with me. I have another option here—I could simply respect Art's privacy and let him just go to it! This was really embarrassing to bring up in our session, but I'm so glad I did. I have a whole different perspective now."

There's no question that it's not easy for couples to talk about sexual concerns. In this next story, Ben and Keith had a very difficult time talking with each other about problems maintaining an erection. They were both frustrated and confused. Over the fourteen years they'd been together, their lovemaking had lost its "shine." And to complicate matters, there were more and more moments of sexual disappointments in bed. When this happened, they'd lie side by side in the darkness, losing connection, each so immersed in disappointment that neither could talk about how they felt. They didn't speak, they didn't touch, and the silence between them became a great wall. They just lay next to each other, retreating to some private hurting place, until sleep came. If they could have talked, it might have been a relief for both of them to release their feelings and their love for each other. But they didn't know how to move past the hurt and disappointment. Each one had such a hard time moving out of his own space enough to join the other. And the space between them became a chasm.

As you may have noticed, these stories about misunderstandings have to do with hoping someone will read lips or minds. This expectation is a guaranteed path to disappointment.

If You Love Me, You'll Read My Mind

Do you believe that if someone loves you enough, they'll read your mind—anticipating your wishes, knowing you want yellow roses, surprising you with dinner reservations at that little place you've been wanting to try? And if they don't read your mind, do you tell yourself that proves they don't love you enough. At least not the way you want them to love you.

The whole thing turns into some sort of test, but not a terribly fair or accurate one, because the other person doesn't know what the rules are. What a setup for you to be disappointed! And you'll most likely get continued reinforcement of any old beliefs that others don't care about you, don't respect you, and will usually disappoint you.

Francine married Roy because she was tired of taking care of other folks her whole life, and he seemed just the ticket to take care of her for a change. When she was eighteen, she decided it was time to get away from home, and she and Roy were married. Since she was a little girl, she had to be the "responsible one" in the family, taking

> Do you believe that if someone loves
> you enough, they'll read your mind?

care of things, making sure they flowed smoothly. Everyone depended on her.

Other family members were pretty inept. Her mom was so "helpless" that she could barely get herself dressed in the morning. Francine would have to remind her mom about a lot of things—to walk Francine to the school bus, or that it was time to cook dinner, or to wash Francine's school clothes. Looking back as an adult, Francine realizes how depressed her mom was.

Her dad was a piece of work, too. He got up and went to his job every day, but in the evenings he would zone out, just sitting around, drinking beer, and reading the newspaper. He often made promises he didn't keep, for example, promising to teach Francine to ride her new bike, then repeatedly forgetting. Promising to take the family out on Sundays, then making other plans. Francine would think, "Maybe all those beers did something to his brain."

Francine's "escape" marriage to Roy didn't last long. A couple of years later she met and married Chuck. He was a big hulk of a man, teddybear-ish, with a soft, monotone voice that Francine initially found soothing and reassuring. But soon she came to recognize his demeanor as depressed. And she wondered how she had missed it early on.

But there's a funny thing about missing depression: If you're around it growing up, as Francine was, it becomes a way of life. You begin to assume that everyone is like Mommy or Daddy and you can't seem to spot depression in other people. We just take that sadness or isolation or slowness or lack of energy for granted.

When Francine married Chuck, she liked his quiet, solid way of handling things. She felt secure in his arms. She felt "at last, here is someone who could take care of me." But what she saw as a deliberate way of moving through life often turned into foot-dragging. She had hopes that he'd take some initiative and take care of things around the house that needed to get done. However, she usually didn't tell him directly which projects she wanted done—she more or less hoped he would read her mind. Surely if he did, it would be a sign that he *really* cared about her.

Well, he never was a very good mind reader. And Francine found herself getting hurt by his inability to guess what she had in mind. And, needless to say, those projects never seemed to get done. Things came to a head upon her return from a trip back East. She had asked him to be sure to water the plants while she was visiting her family. "I was furious when I returned to half-dead plants. He 'forgot.' I was fuming and told myself that he didn't care about me because he didn't care about my plants." (Quite a leap in logic there, but we do tend to make those leaps sometimes, don't we?)

I know that for some of you, whether the plants were watered may seem insignificant, but it became a big deal for Francine. Something happened to her trust in Chuck. That space of openness and trust began to close up a little. No real harm done, but she began to expect that she couldn't depend on him.

Realizing that the relationship was in need of some repair work, she suggested that they have a romantic weekend getaway. She told him how important this was to her. He said fine with him and would she please make the plans. Of course, she would have preferred if *he* offered to make the plans (yes, you guessed it—proof of how much he cared), but she went ahead and made the advance arrangements and then told him of the game plan.

Well, the weekend was approaching, and Francine reminded him of their plans. Chuck stared back blankly. He had "totally forgotten" and had made other plans with business associates.

"Sure I was hurt, but I was also mad as hell," she recalls. "I could actually feel the resentment taking hold and hooking onto the walls of my stomach. I knew at that point we really were in trouble."

Francine asked Chuck to join her in therapy for some couple's sessions. She tried to explain how his "forgetfulness" was way too familiar. As a child she had lived with so many promises and disappointments, when her dad would be forgetful just as Chuck had been. While they talked in the session, Chuck seemed to understand why Francine got so upset, but his compassion was short-lived. He just couldn't seem to hold on to the idea for very long and would revert to his old behavior. Perhaps he simply "forgot" again.

Francine began to tell herself that she could not depend on Chuck. She began to take responsibility for managing the household and the total care of their children. She became the pivotal person in the home. And she'd tell anyone who would listen how she "really resented the hell out of it."

What had once been a comfortably soft space between them, holding trust and hope and caring, soon became filled with shards of resentment, bitterness, ill will, and animosity. And the hurt and pain just kept intensifying for Francine.

But what about Chuck? From his perspective, nothing really seemed amiss. True enough, he was often adrift in his own world. He frequently did not listen carefully, and he knew he could be forgetful.

But he was not being mean-spirited or malicious—even though Francine believed he was.

Chuck found himself becoming resentful as well. He felt Francine was treating him as if he were a helpless infant, especially when she spoke to him in her particularly patronizing way. He didn't like it at all. And the more he didn't like it, the more he tended to drag his feet whenever she asked him to do something for her. You may recognize this type of passive anger. The official word for it is "passive-aggressive behavior"—a fancy phrase for "foot-dragging" and "yes, butting."

What could this couple have done to improve their situation? First of all, Francine could have stated exactly what she wants and needs from Chuck—clearly and definitively. This would give Chuck the space to state whether he is comfortable in honoring her requests. And, importantly, it gives him the space to practice saying "no." Perhaps he could say to Francine, "I can't do that, but here is what I can do." And, concurrently, Francine could practice *allowing* enough room for Chuck to say "no" to her requests. As long as he feels he is expected to say "yes," he will find an indirect way to say "no," as we saw from his foot-dragging and "yes-butting." And this kind of indirect communication surely interferes with intimacy.

How much room do you leave for the other person in your communications? Do you leave enough space for them to say "no"? Can they check things out with you? Can they freely ask questions to clarify things, or do you tend take a stance that protects your position? Do you leave room for them to share their feelings? Do you acknowledge their feelings? We can take up space by the way we communicate. How we bring up issues is important. Whining takes up lots of space. Stonewalling takes up a huge chunk. Demands, intrusions, and neediness all take up more than their share. Some guidelines to avoid these missteps and practice good communication follow.

What Is Clear Communication Anyway?

Good communication is more than understanding each other's words. It also means communicating feelings, as well as experiences and history. It entails making an attempt to understand the meaning behind the words, as well as why someone might be overreacting.

By communicating clearly, you can avoid misunderstandings. And clear communication means using "I" statements (statements about how something affects you and the relationship), instead of using "you" statements (criticizing or complaining about what the

> Good communication means communicating
> feelings as well as experiences and history.

other person did wrong). This way you can reflect your perceptions and feelings and send a nonblaming message. For example, saying, "You imbecile, how dare you scream at me!" isn't going to get you very far. But saying, "I'm upset that you raised your voice to me," is a clear statement of the speaker's feelings, said in a nonblaming way. This addresses the behavior rather than shaming the person.

When using these guidelines, don't hesitate to say you want to go through these steps without interruption. There's plenty of opportunity for the other person to respond. And by the way, this isn't about confronting a person—it's about confronting a *situation*. And by the way, it's a nice idea to ask, "Is this a good time to talk?"

- **Step one:** Describe the behavior that you have a problem with in *observable, nonblaming terms*. "Yesterday, I noticed that while I was talking with you, you wandered out of the room." (This frames the interaction from *your* perception in a way that helps the other person feel less defensive and less likely to argue.)

- **Step two:** Describe how you felt about the action. "I felt hurt (angry, upset, confused)." you may want to read more about describing your feelings in chapter 14.

- **Step three:** Describe how you explained the action to yourself. For example, "When you walked out, I told myself, 'I guess I'm not worth listening to.'" In appropriate situations, you might add how the behavior recreates old messages from childhood. "This is what I used to tell myself when my mom dozed off as I was talking to her." (Use this step selectively— only in situations where it feels safe. For instance, maybe with a partner, but probably not with an employer.)

- **Step four:** Clearly describe what you want to change in the relationship and how you would like the interaction to go next time. "Next time I would like you to stay with me and hear me out, or excuse yourself momentarily, if you must, then come back to hear me finish."

By the way, it's helpful to make sure the other person understands your meaning. Don't be timid about asking them to repeat back the gist of your request—what they heard you say. This gives you a chance to clarify your intended meaning in case there's a misunderstanding.

Good communication means practicing being empathic—putting yourself in the shoes of the other person. Sometimes it's useful to try to hypothesize what might be going on with them. What might they be feeling? Or better yet, ask them. But remember that empathy is not about how you might be feeling in their shoes. It means imagining how *they* are feeling.

Empathy isn't only about how you
might be feeling in your partner's shoes.
It means imagining how <u>they</u> are feeling.

So often we are tempted to sit on our feelings and not say anything. But by withholding, even if you're trying to spare your partner's feelings, you can actually really hurt the other person in the long run. By saying something to your partner, you show that you care about them, and your honesty and forthrightness show your respect for the relationship.

What if you do get your nerve up and bring up an important issue with your partner but it doesn't get resolved? Well, once you have brought a matter up, it's a lot easier to move right back into that space and bring it up again. What if you bring up a subject and your partner says something like, "I don't want to talk about it." You could ask, "What do you want me to do with my feelings about this? If I can't express them to you, I'm afraid I'll shut down and withdraw from you."

By improving communication skills you can sort out misunderstandings stemming from the unrealistic expectations that we've been discussing. However, there are other kinds of unrealistic expectations—ones that come from being unable to separate fantasy life from day-to-day existence. Read on.

11

Abracadabra

Fantasies and
Wishful Thinking

Have you ever found yourself craving an intimate relationship with someone? Do you feel sorry for yourself that you're not having one? When you see couples on the street who are walking arm in arm or hugging or kissing, do you wish you could have someone to hug or kiss, too? You may find yourself wanting a close, caring relationship so badly that the fantasies take over, you jump in too fast, and feel foolish.

Wishing is one thing and *readiness* is another. Sometimes we get the two confused. Readiness means being able to make that important shift we talked about in chapter 2—from an individual way of thinking to a relational way of thinking. But lots of us do lots of wishing and hoping that comes packaged as reveries, cyberspace fantasies, long-distance relationships, thinking about long lost loves, and the wishful thinking of secret contracts and hidden agendas.

Reveries

A woman I know tells how she found herself fantasizing about a man she would often see around the neighborhood. Actually, they had talked briefly about a year before. She watched him from afar and often envisioned having a relationship of some kind with him. Then one day she found herself next to him in the post office line. She reminded him where they had met before and was able talk to him long enough to make a connection. And from then on it was easy enough to have a succession of conversations at the neighborhood places: the post office, the supermarket, or the café. Then coffee "dates" turned into dinner dates. "I can't believe I'm actually going out with him," she'd say to herself.

But, in fact, they didn't start at the starting post at the same time. After all, she'd been in a relationship with him for over a year—in her reveries! The relationship didn't last long, of course. It's not possible to compete with a fantasy, and she had idealized him for too long. He was bound to come up short. Her unrealistic expectations could only lead to disappointment. And they did.

A man I know tells this story: "I couldn't believe how fast Marc and I got close. We had so much in common and could talk together so easily; I was envisioning this fabulous relationship. But, little bit by little bit, I realized there were some telltale signs that should have been early warnings. I was so infatuated that I missed all the flashing red lights.

"One day we were in a coffee shop having brunch during a romantic weekend. We were sitting by the window and I couldn't help but notice the constant parade of gorgeous men riding the escalator to the adjacent gym.

"Marc said to me, 'Please don't look at these men when they walk by. I don't like it when you look at anyone else.' I wasn't leering or anything, just sort of glancing in that direction now and then. I didn't mean anything by it, but clearly it bothered him.

"A week or so later he admonished, 'You're doing it again and I don't like it. I don't like you looking at other people when you're with me.' I said, 'I'm here with you. I made the choice to be with *you*.' When Marc told me I couldn't look, I felt like the air had left the room. After all, my fantasies were here long before he was. It was as if he was sucking out my spirit. When I finally decided to stop seeing him, I felt such a rush of freedom!"

We're so quick to get caught up in the fantasy of how we want someone to be. And with the accessibility to cyberspace, it becomes so easy to fuel those fantasies.

Cyberspace

Cyberspace seems to be filling up more and more time and space, as so many of us stay glued to computer screens, sending and answering e-mail, surfing the Web, talking in chat rooms and news-groups, and playing games.

"Cyber" is a term we take for granted these days, but where does it come from? The term "cyber" is from the term "cybernetics," the science of communication and control, which came into usage in the late '40s. In the '60s its principals of information and feedback became popular in the field of family therapy. Here again is that important theory of reciprocity—the effect of behavior on subse-quent behavior. Through recurring sequences of interaction, a per-son influences his or her environment and is, in turn, influenced by it. So, we come full circle: "cyber" evolved from a word that evolved into a family-therapy term that was used to describe relationships. And just look at what a huge impact "cyber" has on our relation-ships now.

Indeed, many of us have a personal relationship with the com-puter, giving over so much time, space, and energy to it. I know how easy it can be to develop a relationship with my computer when I'm working on a book or a magazine piece. When I'm writing or researching something on the Internet, I get completely absorbed in what I'm doing. In fact, if the phone rings and I answer it, the person calling invariably asks, "Are you okay? It seems as if you are some-where else." Yes, I guess I was somewhere else—I was, in fact, orbit-ing around in cyberspace. I was "involved" in an intense relationship with my computer.

But for many people, relationships with computers don't just stop with academic or professional involvement. Chat rooms and pri-vate chat areas are relationships that take up time and space. The Internet is accessible, affordable, and anonymous, and for many peo-ple, "relationships" with the Internet can be special, absorbing, and seductive as well.

Excessive use of the Internet was addressed by Dr. Kimberly Young of the Center for On-Line Addiction in a 1996 paper. Patho-logical Internet use (PIU) is considered as addictive as alcohol or drugs and is equated with another nonsubstance type of addiction—compulsive gambling. Dr. Young found that Internet addicts spend an average of thirty-eight hours per week in cyber-time activities unrelated to employment or academics. If any of these folks have a forty- or fifty-plus hour work week, it surely doesn't leave much time for sleep, much less a romantic relationship.

And that's the point. Even if you are only spending fifteen or twenty hours a week online, wouldn't all this screen time interfere with real-life relationship intimacy? One woman describes how her addiction took over. "When I spent more and more time engaging in online sex, I didn't take care of household chores, I came to bed late every night and lost interest in sex. The Internet added incredible sexual energy to my life, but not to my marriage."

Virtual Infidelity

What happens when cyberspace starts filling up with cybersex? Even a new language develops, as "cyber" becomes a verb—"there he goes, cybering again"—having cybersex, maybe even a cyberaffair with a cyberpartner, and perhaps having a cyberorgasm (unless, of course, it was cyberfaked!). It all adds up to virtual infidelity. But it's important to remember that, just as in any other affair, cyberaffairs don't "just happen." This affair, like others, is usually a symptom of an underlying problem that existed in the couple's relationship *before* the cyberaffair began something is lacking.

It's so easy to tell oneself that this is "not really sex," so "it's not really an affair. No harm done. No one will get hurt." The complaint that I hear most often from couples is that when one partner is over-involved with the Internet in general and cybersex in particular, the other partner feels neglected. When one partner is at the computer, the other is alone in another room. This can choke the life out of relationships.

The lure of the Internet is its anonymity, which allows lots of space to fantasize. In cyberspace, you can be anything you want to be. In fact, people reinvent themselves, assuming a secret identity, often donning "personas" different than their everyday lives. If you're shy, you can be gregarious on the Net; if you're serious, you can be humorous. Role-playing is common in chat rooms—you can choose any age, gender, body type, hair color, or occupation. The Internet executive who was arrested soliciting a thirteen-year-old girl in a chat room said he was only "role-playing." But then again, the male FBI agent who pretended to be the thirteen-year-old girl was role-playing as well.

Relationship.com

It's easy to get involved in intimate conversations online because it feels safer than face-to-face contact. But you're only fooling yourself if you think you're engaging in any real closeness. Any rapid jump to online intimacy is most likely of the "pseudo" variety. And the higher and more unrealistic the expectation, the greater the disappointment and the bigger the subsequent fall. Often some dejection gets thrown in as well when you "lose" the relationship you fooled yourself into thinking was real.

Another way we fill cyberspace is by "reading in" a tone or an inflection into e-mail messages, which just might change the meaning. No wonder the little smiling or frowning faces are used so frequently to punctuate comments.

And where is the privacy? If someone subscribes to a server with a "buddy list" or "instant messenger," they can locate you online any time of the day or night. Whew. You have to go out of your way to not be located. You can use another screen name of course, or you can specify that you don't want anyone to send you instant messages. What a bother! When people creep uninvited into your private space, it feels like a violation.

Long-Distance Relationships

Another great way to replace true intimacy with fantasy going is to have a long-distance relationship. This solution is just the ticket if you have needs for lots of space. You can live the dream, you don't have to live the reality. The distance becomes built-in insulation. It pads the relationship, offering a buffer zone and, as one man says, "It acts as a 'shock absorber' for me—in case there are 'collisions' or other disagreements." After all, you don't *have* to see one another, talk to one another, or even deal with one another on a day-to-day basis. But you can still feel as if you're in a relationship, you can even be a "couple" in your mind. And if you like anticipation, you have lots of that between visits. Best of all, you can keep the fantasy alive.

Long Lost Loves

Fantasizing about and replaying old romantic relationships is a great way to fill up time and space. That "ghost" can certainly take up lots of room in your life, if you let it, filling up all the nooks and crannies of your soul. Trouble is, it can hold you back from connecting to a current lover.

Remember when we discussed feelings of loyalty to parents, modes of being overly connected to them when you actually need to get some separation? Well, some of us tend to stay loyal to old lovers in much the same way. And this loyalty gets in the way of moving on and making a connection to someone new. I've heard people describe how feelings they still have for an old lover can keep them from fully committing—even to the person they marry. This misplaced feeling of loyalty can last for many years, interfering with breaking that old connection and making a new one. Keeping a special place in your heart for a long lost love is one thing, but what if that space is so full that there is just no room for a present relationship? Where can your new partner fit?

I know of a Southern woman who frequently crosses paths with an old flame. Both are married to other people, and both are still attracted to each other. "Well, it's just like running into Rhett Butler at just about every social event I attend," she jokes. "Each time the flame gets fanned." What a powerful, romantic fantasy that must be. And how complicating it must be for her new relationships.

Secret Contracts and Hidden Agendas

A different kind of wishful thinking comes in the form of secret contracts and hidden agendas, which can also confuse and damage relationships. These one-sided, unspoken contracts between two people can lead to disappointments—big time. These expectations are based on a presumption that the other person will cooperate in a plan that has never actually been discussed between the two. All too often, couples enter into partnership with different agendas regarding what they expect to give and what they expect to get from the partner. When they fail to discuss these plans beforehand, somebody gets a big surprise when the partner doesn't uphold their end of the "bargain," and the "deal" doesn't happen.

These presumed agreements can take many forms: when or if to buy a house, have a child, buy a new car, the type of vacation to take, how much to spend or invest, how expenses are shared, whether both continue to work, which friends to keep, how often to have sex and will it be the stuff of which fantasies are made?

Some of these expectations are cultural and societal, some are "because that's the way we've always done it in our family," and some are simply somewhat self-absorbed, wishful thinking. Some of these presumptions are conscious and verbalized, some are conscious but not verbalized, and some are not even in the awareness of the person who assumes them. The person who is expecting something from the partner and doesn't get it will not only be disappointed, but will often be resentful and angry as well.

The problem is, as Clifford Sager describes in the *Handbook of Family Therapy*, edited by Gurman and Kniskern (1981), not only does each partner not have any idea of certain aspects of the other's terms, but in fact, isn't even aware of his or her own terms for the relationship. Sager identifies three levels of awareness of "contracts."

Level 1 includes desires, needs, and expectations that are conscious and verbalized. This is where one person clearly says, "I want _____ , and in exchange I'm willing to do _____ ." However, Sager emphasizes that although the communication may be clearly stated by one partner, the other partner may not hear or register what was said. Level 2 also includes conscious desires, needs, and expectations; however, they are not verbalized to the partner due to embarrassment or to fear of rejection, disapproval, or anger. Level 3 consists of desires, needs, and expectations that are beyond awareness and are often contradictory and unrealistic.

These unspoken or hidden "terms," "contracts," and "agreements" affect all areas of relationships—lifestyle, sex, recreation, values, friends, money, decisionmaking, extended families, childrearing, hopes, and plans.

Perhaps you, too, have stumbled over hidden agendas provided by your partner. And perhaps you have some of your own. If you think they may be lurking around, it's helpful to get them out into the open by discussing them.

Otherwise, resentments develop and you and your partner may start to feel alienated from each other. Isn't it easy to get resentful if you feel you have fulfilled your end of the bargain, but you think your partner has failed to fulfill his or her part?

We've been looking at different forms of expectations and disappointments that interfere in creating and maintaining couples' relationships. Hope as we might that we can make a go of it, sadly, many of us haven't yet learned the necessary skills to be able to be in a committed relationship. One barrier is, of course, those unrealistic expectations and agendas we've just been discussing. But there are numerous factors interfering with being a "couple," and in the next chapter, you'll learn more about how these pesky devils operate.

12

I Want to Be and You Want to Flee

Never Getting to "Couple"

Although we dream about being in a long-term, committed, connected relationship, sometimes two people never make it to "couple." There are of course lots of reasons for this, but let's focus here on three of the most common problems that tend to mess up relationships.

Magical Thinking

First, there's the whole issue of unrealistic expectations that I've described in the last two chapters. I'm a big believer in the power of opening your heart, affirming what you need, and putting it out to the universe. But this is not the same as crossing your fingers and making a wish, or hoping that the other person can read your mind. As we've seen in the preceding chapters, these expectations lead to disappointments, which lead to hurt, resentment, anger, and alienation.

Sometimes as adults, we revert to the magical thinking of our childhood, when we lived midway between the world of magic and the world of reality and all things were possible. Back then we believed we were the center of the world and our wishful thoughts could make things happen. Magical thinking is a normal part of childhood development, but in the adult world it's a setup for disappointment.

> Magical thinking is a normal part of childhood development, but in the adult world it's a setup for disappointment.

I'm Only Flexible Until I'm Not Flexible Anymore

Another problem area is being so easygoing in the early stages of the relationship that, if you decide to shift gears and speak up, it leaves your partner dumbfounded. He or she may get a little angry and possibly feel a little duped. Have you found yourself trying hard to be readily agreeable and maybe even submissive in the early stages of your relationships? Then, once you start feeling a little more secure, you might shift gears, get up some nerve, and ask for (or even demand) what you want or need? Sometimes the other person is stunned at how you've changed. They may interpret this new behavior as you nagging or trying to change them. They might feel angry even a little duped.

One woman says, "Everyone thinks I'm so adaptable. But the truth is, I'm flexible until I'm not. And boy, do people get surprised!" She demonstrated this idea by holding up her thumb. "Notice how flexible it looks," she declared. "See how curved it is? But now take a closer look. If I try to bend it even a little further, it resists. It does not bend any more at all." It only looks flexible.

The "Dance-Away Lover"

This is the big challenge for most new relationships—staying in the relationship long enough to balance closeness and distance. Usually, however, one person gets too close, and the other person gets scared and runs.

The basic conflict here is the need for closeness and the fear of it. You may find yourself really caring for someone, caring more than you ever intended or even imagined you would. You begin to realize that this person is actually important to you. You might find yourself opening up and sharing some childhood memories, maybe even some past hurts. You may surprise yourself by sharing very private thoughts, concerns, fears, or hopes. You might find yourself sharing some feelings! And maybe you start getting nervous—and yes, maybe scared. The developing closeness starts to become disconcerting. You might say to yourself, "Hey, this isn't supposed to happen. I'm supposed to be in *control* of this. How did I let this happen? How did I start caring so much?"

You may find yourself pushing away or pulling back in alarm. You might even bolt and run. Poof. Gone. Perhaps never to be heard from again. Maybe without an explanation, maybe without a good-bye. Frequently the disappearing act comes soon after a heartfelt talk, a closer-than-usual emotional moment, or especially intense sex. You know the kind of moment I mean. Perhaps it's even the kind of intimate moment that I describe throughout this book.

> You may find yourself pushing away ... after a heartfelt talk, a closer-than-usual emotional moment, or especially intense sex.

Suddenly, desperately, there seems to be a need for some breathing room. "I can't stand the anxiety," says one man. "All I know is I want to take off and run. And I usually do. Sometimes I wish I could be like the Invisible Man in the movie. He controlled who gets to see him by wrapping and unwrapping himself, giving form, erasing, giving form, erasing."

And a woman I know adds, "When I find myself getting too close, I get scared and start moving away. I guess you could say I disappear into myself. My lover says he gets very confused—one moment I'm there and the next moment I'm 'gone.'"

Another woman has been becoming aware of how she retreats to a safer place once she finds herself getting a little too open with someone. "I get more surfacy, more shallow in my next interaction with that person. It's as if that earlier conversation never took place—probably because a part of me wishes it hadn't."

Final Score: "Fear of Closeness" = 15; "Desire for Closeness" = 3

Once again, the fear of closeness seems to win over the need for it. "Bolting" can take the form of an emotional leaving or a physical leaving. The emotional kind can be confusing, but the physical can be agonizing. When you're on the receiving end of this performance, you probably don't know what hit you. If you are fortunate enough to get a post-bolt explanation, it may go something like this: "It was what it was. Don't try to make anything out of it," or "Well, we gave it a whirl and it didn't work out," or "I never promised you a long-term relationship."

The "Dance-Away Lover" is magnificently described by psychologist Daniel Goldstine in a book of the same title (1977). "Lover" wants intimacy but can't handle it. "Lover" holds on to the hope of someday having a close, loving relationship, yearning for something *magical* to happen—hoping that each new person will finally be the "right" person. Unfortunately, Lover holds up some pretty highly idealized, romanticized standards, and it's just about impossible for *anyone* to meet them. Even though the bar gets placed exceedingly high, Lover rationalizes that the prospective partner "just isn't right," or "isn't good enough," and drops the person like a hot potato. The poor, unfortunate dumpee doesn't even know what happened.

Imagine that you're dancing with a special someone on the dance floor, moving to the music, getting into the rhythm of it all. You start a turn, facing the other direction for a moment. Then you turn back to your partner . . . and there's no one there. Gone! He or she must have left the dance floor when you weren't looking. If, in fact, you ever get a chance to get an explanation, you will probably hear something like, "I never liked dancing with you anyway—there just wasn't any magic there for me."

"That's an intriguing 'dance-away' example," you say. "But it really doesn't happen like that." Okay, here's another scenario. Picture a dance floor again, or maybe a party. Your partner excuses him- or herself to get some air or a cold drink—and they don't return. They just disappear. Finally you figure out they must have left. There are no good-byes, no explanations, no nothing. Just gone. Has anything like that ever happened to you or to anyone you know? Do you think there might be a message here about Lover's capacity for an intimate relationship? Or is it just one full dance card after another?

The Elusive Butterfly

There is something really seductive about this elusive quality. It draws you in. What's that old saying? "Like a moth to a flame." Well, this dynamic surely lends itself to high drama if you're inclined to that sort of thing. In an elusive kind of relationship, there is nothing tangible to grab on to, so you can make it into anything you want it to be—but only in your mind. It doesn't have substance; it isn't real. But it does fill up empty space. Sooner or later your resentment starts, and the anger can't be far behind. That fills up space, too.

"I'm Just a Guy Who Can't Say 'No'"

What about people who can't say "no" to important people in their lives because doing so might disappoint someone. So, in the name of protecting feelings of others, they always say "yes."

People find these folks very attractive because they appear sensitive, kind, and caring and can make you feel important. Because these people are "pleasers" and charming to boot, others believe they mean what they say when they say "yes." However, because they can't say "no," they end up foot dragging, showing up late or not at all. This is deception in the name of kindness, arousing hopes that can't be met. These folks end up disappointing people anyway, perhaps even more than if they'd said "no" in the first place.

They flit from one relationship to another, like a bee flying from flower to flower, awakening expectations, then disappointing them. Because these actions lead to resentment and anger, it's no surprise that their lovers are sometimes provoked to be cruel. This provides an excuse to leave them in good conscience and move on to the next relationship.

Let's take Neil and Rita as an example. Neil can't say "no" and gets involved with Rita who has unrealistic expectations about the relationship. She wants someone who will read her mind, guessing every little secret desire she has: special gifts, expensive dinners, romantic getaways. Instead, she gets Neil, a "yes-man" who ends up disappointing her every time she has a secret yearning.

She set herself up for disappointment with her unrealistic expectations. But she chose the right guy for the job—Neil is a master of the trade. There was the time she asked him to plan a romantic trip (because if *he* planned it, that would mean he cared about her). If you guessed that he agreed but the trip never materialized, you got his number a lot faster than Rita did! When she finally figured out that the trip wasn't going to happen, her feelings were hurt and she was angry—very angry. He left, of course. He was so afraid of someone being disappointed in *him* that he couldn't stick around. He may not have intended to reject her, but he invalidated the relationship by not being candid about his feelings.

It's not easy to be honest about feelings, even to ourselves. If Neil could have searched around inside and come up with what he was really feeling about the situation, Rita might not have been so disappointed and hurt. There might have been any number of reasons he didn't feel okay about taking the trip. He might have said, "I want to be with you, but I'd rather not go out of town for a weekend, because I'm more comfortable staying at home." But instead he said "okay" and wasn't able to follow through.

Out of Sight, Out of Mind

It can be so unnerving to try to be in a relationship with someone who divides his or her life into neat little compartments. You may be putting him or her at the top of your "to think about often" list, but this person is preoccupied with lots of other matters and you may not be anywhere near the top of their list of "things to do today." This partitioning can drive you nuts. It would only seem fair that if you are thinking about someone, they should be thinking about you as well.

It would only seem fair—if you're thinking about someone, they should be thinking about you as well.

If he or she doesn't call you as often as you think they should, it may mean that they just aren't thinking about you as much as you're thinking about them. It doesn't mean they don't care about you. They just think differently than you do. You're just not in their frame of reference as often as you might want.

"Well, why not," you ask in your self-important way. It might be that they are just self-absorbed. That is, absorbed with the business that pertains to them. There's space in their head to think about one thing at a time, and it's simply not you at that moment.

Yes, it does indeed seem like out of sight, out of mind. Sometimes a phone call from *you* is all it takes to remind them that you're around. But if you let your ego get in the way or let your feelings get hurt, it's hard to be a squeaky wheel. You may simply withdraw, sacrificing another relationship to assumptions and to the expectation that partners do things your way.

13

Tighten Your SeatBelts—
Bumpy Road Ahead

Situational Stressors

Perhaps it's wishful thinking or eternal optimism or naivete, but all too often we find ourselves envisioning a blissful arm-in-arm stroll with our honey along the road of couplehood. Trouble is, there are bumps in the road that we didn't quite anticipate. Many of these road hazards are life situations that may be temporary, but can still cause a great deal of stress. I refer to these stressful situations in relationships as "situational stressors." They arrive in the form of transitional developments, life-cycle changes, or rites of passage. Here is a list of some common situations that, over time, can affect closeness and distance in intimate relationships.

- Work schedules
- Commuting issues
- A change in structured space
- New child
- Traveling together
- Layoffs/Retirement
- Relatives and other houseguests
- Empty nest

- Emotional or physical illness

- Aging parents

Work Schedules

Besides the time spent commuting, there are those ten-hour-plus days at work. For many of us, our place of employment becomes a substitute "family," where we not only share projects and strategies, but also a social life. If there is any kind of void in our lives, work fills it. Even if there isn't a void, work finds a way to fill up space anyway. Then our job becomes the top priority, over relationships, family, and friends. When there is no balance between them, it can lead to hurt feelings, misunderstandings, resentment, and anger.

It doesn't feel good to be considered a lower priority than your partner's career obligations. And, if a grueling commute is part of the work schedule, it can really play havoc with relationship intimacy.

Commuting Issues

What if one or both of you are up and out of the house at 4 or 5 A.M.? Even 6 or 7 A.M.? How does that affect your relationship? Do you have a chance to connect in the morning? Do you find a way to connect during the day by phone or e-mail? And what happens after work? Are you able to find time for each other then, or are you too exhausted? Commuting and the time and energy it takes can surely be a drain on your relationship. It can cause resentment when you hardly have any evening time left for each other.

Commuting does, however, allow you to have much-needed transitional time alone between the hectic, often breathless pace of the office and the demands of family at home. If you can have this time to yourself, it is easier to reconnect with your partner, as we saw in chapter 4. A commute can provide solitude and peace—a little breathing room in a hectic environment. Whether it be by car or public transportation, commuting can provide some peace of mind, time to decompress, to sort things out, or to space out. It can offer time for soothing music or books on tape.

Changes in Structured Time and Space

Changes in structured space refers to sudden shifts in day-to-day activities, some of which can cause a multitude of relationship problems. These transitions would include vacations, a new child, leaves, lay-offs, or retirement.

What readily comes to mind is the shift that goes on for instructors, teachers, and other school personnel. There is the end-of-the-year whirlwind and then summer starts, and the normal routine disappears. This transition leaves lots of unstructured time, necessitating "shifting gears" in order to fill it.

This is true, too, for students finishing a school project, thesis, or dissertation. I remember experiencing this big void after college, after my master's program and again following the completion of my dissertation for my Ph.D. How did I fill up that void? By getting the blues. I would joke that it was a mini postpartum depression, where endorphin levels surge then fall abruptly. But it wasn't anything to joke about. Depression never is.

New Child

Most couples aren't prepared for the infringement on their space with the arrival of a child. Nothing can change your schedule faster than the needs of a new little person in the household. It can be most unsettling to be faced with crying, feedings, and diaper changings, harshly interrupting your sleep, time together, and sex life. I described how children affect your personal space in chapter 4.

Traveling Together

Traveling together works well for some couples because they see it as an adventure and find ways to work as a travel team. But traveling together can be hell for others. This is usually because there is a change in structure that one or both people cannot tolerate. When your routine is changed, and days are no longer predictable and familiar, it can sure throw you off balance. Anxiety can surface, and before you know it, you may find yourself acting out your feelings. You may recall how, in chapter 7, we looked at how we try so hard to control our environment when we're feeling anxious and end up controlling the people around us as well. The couple in the story below demonstrate how traveling together can bring this dynamic to the forefront.

Sally and Hank were visiting old college friends of hers on the East Coast. They had planned to go off by themselves one day and have some time together. But there were a series of miscues about meeting up with each other. Hank was late, Sally waited for a while, and then went off to join her friends. He was hurt and felt left out of the "threesome." What was essentially a simple miscommunication

---

When your routine is changed
it can throw you off balance.

---

put a real damper on the rest of the visit until Sally and Hank made time to talk about what had happened.

"I was upset that you weren't where you said you would be," Hank said.

"You were late," countered Sally. "I didn't feel like waiting around for you, so I went and found my friends."

Hank admitted, "I thought I had become so boring that you didn't want to spend time with me."

"Really?" Sally responded, "I felt like you were late on purpose, like you'd engineered it."

Hank was astonished. "I thought you had! My feelings were hurt. I thought you'd rather spend time with your friends than with me."

Patsy and Nicolas try to avoid these kinds of snafus during their frequent business trips to other countries. "We've worked out a routine where each one is in charge of making plans on alternate days. And it's okay, if either of us wants to go off on our own during the day. We just say, 'I'll meet you at dinner.' and make sure we are clear about the time and place."

And then there are the vacationing-by-car stories. Most of us have one or two, but they are not always of the type we want to entertain our friends with. They are often too painful.

Gena and Nathan fight about directions and map reading. She gives directions to Nathan, but she gives several at a time, and he can only hear step-by-step, one-at-a-time directions. Clearly, her style is different from his and he doesn't have the ability for focus and concentration that she does. Each car trip would end with both of them frustrated and angry with each other. This pattern ended when they found a way to work as a team, including Gena slowing those directions down.

Often people feel trapped in the car during trips—as if there is no way out of that small space. This can conjure up all kinds of images of not being able to breathe. One woman describes getting especially distressed when her partner withdraws instead of acknowledging being angry. "The silence takes over—the air is thick with it. I feel as if I'm suffocating. It's always difficult when I feel shut out at home, but in the car it's positively claustrophobic." If you are feeling stressed or disconnected, sometimes it helps to arrange frequent rest stops to rebalance and reconnect.

But Cassie has come up with a great idea for not feeling ignored during a car trip. "When I travel with my boyfriend, he gets really into the music or deep in thought while he's driving. Sometimes I feel shut out, so I asked myself "What can I do?" I hit upon the 'cake-pan plan.' As a kid, I used to pack a cake pan for car trips filled with a coloring book, crayons, and picture cards. So now I just say to myself, 'I think I'll pack my present-day cake pan for the car trip.' Now I include my Discman, a book, and a crossword puzzle." Cassie has managed to fill up that cake pan so well that there isn't any room to feel ignored.

Layoffs/Retirement

Layoffs or retirement are also sudden shifts in structured time that leave large holes in your day and require you to work out new arrangements with your partner—especially if they are still working. And, if your partner is not working, suddenly you find yourself dealing with twenty-four hours a day of togetherness.

With so much extra time on your hands, your partner may find that you are drifting into their personal space. It may also seem to you that your partner is getting into your face by reminding you to do all those chores around the house that you've both been putting off for so long.

Phil decided to take an early retirement from his thirty years of running the operations of a large company—a high-stress job with lots of daily demands and little free time. He was tired of the grind and the ninety-minute commute, so retirement sounded like a good idea to him. His wife, Margaret, a graphic artist who now works from her home office, was supportive of Phil's decision, looking forward to more time with him. Although they had planned financially for retirement, they didn't plan for the letdown and doldrums that can go along with it.

The biggest problem for Phil was the sudden loss of identity he experienced when he left the company. He saw himself as a person who got things done, an important part of the company team. Because work took up a large percentage of his life, this part of his identity ceased to exist once he retired. Phil didn't know who he was anymore. His experience is a common one. Either a layoff or retirement represents a loss of identity, which can throw us for a loop and leave a very big space in our lives. Phil found himself filling that space with the help of TV and AOL. "I know everything about current events these days," he says. "Between CNN and the computer screen I spend hours in the company of the daily news. It's not helping my marriage one bit." This lament about online activities affecting relationships sounds all too familiar, as we saw in chapter 11.

But retirement can present other problems as well. Couples often make the decision to "downsize" from a larger home to a smaller one, necessitating adjustments and big decisions. Which life mementos to keep, which to discard? And for some, retirement might also mean a downsizing of lifestyle as well, because of reduced income. A move to new quarters, coming right on the heels of retiring, results in three simultaneous losses—loss of professional identity, loss of structure, and loss of familiar surroundings.

Another unexpected situation might take place. A partner who was for many years "too busy" to take part in family activities with children or grandchildren, may find themselves on the outside looking in once they have more time to spend with the family. This exclusion happens because all those years of being "too busy" resulted in family members forming separate alliances.

Although sudden layoffs can't usually be foreseen, retirement *can* be planned for in order to find productive ways of filling up the empty time and space. Sitting down with your partner and talking about how to restructure time and space is a good start. A valuable way to fill space would be by inquiring into community programs where you could volunteer time to share your knowledge from hobbies or work experience.

This is what Horace and Eleanor tried to do when she decided to retire from her high-powered advertising job. The first thing they did was to sit down together and try as realistically as possible to make a plan. During one of their talks, Horace was able to tell Eleanor about how he envied her retirement plans, wishing he could do the same now instead of in two years. But talking about it together helped and he was supportive of her decision. Eleanor did everything she could think of to research retirement issues that might come up. She read some books on the subject and both she and Horace talked to couples they knew who had gone through the experience. And as soon as she decided to retire, she contacted the high schools and the senior centers to see how she might volunteer her advertising know-how. The high school was delighted to have her work with the yearbook advertising staff.

There were a few bumps in the road, of course, but Eleanor and Horace had expected some problems. Their teamwork in preparing for her retirement helped them to do the necessary restructuring of time, space, and activities. Yes, they had a lot of readjusting to do, but they got to know each other in new ways as they embarked on this important life transition.

Those "Outlaw In-Laws" — Relatives and Other Houseguests

Talk about stressful situations, this can be one of the worst. And the smaller the space, the more anxiety seems to fill up every nook and cranny, especially when it's relatives who are visiting. It seems as if they are always doing *something* that gets on your nerves. Taking over in the kitchen, or criticizing the way you set the table, or putting their feet on your coffee table, shoes and all. Up, up, *up* goes the anxiety barometer. I've even heard of situations where the visiting relatives or friends plan to stay in a motel or hotel, and the couple gets upset, taking it personally that their guests are choosing not to stay with them. Are there *any* right answers to this dilemma?

How do people handle these visits without hurting their relationships? One couple I know sits down before the visitor's arrival and strategizes how the weekend will go and how they will each manage to have some alone time (individually and together) during the visit. For example, when the woman's mother is visiting, her partner doesn't always need to hang out with them. He gets to have his own time to do what he needs to do for himself—take a long walk or bike ride, for instance. He joins them some of the time, but not *all* the time. This planning seems to keep the weekend fairly resentment-free.

What if it's the other way around, and you and your partner are the visitors? It's important here, too, that you plan to have some time together. If possible, plan a day trip on your own, away from your hosts. Rent a car if you need one so you're not dependent on your hosts for transportation. Then *you* are in control of your time.

But being a houseguest is not the only way in-law problems arise. Too often one person feels they are treated differently by their partner when the partner's parents are around. "I feel left out, not included around his parents," protests Judith. "It's as if I don't exist, as if they'd rather I not be with them. I feel ignored at dinner, both by Keith and his parents." And in some ways, she's right. Keith feels squeezed into a kind of loyalty bind whenever his parents come to visit, and it's not okay. He hasn't been able to detach sufficiently from his parents and form new relationship bonds with Judith. He hasn't been able to make room for both in his life, and Judith is keenly aware of this. One day when his parents were visiting, they all went shopping together. When Judith called him over to see a sweater she liked, he wouldn't join her at the sweater table. When they finally talked about it later, he told her why he was resistant. Keith and Judith always choose sweaters together and share them as a way of sharing intimacy. By not joining her in choosing the sweater, Keith was, in a way, keeping their intimate act private from his parents. But, without understanding his motives, Judith felt thoroughly rejected by him as she often did in the presence of his parents.

Another "outlaw in-law" situation that contributes to someone feeling like chopped liver is when one partner acts as "advisor" to his or her own family members, taking time and space away from the couple's relationship.

Sonia laments that her partner is frequently "on call" to his divorced sister, who lives in another city. He frequently makes solo visits to see her, and they talk on the phone just about every day. "He's just like a 'stand-in' husband to her," Sonia bemoans. "I feel as if I am second fiddle to his family." Again, this is a situation where one partner has not differentiated from his family of origin, and his primary loyalty seems to be to the family members.

What should you do in situations like these? First of all, look at whether there may be cultural influences on seemingly errant behaviors. Ask questions, check things out. It may not be exactly as it seems to you at first glance. Your investigation also notifies your partner that this is a problem for you in the relationship. While you're discussing it, say what kind of attention you need from your partner so he or she can see whether or not that's do-able. If it's not, you might want to know that. By openly checking out the situation you have all the information and can make an informed decision about the best plan of action to take.

But let's also consider the partner who feels that they must take care of family first. Betsy has an adult daughter and a granddaughter, but is in the first year of a romantic relationship. "I try to fit everyone into my life, but there's just not enough room to balance everyone's needs. My partner wants to spend time with me on the weekends, but that's the only time I can see my daughter and granddaughter. Weeknights are too hard, what with everyone's school and work schedules. I'm trying to work out some sort of rotation system, but somebody's nose always seems to get out of joint about it. It feels like way too much weight on my shoulders."

Is there something old about this feeling? Betsy's answer was immediate. "This is exactly how I felt as an only child. I had to be the responsible one in the family. And to make matters worse, I never felt that *my* needs counted at all." And so the realization hit that this huge feeling of responsibility was not just about her lover or her daughter or granddaughter. It was about her old, familiar, childhood role as well. She was still being the "responsible one." As we talked, it was as if a weight had lifted—along with her shoulders and her spirits.

Empty Nest

Raising children can be stressful, no doubt, but launching them comes with its own special set of stressors. The accomplishment of this transition depends on many factors, especially the family's degree of differentiation (being connected but separate), whether or not the parents are trying to "make right" their own unresolved childhood experiences, and whether the child is the "glue" that holds the parents together. Loyalty and betrayal issues abound, often influencing the adult child's romantic relationship. The emotions experienced at this launching phase of the life cycle are even more complicated if other transitions are going on at the same time: retirement, illness, or death of the parent's own parent.

Emotional and Physical Illnesses

Surely chronic or life-threatening illnesses can have an effect on closeness and distance in relationships. When an illness is present, restrictions affect interactions between partners. What happens if the partner whose job it was to caretake finds him or herself dependent and in need of assistance? This is a very big adjustment to make in the relationship. Some couples grow closer, some couples grow apart. Sometimes these stressors reach a saturation point, as I discussed in chapter 6.

Aging Parents

If you find yourself having to deal with the difficulties of caring for an aging parent, the energy drain can be gigantic. You may have to talk your parent into giving up their private living space, and then comes the task of finding the "right" living situation for them. You could have to move them again if it doesn't work out. And if you are in the same geographical area, there are the daily or weekly visits. Just as you get into the routine of it all, yet another move may be necessary.

All of this can turn your relationship upside down and inside out. With all the time it takes to parent-sit, your partner will most likely feel neglected.

So what to do about it? Good communication between the couple is important so that feelings of guilt, blame, or resentment don't build up. It's important for each to be clear about what they need from the other one, so energy isn't wasted by trying to do fancy guesswork. It's important for the caretaker to find ways to feel taken care of—do they have friends they can ask for support or help or nurturing? And peer support groups are helpful here—both for the ill partner and for the caretaker. Many hospitals offer them because they recognize how important it is not to feel as though you're going through this upheaval alone. And what if you are juggling caring for your own children while you're attempting to make workable arrangements for your parent or parents. No wonder they call it the "sandwich generation"—what a squeeze this can be.

Here is another circumstance where support groups can help you find a community and see how other people are handling the situation. How are they juggling their time? How are they finding ways to make time for their partners? How are they making time for themselves? Yes, I know you might say, "How will I ever find time to go to support group meetings?" But look at it as an investment in the future for yourself. This truly is a balancing act—giving and receiving space.

Having to deal with any of these situational stressors may sometimes feel like slogging knee deep into the Big Muddy. At times the enormity of the stresses can be overwhelming, throwing your relationship off balance.

It's not only important to give space but to be able to receive space as well. In the next chapter we'll look at ways to take care of yourself, getting to understand and respect your own needs in your relationship with your partner. And by now you'll recognize this theme: Knowing yourself is a prerequisite for intimacy with another person. In other words, making space on the inside in order to make space in your relationship.

14

The Space to Give and the Space to Receive

Recognizing Needs for Comfortable Space

At this point in the journey of discovering how personal space affects relationships, you can see how your need for space takes many twists and turns along the road to intimacy. Each of you has your own comfort level where space is concerned. First you must identify your needs, then find a way to negotiate your needs for feelings, your needs for privacy, and your needs to have needs.

Our Need for Feelings

You may not even know that you're having a feeling, much less knowing what the feeling might be. And if you don't know what you're feeling, how can you put words to it? And if you can't give it voice, how can your partner hear you and understand how you feel?

We Need to Have Feelings

"How do you feel about that," someone would ask me.

"I don't know," I'd say. "Nothing comes to mind."

Some of you will understand this little scene because you, too, may have cut off your feelings. And others, for the life of you, won't be able to understand how some people can have no inkling of what their feelings might be. Some children learn that it is okay to befriend feelings as a child, and others learn to push them away because the family rule is: "Don't have feelings." So we were young, we learn to cut them off. After a while, we forget what it's like to have certain feelings: "Anger? I never get angry." "Sad? I don't know what you're talking about." If we dared to express our feelings someone might get upset at us. So we stuffed them and now, as adults, it's not easy to call them back. If you find yourself clenching your jaw, perhaps you're angry. If you find yourself sighing a lot, just maybe you are sad. Feelings generally fall into categories of mad, sad, bad, glad, "had," or scared. The comprehensive list of feelings on this and the next page is from *Couples Skills* (p. 29), by Matthew McKay, Ph.D., Patrick Fanning, and Kim Paleg, Ph.D. (1994). When I read it, I unearthed feelings I forgot I had. Perhaps you will rediscover some, as well.

Feelings List

Affectionate	Furious	Put down
Afraid	Generous	Relaxed
Amused	Glad	Relieved
Angry	Gloomy	Resentful
Annoyed	Grateful	Resigned
Anxious	Great	Sad
Apprehensive	Guilty	Safe
Bitter	Happy	Satisfied
Bored	Hateful	Secure
Calm	Helpless	Sexy
Capable	Hopeless	Silly
Cheerful	Horrified	Strong
Comfortable	Hostile	Stubborn
Competent	Impatient	Stuck
Concerned	Inhibited	Supportive
Confident	Irritated	Sympathetic
Confused	Isolated	Tender
Contemptuous	Joyful	Terrified
Controlled	Lonely	Threatened
Curious	Loved	Thrilled

Defeated	Loving	Touchy
Dejected	Loyal	Trapped
Delighted	Melancholy	Troubled
Depressed	Miserable	Unappreciated
Desirable	Muddled	Uncertain
Despairing	Needy	Understood
Desperate	Nervous	Uneasy
Determined	Out of control	Unfulfilled
Devastated	Outraged	Unloved
Disappointed	Overwhelmed	Upset
Discouraged	Panicky	Uptight
Disgusted	Passionate	Used
Distrustful	Peaceful	Useless
Embarrassed	Pessimistic	Victimized
Enraged	Playful	Violated
Exasperated	Pleased	Vulnerable
Excited	Powerful	Wonderful
Fearful	Prejudiced	Worn out
Frantic	Pressured	Worried
Frustrated	Proud	Worthwhile
Fulfilled	Provoked	Yearning

From *Couple Skills*, Matthew McKay, Patrick Fanning, and Kim Paleg, 1994.

And, because of my special interest in rejection and taking things personally, I would add a few more to the list: ashamed, rejected, disrespected, and ignored. Perhaps you, too, can think of some of your own unique feelings to add.

It's not easy to identify your feelings if you've been pushing them aside for a long time, but it *is* possible, with practice. First it helps to identify where the feeling is in your body. For example, it may be caught in your throat, or feel like a tightening across your chest, or a chill in your lower back. Using a journal to write about your feelings as they come to consciousness helps as well.

We Need to Communicate Feelings

Once you can begin to identify a feeling to yourself, you can give yourself the space to take a look at it and the permission to voice it. You can try to understand what the feeling means to you and how it affects and is affected by your relationship. Then you can choose when and how to communicate how you feel to your partner. Sometimes we continue as adults to "stuff" our feelings out of the same fear we had as children: if we dare to speak up, someone will get angry at us, reject us, or abandon us. So often we learned somewhere along the way that expressing feelings (especially strong ones, such as anger) can only be done in an either/or way: either not at all or as an outburst. As suggested in chapter 6, you can use the idea of a continuum to find a way of seeking a middle ground. And the role of feelings in developing communication skills is described in chapter 10. Giving yourself permission to express feelings isn't easy because it's scary to tell these things to your partner. Looking at it from your partner's perspective, it's also difficult to be on the receiving end of feelings.

We Need to Have Our Feelings Heard

After you identify your feelings it's important that your partner allow you the space to put them into words. After all, it takes so much energy to get up the courage to say what's on your mind, it's helpful if your partner is receptive to hearing what you have to say. Trouble is, sometimes there are barriers to this happening. There may be times when the other person thinks they have to jump right in and "fix" things, and instead of listening attentively to what you're saying, they're busy strategizing: "What can I say in response?" or "How can I make it better?" At other times listening to the poignancy of your feelings may bring up their own experiences, making it hard to listen receptively. If, in fact, there seems to be a barrier to either one of you listening to the other, it would be important to discuss this together to see what it might be about.

All of this—needing to have feelings, to communicate your feelings, and to have your feelings heard by your partner—requires space, trust, and energy. But isn't this what real intimacy is all about? An honest expression of feelings is essential. If there's no room for vulnerability, how can there be room for intimacy?

If there's no room for vulnerability,
how can there be room for intimacy?

Our Need for Privacy

Our need for private space is sacred. If we feel it is not being respected, we may very well find ourselves overreacting.

A woman I know was really embarrassed when she found out her husband brought someone home for lunch while she was at work. She likes the house to be "picked up" for company, and it really upset her that someone had been there at a time she considered it "a little messy." That's because she's a very private person. However, the situation reversed when her husband told her to "call before you pop into my office." She took it as a personal affront, telling herself all the reasons he didn't want her there. But forgot to add to her list that he, also, is a very private person.

Our Need for Needs

Just as your feelings may have gotten lost somewhere back there, so did recognition of your needs. You may have learned to compromise them by putting others' needs ahead of your own, perhaps a brother or sister or a parent. You may, in fact, put lots of people's needs ahead of your own. One reason this can happen is because you often don't have the foggiest idea what your needs *are*. If someone were to ask, you might automatically say, "I don't know."

What Do You Long For?

"I'm afraid I'll be ridiculed if I say I have needs," Sandy said. "There was never room for my own needs when I was growing up. If I asked for anything, I felt I was taking up too much space, being too obvious, too needy. And it only got me into trouble. I was never important enough to have any needs that counted. So I came to believe that I don't count either. It's the same now, too. I'm afraid to ask my partner or my friends or my supervisor at work for anything. Sometimes I wish my pa+rtner would offer to do certain things for me so I wouldn't have to ask, like rub my back. That would be great."

One woman puts it this way: "I know he does most of the grocery shopping, and he picks up the dry cleaning and the coffee and the toilet paper, but what I *really* want is a big hug—and I don't get that very often."

Confusing Needs with Neediness

If, as a child, you were made to feel ashamed or bad for having needs, you most likely did not learn to ask directly for what you needed, instead learning to use ploys or manipulations. You may have felt needed by others but didn't get what you needed from them. Perhaps you got the message that there was no space in your family to have needs.

This experience can leave a big hole that may feel like a bottomless pit and it's easy to fear that your neediness will overwhelm people. At times like this, you'll probably confuse having needs with neediness.

You may not always able to distinguish those childhood feelings of desperation from appropriate adult recognition that you do, need something from your partner. You may find yourself getting "This is what I need from you" confused with "I need you."

It can be hard to recognize needs, even harder to be specific. You may only have a vague idea of what will make you feel better, and the more undefined the hole is, the harder it is to fill. If you are not supposed to have needs, how can you even begin to find the words to express them? And if you don't know what it is you're trying to fill, how can you know when the need is satisfied?

Practice, Practice, Practice

If someone were to ask you what you want, what you yearn for, could you give a clear answer? Or would you find yourself saying, "I don't know." How can you communicate your needs to someone else if you can't identify them to yourself first? Because this identification is hard to do without practice, I frequently give clients the following assignment to do each morning upon awakening. I suggest they ask themselves some form of this series of questions. Simple questions to be sure, but not always easy to answer. Don't be surprised if you find this a very difficult exercise to do at first:

- "What would make me feel good today?"

- "What do I want? What do I need?"

- "From whom?" (Yourself? Someone else?)

- "In what way? What form would it take?"

How can you communicate your needs to someone else if you can't **identify** them to yourself first?

Are you in a relationship that fills space but doesn't fill your needs? After all, waiting for someone to fill your needs can mean a very long wait. As one woman says, "I feel more lonely when I'm with him than when I'm by myself. He just doesn't seem to have any idea what I need, and that makes me feel so alone."

When I think of how we look "out there" to get our needs met, I'm reminded of this Indian folk tale. Up in the foothills of the Himalayas, there is a shy, elusive creature known as the musk deer. This deer seeks out the smell of musk its whole life—without realizing the scent comes from its own navel. Sometimes the answer is closer to us than we suspect, and we just aren't recognizing it. You might ask yourself how you would recognize when a need is met, because the answer could be right under your nose.

Defining your needs, putting words to them, may be a new experience for you if no one gave you permission to do it before. Don't be surprised if you struggle with it at first. Doing the above exercise regularly could change your perspective. Practice checking in with yourself throughout the day about how you feel and what would make you feel better. You will develop a more defined sense of yourself—and new respect for both yourself and your needs.

Once you begin to recognize your own wants and needs, how do you go about communicating them to another person? Here are a couple of ways to phrase your request:

- Sometimes I find myself hinting around about something I want or need from you, but I'd really like to just tell you directly. I need for you to _____ .

- I have a request to make of you. It's important to me that you _____ .

Asking for What You Want

Hearing yourself speak your needs out loud works wonders. Be aware that you may have a tendency to say what you *don't* want from someone instead of what you *do* want. Negatives seem to be the first things that come to mind—it's often easier to say, "I don't want you to keep reading the paper when I'm talking about a problem." Instead, emphasize what you want, rather than what you don't want: "I would really like to look into your eyes when we talk. But to do this, I need for you to put the paper down." Sometimes it may be a more complicated need. It took one man quite a while to define what was troubling him. Finally he realized it wasn't okay with him when his wife worked into the evening several days a week. "I long for a regular kind of home life," he told her.

In other words, you will be framing your statements as "this is what I need from you." You can practice doing this by standing in front of a mirror, making eye contact with yourself, and saying the words out loud. Start out with small requests; they can be real or hypothetical. Just listen to the sound of those words coming out of your mouth. You can practice with a therapist or perhaps corral a friend. By practicing with someone, you get the added bonus of hearing a "yes" or "no." You can take turns, too, having the other person do the asking, while you practice accepting or declining.

> Emphasize what you want,
> rather than what you don't want.

Giving Yourself the Space to Love Without Conditions

The phrase "unconditional love" gets tossed around, but there is much misunderstanding about its meaning. Unconditional love means being accepted without conditions—that you don't have to fear someone will withhold love unless you act or perform in a certain way. It does not mean, however, there must be blind acceptance of inappropriate, harmful, or destructive behaviors.

As a child, you may have believed your parents wouldn't love you unless you made good grades, had the "right" friends, or won awards. Now that you're an adult, you may find yourself getting caught in the same trap, expecting someone to keep raising the bar. It happens in relationships, too—you may feel someone will only love you "on condition."

Conditional love is a rejecting kind of love, rejecting the real person. It robs you of who you are, expecting you to be what someone else wants or needs you to be.

But what if you find yourself in a relationship where you are constantly molding yourself to your partner's needs? How can you best deal with this situation? Keeping in mind that real intimacy means being your authentic self, ask yourself if it's really okay that you are not allowed to be yourself. Do you want to continue to be in a relationship where there is probably no chance of real intimacy because you cannot be yourself? What can you do to stay in the relationship and still be true to yourself?

Could it be possible that, because of your childhood experiences, you are so afraid of being judged or rejected that you're reading "conditional love" expectations into your partner's intentions? Talking with your partner may be productive for discovering that each of you has a different perception of the situation. And, too, if your partner isn't aware of your feelings, how can they work with you to change things?

Giving Yourself the Space to Have an Adventure!

Can you make room for filling your life with new adventures—enjoying the here and now, instead of filling the space with worry about the outcome or what others may think? It's all too easy to look at all the reasons why you "can't" rather than all the reasons you "can."

I can think of so many times when the first words out of my mouth were "I can't." Many years ago, my then-husband proposed we take a three-month trip to Europe. At first, I couldn't imagine finding a way to take such a long leave from work, and it caused several sleepless nights. I finally agreed to make space for that adventure, but I almost missed out on it.

Have you missed out on some wonderful adventures because you jumped too fast to "I can't" instead of "I will"? By telling yourself, "I can handle it," you can move past fears that arise. And Susan Jeffers' wise counsel from *Feel the Fear and Do It Anyway* has been instrumental in developing my willingness to try new adventures. But what if that "adventure" doesn't work out as you had hoped and turns into a misadventure? You can still choose to look at it as information-gathering. There is always something to learn if you stay open to that possibility.

Giving Yourself the Space to Have Fun

I think the word is "uptight," isn't it? You know, when you are wound up so tight that you can't let go and have fun. Some of us are just too negative about things, always having lots of good reasons *not* to do something fun, worrying that it will have a negative outcome, afraid to just lighten up let go and enjoy life.

One woman I know seemed to believe it simply wasn't okay to have fun—not at work, not on weekends, not on vacations (well, she hardly took any anyway). It turns out that her parents didn't have much fun either, and somehow she got the idea that she would be disloyal to them if she did things any differently. But something quite miraculous happened. She began saying to herself, "My parents would have complained about this, but guess what—I'm not my parents." Yes, indeed. She's becoming her own person!

Making Transitional Space

Another way to make comfortable space for yourself and for your relationship is to look at some situations as "transitional." This useful "labeling" can be a relationship saver. Let's face it—many occurrences in life can knock the wind out of you and require some sort of accommodation. Some of these are life-cycle changes discussed earlier such as a new marriage, new baby, new job, lost job, illness, retirement, and an "empty nest."

Others are of the daily variety, such as morning goodbyes or unwinding after a day's work. Yes, I know these seem insignificant, but they contain their share of stress and anxiety. And when anxiety starts filling up the space, we tend to act out by getting irritable, critical, angry, or by withdrawing.

I have found it personally helpful to label these seemingly inconsequential things as "transitional." It creates a "container" and gives me a sense of a beginning and an end—reminding me it's "time-limited." It allows me the choice of seeing things as "recovery time" or "recharge time." It provides me space to reorganize my thoughts or plans and to reconstitute, if need be. It gives me room to breathe.

Couples may experience different kinds of daily or weekly transitions, but because they don't identify them as such, these experiences can be bumpy. Richard Carlson, Ph.D., and Kristine Carlson in *Don't Sweat the Small Stuff in Love* (1999), say it so well: "Transitions are like speed bumps. You need to slow down while approaching" (49).

Let's take a look at the act of saying goodbye when one or both of you are going off to work. When I ask about leave-takings, quite a few couples realize that they pick a fight shortly before that moment of departure. The anger from the fight stays with them for a while, with the effect of carrying the essence of their partner with them into the day. In other words, they are staying connected through the anger. Perhaps it would be more productive to identify the leave-taking as a transitional time, recognizing that a shift is occurring from one mode of functioning to another. There must be a better way to stay connected to their partner than fighting. What about a lingering kiss, instead, or a nice, long hug. Now, that's a sweet memory to take to work with you.

People need their transitional time at the end of the workday as well. All too often, before they can recover from one set of demands, they are confronted by another batch. They need a period of time to relax and unwind before shifting gears into interacting with their partner or children.

Freddie, a teacher, needed this kind of time. "My need for alone time is from childhood, and it existed long before my partner came along. I'm not by nature a social person, and I've always been partial to solitude. Because I'm 'exposed' all day in my teaching job, I want some time alone when I get home." Freddie's partner was feeling neglected by this need for alone time. So they experimented with some ways to make initial contact before Freddie went off by himself. A warm hug accompanied by "I'll be back in twenty minutes" seemed to work best.

Time-outs

One of the best ways to negotiate comfortable space is to devise and use creative "time-outs." Time-outs soothe souls and save relationships. Time-outs mean taking time out from the intensity of a disagreement with your partner. But in order to be able to do this, it's helpful to first be able to know how to disengage enough from the intensity to step back and sort through your confused emotions. Let's first take a look at personal time-outs, then move into how to develop skills for time-outs in the heat of battle with your partner.

Personal Time-outs

Okay, let's face it. Some things are just hot-button issues and your partner just said or did something that pushed the button. Perhaps it was something insulting, dismissive, condescending, or annoying. You may feel irritated, hurt, or even betrayed in some way. Those feelings start taking over, and begin to overwhelm you. What can you do to stop the emotional flooding? How can you sort out your feelings, think more clearly, and stay centered?

In *Don't Take It Personally!* I describe how, when I feel flooded, it feels as if my feelings are fine gold chains all tangled up. I describe how I once read a household hint that suggested putting those knotted chains on waxed paper and adding a few drops of mineral oil. Then you gently move them around with two straight pins until they untangle. And they *will* untangle. It works for feelings as well—try visualizing this image the next time your feelings are all jangled and tangled.

Time-outs work great and they come in all sorts of flavors. The point is to create enough emotional and physical space between yourself and your partner to catch your breath and untangle.

By experimenting with ways to do this, you will be able to walk alongside yourself, creating just enough objectivity that you won't be so immersed in the intensity of it all. This space gives you the ability to see that you have a choice here—to continue the fight with your partner or not, to continue to say hurtful things or not, or to continue to be hurt by your partner's words or not. Instead, you can take a time-out, either using your cognitive skills to disengage or actually physically leaving the room for a while.

Fighting Time-outs

I'm not going to pretend that it's easy to take this distance in the heat of battle. But there are some ways to get started. Try counting to ten or breathing ten long breaths (or both at the same time) to get the distance you need to calm down. It really does work to count to ten, slowly. Ten seconds is often sufficient time to regain just enough composure to attain some objectivity. But there are some other techniques you can experiment with as well. You can remind yourself that you can always push the "save" button and deal with it later, like an instant replay. You can visualize a plastic shield in front of you or a pliable bubble around yourself to keep you protected from the words of the other person.

Try counting to ten or breathing ten long breaths
to get the distance you need to calm down.

Taking physical time-outs is another way of gaining much-needed space for yourself. A good way to do this is to say you want to take some time to "collect your thoughts," or "think it through." You might want to say that you want to go into the other room or take a walk, and that you'll be back in twenty minutes (it takes at least twenty minutes to self-soothe and calm yourself down). But always *say you'll be back*—and be back when you say. Abandonment issues might be lurking around, and it doesn't help to aggravate them. Another useful technique for stopping the escalation is agreeing on some words, phrases, or signals that both of you can recognize and relate to. For example, you could try using the easily recogniz-able "time out" (T-shaped) (*t*-shaped) signal from football.

And, of course, respectful humor (if you can muster it) can work wonders and cue words can work as well, for example, "touché," or "cease-fire." My favorite is *"ouch."* It seems to get the message across.

Sometimes a time-out means allowing necessary space by post-poning a discussion until the next day. This is often a good idea if a disagreement flares up at night and both of you are too tired to give the problem and your partner your full attention. If you're like most of us, when you're tired, you may get cranky, and we all know how easy it is to disintegrate under stress. This isn't about postponing that talk indefinitely, but, rather, dealing with the issue in a fresh way the next day. I'm reminded of an old Russian saying: "The morning is wiser than the evening." Sometimes a hug goodnight and the prom-ise "let's talk about it in the morning when we're fresher" is the best strategy.

"The morning is wiser than the evening."
—Old Russian saying

Time for Yourself

Unless you let yourself have a relationship with yourself first, it's pretty hard to have a relationship with someone else. The exhorta-tions go "know yourself," "be intimate with yourself," "understand yourself." It's all about making room to take time for yourself—time to breathe, time to self-soothe, time to take space.

Make Room to Breathe

On the flyleaf of this book is a quote by Thich Nhat Hanh. I'd like to repeat it here because after contemplating the various mean-ings about space and breathing room, it may take on a more intricate meaning for you.

We have a room for everything—eating, sleeping, watching TV—but we have no room for mindfulness. I recommend that we set up a small room in our homes and call it a "breathing room," where we can be alone and practice just breathing and smiling, at least in difficult moments. That little room should be . . . respected and not violated by anger, shouting, or things like that . . . every home should have one room for breathing.

Coming Up for Air

It helps to breathe. But you knew that. So why is it that so many of us under stress seem to hold our breath, or breathe so shallowly that we might as well not be breathing at all? Maybe being under stress is like being under water—we've gotta come up for air.

Sometimes you may have to remind yourself to breathe. You may find yourself anxious, or hyperventilating, or feeling like the proverbial deer in the headlights. At times like these, what about trying to remember to remind yourself to take a few, slow, deep breaths, and then ten more. Be aware of your breathing, but don't try too hard. See if you can let go enough to let your breath flow. You might have forgotten momentarily to breathe, but it's just a temporary lapse of memory.

In one of Ed Brown's wise and witty Zen talks, he observes, "You really don't have to tell the breath how to breathe. It knows how to be breath! It knows even better than our conscious self knows, and it says, 'Excuse me, I know how to do this.'"

But your breath *can* use some room. It's helpful to allow space for the air and energy to circulate, which means sitting with arms and legs uncrossed. Just sitting quietly and clearing your mind or following your breath during meditation is one way to make room.

Again, I want to say that allowing space to create a relationship with yourself is an important prerequisite for creating space that allows rich relationships with others. The best way to learn about space is to practice making it in yourself. When we open our bodies we open our hearts. There are lots of ways to create space and awareness by making the mind-body connection, working from the inside out. There is meditation of course, yoga posturing and the various martial arts also allow the kind of space I'm talking about. There are other practices to discover as well, all of which can be meditative, mindful, and space enhancing. The NIA technique is a non-impact aerobic technique that blends the rhythms and movements of modern and ethnic dance, yoga, tai chi, tae kwon do, and aikido. Pilates, a series of precise, subtle movements, focuses on one muscle group at a time. Another way to develop a relationship with your body is through body rolling, a muscle release technique, using a ten-inch ball to stimulate your bones and elongate muscles, letting go of tension, feeling the connection with the breath and the body, and creating space.

One of my favorites is a simple one—to remind myself to breathe through my collarbones. Yes, collarbones! And maybe it's just my imagination, but it feels as if my heart is opening up with each breath. As I sit, I find myself opening and expanding without even trying, making space to listen to what my body may be telling me.

Listening to Your Body

The energy of our bodies can tell us a lot about our needs for taking and giving space. This is the language of body sensations (kinesthetics), as we saw in chapter 6. For example, what if you notice that your throat seems tight? Perhaps the next step is to say to yourself, "I think I need to take a day for myself, focusing on my inner world and how to express myself." What if you are experiencing a crowded sensation in your chest? You might say to your partner, "I'm really feeling tension in my heart. I wonder if it's connected to a fear that you'll leave me. Could you hold me close for awhile? If you can't do that right now, then I need to find space to hold and be close to myself."

Self-Soothing

Self-soothing is a way to find your center in the midst of pressures from others. It is a way to tap into your needs and resources by quieting yourself. One way to calm yourself is through repetition of movement. This has an autohypnotic effect, and you may already be doing it without even knowing. Do you ever find yourself touching or rubbing your hand, arm, shoulder, chin, or hair? You may have dismissed this repetitive touching as "just a nervous thing I do." You may even be critical of yourself for doing it, but it is, in fact, a creative way of calming yourself. Next time you find yourself stroking your hair or your shoulder or your knuckles, try doing *more* of it and notice how well you are making space for yourself.

This "holding on to yourself" can also bring connection with your partner, in what David Schnarch calls "hugging till relaxed." This isn't about leaning on the other person, this is about differentiation, "the ability to stand on your own two feet, both physically and emotionally, when you are close to others."

Here are the basics:

- Stand on your own two feet.

- Put your arms around your partner.

- Focus on *yourself.*

• Quiet yourself down—way down.

This idea reminds me of a saying I've often heard: A dependent (leaning) relationship is like the letter "A" (leaning on each other) while a differentiated yet connected relationship is like the letter "H" (each standing on their own two feet).

Even though you may feel solid and balanced when you're on your own, when you are in a relationship, the unexpected tendency to "lean" can knock you off your feet.

> A dependent relationship is like
> the letter "A"; a differentiated yet connected
> relationship is like the letter "H."

Space needs begin with the awareness or denial of energy within the body. And when you can transfer these energetic needs into verbal communication, you can begin to balance closeness and distance, creating the right amount of space to be a couple. Yes, it can work, and as you'll see in the following chapter there are effective ways to create comfortable space for the two of you.

15

My Space, Your Space, Our Space

Closing the Gap in Your Relationship

We've been looking at some of the important stepping-stones to intimacy—giving and accepting respect, establishing honesty, building trust, and allowing vulnerability. Now let's focus in on how to get this information to work for you and your partner. I'd like to remind you that this work can come naturally, just as working in the garden is joyous and not painful work. But with any kind of endeavor, a plan is helpful.

Building relationships is similar to working on a jigsaw puzzle. Some people work from the outer edges inward. Some people work outward to the edges. As one woman says, "I've always enjoyed finding where the proper piece went. Nobody ever explained to me before how to go from here to there. I always got stuck in the parts that were missing."

And that's the point for relationships, too. It's a matter of building what is missing. For example, anger can be valuable because the making up part is often good. Perhaps it takes being angry to allow your partner to be tender afterwards. Perhaps it takes being angry to allow you to be receptive. Can you substitute something else for the anger? Can you build what is missing? What else can bring feelings of closeness, tenderness, or receptivity? The following stories are an introduction to looking at what works in relationship-building.

Looking at What Works

Marjorie feels left out when Nick comes home from the office. He goes into his study, shuts the door, and "disappears" for an hour or so. Marjorie tells herself that Nick doesn't want to be with her. But actually Nick goes into the study because he needs a breather, some time and space to himself. He needs transition time between office and home responsibilities.

Well, how much time does Nick really need? Does he need a whole hour? What if he took space for himself for thirty minutes or so? Is that enough time for him? Could Marjorie tolerate this time alone without feeling left out and rejected by Nick? What does she need from him before he goes into his study?

Here is another situation where solutions can be negotiated. Joel feels left out when Sam spaces out in front of the TV. Joel wants contact—to touch and talk. There are times when Sam is okay with this, but at other times he needs some room to space out. In our sessions, we speculated on how they could be with each other, stay connected, but not request or expect the other person's direct attention. What are the bottom line needs that would enable Joel to feel secure in the relationship? What are the bottom line needs for Sam? Could Joel stay in the same room while Sam watches TV or reads without demanding his direct attention? Perhaps Joel could also read or work on his laptop. This is an example of sharing space but not time.

Does this kind of situation sound familiar to you? How can you find some common ground with your partner? You've made a good beginning by realizing that you both want different forms of the same thing—*contact*. Can you put words to the kind of physical or emotional closeness you really want? By assessing and defining your individual needs, a workable deal can usually be negotiated. You can most likely get some of those needs met, but first you'll have to know what they are. What do you want from the other person? What do you really have in mind? What do you want him or her to do or say?

Calling Ahead

Here is Joe's solution designed to get much-needed space and avoid misunderstandings. "If I'm having a particularly stressful day at the office, I call my partner before leaving and say, 'I'll be home soon, but I'll need some time to wind down. I won't be able to carry on a decent conversation with you tonight.' This 'early warning system' works great. This way, there won't be expectations that I can't meet, and most of the time, there are no hard feelings."

Overlapping Images

You've probably noticed how images in television commercials sometimes morph one into another. For example, a human face will change into a lion's face or an antelope will transform into a car—right before your eyes. Well, this is what happens with interactions as well. One contextual experience that may be old may be replicated by another experience in the present. Or two present-day situations may be similar to each other. This is "isomorphism," when one process takes on the same properties as another.

For example, an event or process that occurs in the present relationship of a couple may also have occurred in the childhood experience of either or both, or in the couple's early history together. In other words, there is a parallel process that goes on, a replication across contexts. By looking at a small segment of a couple's interaction, a theme often emerges regarding the wider view of the couple's process together. Throughout this book there have been examples of isomorphism, but let's take a close-up look at the process that goes on between Randall and Brenda.

When Randall asks Brenda if she would like to eat at home or go out, she says, "Let me think about it," but can't give him an answer. He repeats the question—still no answer. Then he starts getting angry, thinking she is "dissing" him by not responding. The angrier he gets, the more she clams up; the more she clams up, the angrier he gets. And on it goes.

This exchange doesn't just occur around dinner plans. It happens around all kinds of situations—whether to stay home on Sunday or take a drive to the country, what to order from a menu, whether to buy a red car or a beige car, and even which mail to keep and which to toss. Each partner waits for the other to make the decision, and no decisions get made.

By looking back at a childhood experience through your adult eyes, you can put things in their proper perspective. If the original context can be established, it becomes easier to understand why someone reacts the way they do. Let's look in on Brenda and Randall again. "I just can't make a decision," says Brenda. "Any choice I make might turn out wrong." Is there an earlier context for that? "When I was a child, any choice I made would always be the wrong choice. I never could do anything right and always got into trouble. I don't ever want to be put in that position again, and that's exactly how I feel every time Randall asks me to make a decision."

Does Randall know why he gets so angry with Brenda? "I guess it's from my childhood, too," he reflected. "My mom always depended on me to take care of things. She seemed so helpless much of the time, and I had to take over for her. I felt I couldn't ever make a mistake." Isn't it interesting how Brenda felt she was always going to be wrong, and Randall felt he had no space to be wrong. She clams up and he blows up.

Both Brenda and Randall better understood each other and how their styles fit together since that eye-opening exchange of information. You and your partner can also benefit from understanding the importance of your process together from context to context. Instead of letting your history cause a reaction, why not let it become a resource? After all, we do tend to repeat those childhood dramas—"it ain't much but it's home!"

Whose Words Are Those?

I believe our history influences our present relationships. When we consider the backdrop of early experiences, beliefs, and rules, the meanings and intentions of present interactions become much clearer. In fact, when two people are in a room together having a talk (or even an argument) there are many more folks there with them, perhaps dozens. Each of them has several people sitting on their shoulder—parents, siblings, grandparents, aunts, and uncles. Each has to have their say, each has to get a word in, or an opinion, or a judgment. And sometimes one partner or other opens their mouth and doesn't know where on earth thier words came from, but it sure sounds like something Grandma would say.

It's really wonderful when couples have the benefit of hearing about each other's early experiences. They get the opportunity to understand how repetitive patterns and family messages get passed down from generation to generation. This gives each partner a context in which to understand the other's motivations, actions, reactions and especially, overreactions. It is often a special and rewarding experience to look at ancestral influences—both joys and struggles—as well as your family of origin experiences in the presence of your partner. And sometimes new memories or insights arise during this exploration. Remembering and sharing the origins of these experiences during couple's therapy can create openness and understanding, which benefits a couple's capacity for intimacy.

> Instead of letting your history cause
> a reaction, let it become a resource.

Here's an example of how this works. Let's say the couple enters therapy because one complains about not getting enough attention from the other. Resentment has built because of hurt feelings and misunderstandings. One of them is frequently working late at the office, stopping off for a drink with friends, or retreating behind a closed door.

Does the partner who is waiting feel invisible or left out? Could there be feelings of rejection or abandonment? Is there anything familiar about this situation, maybe from childhood? Was either parent frequently preoccupied or unavailable? Did the parent say, "I'm too busy now," and did the child translate this to mean, "He's too busy for me, therefore I don't count, which means I'm unlovable"? Is this couple's rift a re-creation of experiences in the family of origin? And was this childhood drama carried into the marriage? Frequently in the past, the then-child felt helpless to make choices about how to respond to these messages. An important goal of therapy is to help a client recognize that, as a capable adult, they have options they may not have had in childhood.

Let's look at still another situation, one in which dependence or lack of autonomy is an issue in the relationship. It is helpful to work toward each partner differentiating from their family of origin (even if they insist they *did* separate—after all, didn't they move across the country?). The problem is, in many instances the "leaving" may be more like a running away, cutting off from the family without doing the work of differentiating. In these situations, the leaving was often dramatic, and the "charge" is still there, in spite of the physical distance and infrequent visitations. Murray Bowen makes the important point that an individual who runs away in his or her own family will also run away in marriage—usually by creating emotional distance.

Some of this differentiation work can be done during couple's therapy, enabling each partner to assist one another in the task of differentiating from their family of origin in order to form intimate bonds with each other. I educate the couple about how experts agree that unless we appropriately disengage from our families, we are often not able to form new connections with a romantic partner. Clients are often surprised to hear that the emotional overconnection can be just as powerful when a parent has died. When there is such an intense connection, it's pretty hard to make room for connecting to your partner.

No-Fault Assurance

Can you try to imagine how much energy and space is taken up by blame, resentment, and anger? Would you then like to find some way of letting go of it to make room for other aspects of your relationship to flourish? Are you willing to try a brief activity to get some idea of how much space gets used up?

Close your eyes and picture what your own style of blame looks like. What form does it have? What texture? What color? What else do you know about it? And now try doing the same visualization for your resentment. What does it look like? How much room does it take up? And what about your anger? Can you describe its properties to yourself as well? Does it take up less or more room than the blame? Less or more room than the resentment? And all together, how much space do these three take up in your heart? Is there room to breathe? Would you like to make more breathing room for yourself? One way to do this is to let go of the blame, resentment, and anger.

Perhaps the most constructive way to do this is through compassion. I see compassion as empathy, putting yourself in your partner's shoes. Trying to see his or her vulnerabilities and how family history may have contributed to words or actions that may have hurt your feelings. Compassion does not necessarily mean forgiveness. It's nice if you can get to forgiving, but it's not always possible for everyone. Remember, you can have compassion even if you can't forgive—they are not the same thing.

After the resentment is cleaned out a little, what would you like to use it for? Would you like to keep the space clear? This would be in the tradition of Zen or minimalist art. This would be empty space rather than the clutter that blame and resentment provide. Because resentment and blame are often reactions to disappointment from unrealistic expectations, what about cutting way back on expecting your partner to make sure your needs get met? Can you give yourself permission to take full responsibility for creating the result *you* want? This means asking for what you want instead of hoping they will read your mind. The following story is a good illustration of this.

Lucy started thinking about her upcoming fifteenth anniversary with Brad over a month ago. She envisioned Brad surprising her with dinner at that new, hard-to-get-into restaurant. He knew she wanted to go. But she didn't say a word to him until the night before their anniversary, asking Brad what plans he'd made. Plans? To be honest, he hadn't given it a thought. He didn't really forget; he just hadn't thought about it. And it turned out that he had to work late, so dinner would be out of the question. He didn't see a problem—they'd just celebrate another night.

But Lucy didn't like that idea one bit. This wasn't any old anniversary. After all, fifteen years is a long time. But had Lucy approached Brad early on about clearing his work schedule? Had she taken charge of making the dinner reservation herself? Who said it was her partner's job to do it? Sure, she felt Brad should take on these responsibilities, because it would show he cared. But what about if Lucy shows *she* cares—for herself, for her partner, and for their relationship?

Maximizing Your Time Together

No question that relationships take a whole bunch of work. Here are some suggestions for keeping that spark going.

- Every other week (or even once a week), have a standing "Date Night." If you have children, prearrange for a standing sitter.

- Before you return home from your "date," take an arm-in-arm stroll.

- Flirt with each other often. Touch hands at dinner. Whisper sexy things. One woman moves in close to her partner at parties and whispers, "I'd love to make love to you" (or some equivalent). His response is a blush and a broad smile.

- Take the same day off from work once in a while, and do something romantic together.

- Or even on a workday, meet each other for a romantic lunch somewhere.

- Try to have a few moments of time together before going to sleep, even if one of you generally goes to bed before the other. In fact, this can provide an opportunity for a special moment of closeness—the night owl gets a chance to "tuck in" the early bird.

- Think "variety." When I was in college everyone lined up to take a sexy class on sex and relationships. The instructor's favorite expression was, "Sex is the spice of life and variety is the spice of sex." His favorite suggestion for variety was, "No matter how long you've been a couple, try 'doing it' in the backseat of the car once in a while."

I guess you could call this the "grown-up" list for how to keep the shine in your intimate relationship. But take a look at the list below from *Advice for a Happy Marriage* (Crawford 1997). These are sound recommendations from third-graders to their teacher on the occasion of her marriage. Here are some of my favorites:

- "You need to kiss every once in a while."

- "If someone comes home late from work, don't make a fight about it because they probably have been working too hard."

- "Have a fun time with celebrations. Make *sure* to celebrate days like Halloween."

- "On holidays, give presents and love."

- "Don't ever get in fights; it could cause something bad to happen."

- "Kiss and make up when you get into a fight."

- "Mostly say yes. (Like if you're going to have hot dogs for dinner and you really don't like hot dogs, it's okay to say no.)"

- "Take breaks from each other once in a while."

- "Give lots of love to each other and respect one another."

Good advice, wouldn't you say? And now let's move from the very specific (Halloween?) to the more general—summarizing some key points of *Breathing Room*.

Becoming a Couple

Here are some questions you can ask yourself: What does closeness mean to you? And specifically, how would you know when you were feeling close to your partner? What would the indicators be? Chances are you will mention some form of "respect"—here we are back to the importance of respect again. Respect for your own needs, respect for your partner's needs, and the ability to make a shift in thinking from an individual framework to a couple's framework, to think *relationally*, instead of *individually*. Let's review some of the ways you can respect each other's feelings, desires, and personal space in order to become a couple.

One important way of thinking relationally and respecting the other person's feelings is to be empathic, putting yourself in your partner's shoes. And, if you recall from our earlier discussion, this is more than imagining how you might feel. It means imagining how your partner feels. You'll need to remind yourself that there are two realities, and neither is right nor wrong, only different. And this is connected to the usefulness of recognizing that though it often seems as if your partner has the problems with intimacy, you, too, are a player in the intimacy dance. Ask yourself what part you play. This recognition will help you feel more in control of the situation and not so "done to."

There are lots of times you might feel helpless or helplessly reactive. But if you can possibly find ways to be proactive instead of reactive, you'll feel more in charge of your life. You do have a lot of power—when you get right down to it, no one can make you as happy as you can make yourself. In fact, the quickest way to change your relationship is to change yourself. It's a whole lot easier than trying to change the other person. And, because everything is relational, if you change, it's not possible for your partner to continue to relate to you in the same way. Your relationship will also change. Relationships improve not only by decreasing the negatives, but by increasing the positives. My favorite question to ask couples has to do with noticing any shades of difference in their relationship. "What's different about this week" or "What's different about this interaction?" There is so much to learn from all the changes.

You may have noticed that the trigger for most of the problematic behavior I've described here stems from anxiety. A good question to ask yourself is, "Am I feeling anxious? What might I be feeling anxious about?" Reminding your partner, "Please try to hear this. This is not about you, this is about my needing space," can circumvent a lot of hurt feelings. And while you are at it, it wouldn't hurt to remind yourself, "This is not about *me*, this is about *you* needing space."

Are you able to notice how you sound when you "lose it" and say hurtful things? Can you stop the action, step back, and say, "I didn't mean for it to sound like that. I realize that was hurtful. Let me start again"? Taking emotional or physical "time-outs" helps you become a more objective observer. And unless you can step back and notice what is happening, you won't be able to change it.

Another way of honing your observation skills is by giving attention to the events leading up to hurt feelings or overreactions. What comes before? What comes after? And what about before that? The same goes for the sequences leading to positive, validating, enjoyable interactions. We can learn from both the negative and the positive.

Speaking of the positive, you might want to practice thinking in terms of what you want rather than what you don't want. It's all too easy reciting a litany of disappointments. It can be a challenge to think through how you want things to be and to put this into words. Related to this, are you able to recognize your needs and longings and communicate them to your partner? This kind of directness allows you to make room for what you want in the relationship.

Are you able to leave space for the other person in your communications? By this I mean the space to say "no" or to ask questions, the space to clarify or check things out with you? Are you able to leave space for your partner to share feelings? And what about leaving space for disagreements? Can you let it be okay for both of you to be honest about your feelings, without fear of being dismissed, ridiculed, or abandoned. Can you "agree to disagree"? By the way, before you initiate a "heavy-duty" conversation with your partner, you might consider asking first, "Is this a good time to talk?" And here's another thought—looking into someone's eyes is one of the best ways to connect with someone, yet it takes practice for most of us. If you get a chance to experiment, you may get some great results.

Another place to experiment with results is to keep in mind that defining the problem is 50 percent of finding a solution. It's pretty hard to solve a problem if you don't first know what it is.

Remind yourself that you and your partner may have different styles of feeling, thinking, and doing things. This is primarily because you grew up in different families, with different backgrounds and values. Recognizing these understandable differences can prevent hurt feelings, especially if your partner isn't showing that they care about you the same way you would show your caring for them. Here is a bit of "author unkown" wisdom I'd like to pass on to you: Just because someone doesn't love you the way you want them to, doesn't mean they don't love you with all they have.

Just because someone doesn't love you the
way you want them to, doesn't mean they
don't love you with all they have.

Each of you has different strengths as well. Perhaps each of you will be able to say to the other, "I'm good at some things, and you are good at others. Together we make a great team. I don't have to fault you for the things you're not good at. Who says it has to be half and half?"

The way I see it, if you could find a way to replace resentment with respect for individuality and feelings, your relationship could open up to new dimensions. When I'm working with a couple, I like to help them find a way to get past the rough and jagged edges of accumulated distrust and resentment, making room for the soft cushion of yearning underneath.

This softness can open the door for each of you to trust that you are loved. This means getting past any old messages of "I'm unlovable or unworthy." It means being able to take in and accept validation, rather than pushing it out of your orbit—this flow of energy between you allows each of you to touch something meaningful in the other. And finally, it means creating space to be a couple.

References

Aron, Elaine. 2000. *The Highly Sensitive Person in Love.* New York: Broadway Books.

Baron, Renee, and Elizabeth Wagele. 1995. *Are You My Type, Am I Yours? Relationships Made Easy Through the Enneagram.* San Francisco: Harper San Francisco.

Bowen, Murray. 1978. *Family Therapy and Clinical Practice.* New York: Jason Aronson, Inc.

Carlson, Richard, and Kristine Carlson. 1999. *Don't Sweat the Small Stuff in Love.* New York: Hyperion.

Clinebell, H. J., and C. H. Clinebell. 1970. *The Intimate Marriage.* New York: Harper & Row.

Crawford, Debi Dietz, and Friends. 1997. *Advice For a Happy Marriage.* New York: Warner Treasures

Daniels, David, and Virginia Price. 2000. *The Essential Enneagram.* San Francisco: HarperSanFrancisco.

Erikson, Erik. 1950. *Childhood and Society.* New York: Norton & Company

Fain, Audrey. 1989. An Exploratory Study of Couples for Whom The Enneagram Has Been an Important Factor in Their Relationship. Ph.D. diss. California Graduate School of Family Psychology.

Fogarty, Thomas. 1976. Marital Crisis. In *Family Therapy: Theory and Practice,* edited by Philip Guerin. New York: Gardener Press.

Friday. Nancy. 1997. *My Mother/My Self.* New York: Delta.

Friel, John, and Linda Friel. 1990. *Adult Child's Guide to What's "Normal."* Deerfield Beach, Fla.: Health Communications, Inc.

Gendler, J. Ruth. 1988. *The Book of Qualities.* New York: HarperPerennial.

Giordano, John K., and Monica McGoldrick. 1996. Italian Families. In *Ethnicity & Family Therapy*, edited by Monica McGoldrick, John K. Giordano, and Joe Pearce. New York: The Guilford Press.

Goldstine, Daniel et al. 1977. *The Dance-Away Lover and Other Roles We Play in Love, Sex, and Marriage.* New York: Morrow and Co.

Gottman, John. 1999 *The Seven Principles for Making Marriage Work.* New York: Three Rivers Press.

Hall, Edward T. 1982. *The Hidden Dimension.* New York: Anchor Books.

———. 1983. *The Dance of Life.* New York: Anchor Books.

Hanh, Thich Nhat. 1992. *Peace Is Every Step.* New York: Bantam.

Jeffers, Susan. 1987. *Feel the Fear and Do It Anyway.* New York: Fawcett.

———. 1989. *Opening Our Hearts to Men.* New York: Fawcett.

———. 2000. *I'm Okay . . . You're a Brat.* New York: Renaissance

Karpman , Stephen B. 1968. Fairy Tales and Script Drama Analysis. *Transactional Analysis Bulletin* VII(26):39–43.

Kerr, Michael. 1981. Family Systems Theory and Practice. In *Handbook of Family Therapy*, edited by Alan Gurman and David Kniskern. New York: Brunner/Mazel.

Lerner, Harriet Goldhor. 1985. *The Dance of Anger.* New York: Harper & Row.

———. 1989. *The Dance of Intimacy.* New York: Harper Perennial.

Mellody, Pia, and A. W. Miller. 1989. *Facing Codependence.* San Francisco: HarperSan Francisco.

McGoldrick, Monica, and John K. Giordano. 1996. Overview, Ethnicity and Family Therapy. In *Ethnicity & Family Therapy*, edited by Monica McGoldrick, John K. Giordano, and Joe Pearce. New York: The Guilford Press.

McKay, Matthew, Patrick Fanning, and Kim Paleg. 1994. *Couple Skills.* Oakland, Calif.: New Harbinger Publications.

Napier, Augustus. 1978. The Rejection-Intrusion Pattern. *Journal of Marriage and Family Counseling.* January. 5–12.

Nisker, Wes (Scoop). 1999. *Crazy Wisdom.* Berkeley, Calif.: Ten Speed Press.

Palmer, Helen. 1991. *The Enneagram: Understanding Yourself and Others in Your Life.* San Francisco: HarperSan Francisco.

Page, Susan. 1990. *If I'm So Wonderful, Why Am I Still Single?* New York: Bantam.

———. 1994. *The 8 Essential Traits of Couples Who Thrive.* New York: Dell.

———. 1997. *How One of You Can Bring the Two of You Together.* New York: Broadway Books.

Rilke, Rainer Maria. 1993. *Letters to a Young Poet.* Trans. M. D. Herter Norton. New York: W. W. Norton & Company.

Rosen, Elliott J., and Susan F. Weltman. 1996. Jewish Families: An Overview. In *Ethnicity & Family Therapy,* edited by Monica McGoldrick, John K. Giordano, and Joe Pearce. New York: The Guilford Press.

Rubin, Lillian. 1983. *Intimate Strangers.* New York: Harper & Row.

Savage, Elayne. 1989. Perception of Acceptance or Rejection in Childhood and How It Impacts Adult Intimacy. Ph.D. diss. California Graduate School of Family Psychology.

———. 1997. *Don't Take It Personally! The Art of Dealing with Rejection.* Oakland, Calif.: New Harbinger Publications.

Sager, Clifford. 1981. Couples Therapy and Marriage Contracts. In *Handbook of Family Therapy,* edited by Alan Gurman and David Kniskern. New York: Brunner/Mazel.

Scarf, Maggie. 1988. *Intimate Partners.* New York: Random House

———. 1995. *Intimate Worlds.* New York: Ballentine Books.

Schnarch, David. 1998. *Passionate Marriage.* New York: Owl Books, Henry Holt and Company.

Williamson, Marianne. 1994. *Illuminata.* New York: Riverhead Books.

Young, Kimberly S. 1996. Internet addiction: The emergence of a new clinical disorder. Paper presented at the 104th Annual Convention of the American Psychological Association, Toronto, Ontario, Canada.

Zuckerman, Marvin. 1994. *Behavioral Expression and Biosocial Bases of Sensation Seeking.* New York: Cambridge University Press.

Suggested Readings

TRANSITIONS

Bridges, William. 1980. *Transitions: Making Sense of Life's Changes.* Menlo Park, Calif.: Addison-Wesley.

Elizabeth A Carter and Monica McGoldrick, eds. 1998. *The Expanded Family Life Cycle: Individual, Family and Social Perspectives.* Boston: Allyn & Bacon

Sheehy, Gail. 1996. New Passages: *Mapping Your Life Across Time.* New York: Ballantine Books.

RELATIONSHIPS

Ellenberg, Daniel and Judith Bell. 1995. *Lovers for Life: Creating Lasting Passion, Trust and True Partnership.* Santa Rosa, Calif: Aslan Publishing.

Kantor, David. 1999. *My Lover, Myself: Self Discovery Through Relationship.* New York: Riverhead Books.

Kasl, Charlotte. 1999. *If The Buddha Dated.* New York: Penguin.

McKay, Matthew, Patrick Fanning, and Kim. Paleg, 1994. *Couple Skills.* Oakland: New Harbinger Publications.

CYBERSPACE/CYBERSEX

Locke, John. 1999. *Why We Don't Talk to Each Other Anymore: The De-Voicing of Society.* New York: Touchstone.

Young, Kimberly S..1998.*Caught in the Net: How to Recognize the Signs of Internet Addiction-And a Winning Strategy for Recovery*. New York: John Wiley & Sons.

PERSONAL BOUNDARIES

Black, Jan and Greg Enns. 1998. *Better Boundaries: Owning and Treasuring Your Life*. Oakland, Calif: New Harbinger Publications.

Whitfield, Charles. 1993. *Boundaries and Relationships*. Deerfield Beach, Flor: Health Communications, Inc.

THE MIND/BODY CONNECTION

Davis, Martha, Elizabeth Robbins Eshelman, and Matthew McKay. 2000. *The Relaxation & Stress Reduction Workbook*, 5th Edition. Oakland, Calif: New Harbinger Publications

McKay, Matthew and Patrick Fanning *The Daily Relaxer*. Oakland, Calif: New Harbinger Publications.

Mehta, Silva, Mira Mehta, and Shyam Mehta. 1990. *Yoga : The Iyengar Way*. New York: Knopf.

Scaravelli, Vanda. 1991. *Awakening the Spine*. San Francisco: HarperSanFrancisco.

Suzuki, Shunryu. 1988. *Zen Mind, Beginner's Mind*. Tumbull, Conn. Weatherhill.

Zake, Yamuna and Golden, Stepahanie. 1997. *Body Rolling: An Experiential Approach to Complete Muscle Release*. Rochester, Vermont: Healing Arts Press.

RELATIONSHIP TYPOLOGIES

Arroyo. Stephen. 1993. *Relationships and Life Cycles: Astrological Patterns of Personal Experience*. Sebastopol, Calif: CRCS Publications.

Baron, Renee and Elizabeth Wagele. 1995. *Are You My Type, Am I Yours? Relationships Made Easy Through The Enneagram* San Francisco: HarperSan Francisco.

Davison, Ronald. 1983. Synastry: *Understanding Human Relationships Through Astrology*. Santa Fe, New Mexico: Aurora Press.

Kroeger, Otto and Janet M. Thuesen. 1989. *Type Talk*. New York: Delta

Tieger Paul D. and Barbara Barron-Tieger. 2000. *Just Your Type: Creating the Relationship You've Always Wanted Using the Secrets of Personality Type*. New York: Little Brown & Co.

ADDICTIVE BEHAVIOR AND INTIMACY

Federman, Edward J., Charles E. Drebing, and Chistopher Krebs. 2000. *Don't Leave It to Chance: A Guide for Families of Problem Gamblers.* Oakland, Calif.: New Harbinger Publications.

Roth, Geneen. 1993. *When Food Is Love :Exploring the Relationship Between Eating and Intimacy.* New York: Plume

Woititz, Janet Geringer. 1986, *Marriage on the Rocks.* Deerfield Beach, Fla.: Health Communications.

JEALOUSY

Buss, David M. 2000. *The Dangerous Passion: Why Jealousy Is As Necessary As Love and Sex.* New York: Free Press

Friday, Nancy. 1997. *Jealousy.* New York: M Evans & Co.

Pines, Ayala Malach. 1998. *Romantic Jealousy*: Causes, Symptoms, Cures. New York: Routledge;

TRUST/BETRAYAL

Jampolsky, Lee. 1994. *The Art of Trust: Healing Your Heart and Opening Your Mind.* Berkeley, Calif.: Celestial Arts.

Lusterman, Don-David, *Infidelity: A Survival Guide.* Oakland, Calif.: New Harbinger Publications.

Pittman, Frank. 1990. *Private Lies: Infidelity and Betrayal of Intimacy.* New York: W.W. Norton & Company.

EMPTY NEST/RETIREMENT

Lauer, Jeanette. C. and Robert H. Lauer. 1999. *How to Survive and Thrive in an Empty Nest: Reclaiming Your Life When Your Children Are Grow.* Oakland, Calif.: New Harbinger Publications.

Polston, Betty L. and Susan K. Golant. 1999. *Loving Midlife Marriage: A Guide to Keeping Romance Alive from the Empty Nest Through Retirement.* New York: John Wiley & Sons.

About The Author

Elayne Savage, Ph.D. is also the author of the popular book *Don't Take It Personally! The Art of Dealing with Rejection.* As an expert in the field of relationships, she has over twenty five-years of experience working with couples and families and is a popular workshop leader, trainer, consultant, and graduate-level college instructor. Her early background includes many years of social work experience—as a Medical Social Worker in Baltimore and a Child Protective Ser vices Worker in San Fran cisco. She received her BA in Sociology from the University of Alabama, her MA in Psychology from John F. Ken nedy Uni ver sity, and her Ph.D. in Fam ily Psy chol ogy from the California Graduate School. She is a member of the National Speakers Association and is frequently interviewed in newspapers, magazines, radio, and TV.

Dr. Savage is a nationally recognized expert in managing mis un der standings and get ting beyond rejec tion. You can con tact her for infor ma tion about consulting, keynotes, workshops, and seminars.

Your ideas, com ments, and ques tions are wel come. You can reach Dr. Savage through her website:

www.elaynesavage.com

Some Other New Harbinger Self-Help Titles

Family Guide to Emotional Wellness, $24.95
Undefended Love, $13.95
The Great Big Book of Hope, $15.95
Don't Leave it to Chance, $13.95
Emotional Claustrophobia, $12.95
The Relaxation & Stress Reduction Workbook, Fifth Edition, $19.95
The Loneliness Workbook, $14.95
Thriving with Your Autoimmune Disorder, $16.95
Illness and the Art of Creative Self-Expression, $13.95
The Interstitial Cystitis Survival Guide, $14.95
Outbreak Alert, $15.95
Don't Let Your Mind Stunt Your Growth, $10.95
Energy Tapping, $14.95
Under Her Wing, $13.95
Self-Esteem, Third Edition, $15.95
Women's Sexualitites, $15.95
Knee Pain, $14.95
Helping Your Anxious Child, $12.95
Breaking the Bonds of Irritable Bowel Syndrome, $14.95
Multiple Chemical Sensitivity: A Survival Guide, $16.95
Dancing Naked, $14.95
Why Are We Still Fighting, $15.95
From Sabotage to Success, $14.95
Parkinson's Disease and the Art of Moving, $15.95
A Survivor's Guide to Breast Cancer, $13.95
Men, Women, and Prostate Cancer, $15.95
Make Every Session Count: Getting the Most Out of Your Brief Therapy, $10.95
Virtual Addiction, $12.95
After the Breakup, $13.95
Why Can't I Be the Parent I Want to Be?, $12.95
The Secret Message of Shame, $13.95
The OCD Workbook, $18.95
Tapping Your Inner Strength, $13.95
Binge No More, $14.95
When to Forgive, $12.95
Practical Dreaming, $12.95
Healthy Baby, Toxic World, $15.95
Making Hope Happen, $14.95
I'll Take Care of You, $12.95
Survivor Guilt, $14.95
Children Changed by Trauma, $13.95
Understanding Your Child's Sexual Behavior, $12.95
The Self-Esteem Companion, $10.95
The Gay and Lesbian Self-Esteem Book, $13.95
Making the Big Move, $13.95
How to Survive and Thrive in an Empty Nest, $13.95
Living Well with a Hidden Disability, $15.95
Overcoming Repetitive Motion Injuries the Rossiter Way, $15.95
What to Tell the Kids About Your Divorce, $13.95
The Divorce Book, Second Edition, $15.95
Claiming Your Creative Self: True Stories from the Everyday Lives of Women, $15.95
Taking Control of TMJ, $13.95
Winning Against Relapse: A Workbook of Action Plans for Recurring Health and Emotional Problems, $14.95
Facing 30: Women Talk About Constructing a Real Life and Other Scary Rites of Passage, $12.95
The Worry Control Workbook, $15.95
Wanting What You Have: A Self-Discovery Workbook, $18.95
When Perfect Isn't Good Enough: Strategies for Coping with Perfectionism, $13.95
Earning Your Own Respect: A Handbook of Personal Responsibility, $12.95
High on Stress: A Woman's Guide to Optimizing the Stress in Her Life, $13.95
Infidelity: A Survival Guide, $13.95
Stop Walking on Eggshells, $14.95
Consumer's Guide to Psychiatric Drugs, $16.95
The Fibromyalgia Advocate: Getting the Support You Need to Cope with Fibromyalgia and Myofascial Pain, $18.95
Working Anger: Preventing and Resolving Conflict on the Job, $12.95
Healthy Living with Diabetes, $13.95
Better Boundries: Owning and Treasuring Your Life, $13.95
Goodbye Good Girl, $12.95
Fibromyalgia & Chronic Myofascial Pain Syndrome, $19.95
The Depression Workbook: Living With Depression and Manic Depression, $17.95

Call **toll free, 1-800-748-6273,** or log on to our online bookstore at **www.newharbinger.com** to order. Have your Visa or Mastercard number ready. Or send a check for the titles you want to New Harbinger Publications, Inc., 5674 Shattuck Ave., Oakland, CA 94609. Include $3.80 for the first book and 75¢ for each additional book, to cover shipping and handling. (California residents please include appropriate sales tax.) Allow two to five weeks for delivery.

Prices subject to change without notice.